HEURETICS

HEURETICS

The Logic of Invention

GREGORY L. ULMER

THE JOHNS HOPKINS UNIVERSITY PRESS

Baltimore and London

© 1994 The Johns Hopkins University Press
All rights reserved
Printed in the United States of America on acid-free paper

The Johns Hopkins University Press
2715 North Charles Street
Baltimore, Maryland 21218–4319
The Johns Hopkins Press Ltd., London

Library of Congress Cataloging-in-Publication
Data will be found at the end of this book.

A catalog record for this book is available from the British Library.

CONTENTS

CONTENTS

ILLUSTRATIONS

1. Method. Woodcut designed by Albrecht Dürer for Sebastian Brant's *The Ship of Fools,* 1494. Reprinted with permission, Dover Publications, New York City.

2. Atlantis. L. A. Huffman collection, in Mark H. Brown and W. R. Felton, *The Frontier Years.* "Looking east on Main Street during the 1881 flood, Miles City, Montana. Charlie Brown's place left foreground; Cottage Saloon opposite." Thanks to Coffrin's Old West Gallery, Bozeman, Montana.

3. Francophilia. From *Stories by Famous Authors Illustrated,* New York: Seaboard Publisher, n.d.

4. Identification. "Entry in the Tall Ships Race, New York, 1976." From Peter Kemp, *The History of Ships,* London: Orbis, 1978. Reprinted with permission, Little, Brown, London.

5. Commemoration. "Tyson Ulmer as Columbus." Fifth-grade school project in the exhibition, *First Encounters — 1492,* Gainesville, Florida, 1989. Photograph by Greg Ulmer.

PREFACE

Heuretics continues a project of invention in progress for two decades now, applying to academic discourse the lessons arising out of a matrix crossing French poststructuralist theory, avant-garde art experiments, and electronic media in the context of schooling. My goal has been to find forms appropriate for conducting cultural studies research in relation to the electronic media. Logically, the electronic apparatus does not come "after" print but "between" print and oral "literacy," making technically possible a greater ease of circulation of knowledge through the different institutions of culture. One of the responsibilities of Discipline discourse now is to invent the representational means and the institutional cooperation for this circulation.

In *Applied Grammatology* (1985) I described a "picto-ideo-phonographic" writing theorized by Jacques Derrida and practiced in the films of Sergei Eisenstein, the performance art of Joseph Beuys, and the psychoanalytic seminars of Jacques Lacan. That writing, I suggested, was the basis for academic work in electronic media. In *Teletheory* (1989) I addressed the problem of a "genre" capable of organizing this picto-ideo-phonographic writing. My book was an experiment derived from Hayden White's challenge to contemporary historians to reinvent historiography using the arts and sciences of today as models in the same way that the nineteenth-century historiographers drew upon the models available to them in their period.

Placing White's proposal in the context of video technology, I outlined and tested a genre called "mystory," designed to simulate the experience of invention, the crossing of discourses that has been shown to occur in the invention process. Realizing that learning is much closer to invention than to verification, I intended mystoriography primarily as a pedagogy. The modes of academic writing now taught in school tend to be positioned on the side of the already known rather than on the side of wanting to find out (of theoretical curiosity) and hence discourage learning how to learn.

Heuretics picks up where *Teletheory* left off, taking into account the technology of hypermedia (the digitalized convergence in one "text" of words, images, and sounds) and placing White's experiment in the larger context of the history of method itself. As an "experimental" humanities, heuretics appropriates the history of the avant-garde as a liberal arts mode of research and experimentation. The avant-garde has served until now as an object of study, although it has demonstrated from the beginning an alternative way to use theory as research. Without relinquishing the presently established applications of theory in our disciplines (critique and hermeneutics), heuretics adds to these critical and interpretive practices a generative productivity of the sort practiced in the avant-garde. Vanguard artists, like their counterparts among academic critics, often base their projects on the important theoretical texts of the day. The difference between the two applications had to do with their respective modes of representation: the artists demonstrate the consequences of the theories for the arts by practicing the arts themselves, generating models of prototypes that function critically as well as aesthetically. The vanguardist does not analyze existing art but composes alternatives to it (or uses it as a step toward achieving alternatives).

How are these alternatives invented? One element of the practice is the manifesto, amounting to a discourse on method—a rhetoric or poetics—for a new genre or mode of production: a program of experimentation. In teaching theory heuretically a seminar tries out some of these vanguard poetics, considered as experiments in representation, in the same way that a composition course presents models of the essay to teach the poetics of academic writing. The goal of heuretics is not only to reproduce historical inventions (to learn about the vanguard or any other rhetoric/poetics from the inside, through the experience of making works in those styles) but also to invent new poetics. It turns out that it is possible to learn to write a theory of poetics in the same way that one learns to write interpretations or critiques. Undergraduates have been learning to write "critically" for several decades now, but the production of theories on which criticism is based remains as mysterious as once were the techniques of interpretation and critique. In an experimental humanities, students (and teachers) learn to write original poetics. The value of these poetics may then be tested by using them to see what sorts of work they help the students (or any investigator) to generate. In the heuretic classroom, students become producers as well as consumers of theory.

I want to acknowledge the support and inspiration of friends, colleagues, and students at the University of Florida who have contributed to the genesis of this study. My biggest debt is to Robert Ray and the other members of the Florida Research Ensemble for discussions and projects from which I have been learning a distinctive approach to cultural studies. Thanks also to the members of the Florida Media Arts Center (Gainesville), Public Domain (Atlanta), and the Critical Art Ensemble (Tallahassee). *Heuretics* was written during a sabbatical leave funded by the University of Florida. None of my work would be possible without the support of my family, especially my wife, Kathy, our boys, Ty and Lee, and even our *cattt,* Foster.

P A R T   O N E

HOW TO MAKE
A THEORY OF METHOD

*It could be said that the social is given immediately with a phrase universe
(be it the one presented by the tail of a cat).*

Jean-François Lyotard

1

GRAMMATOLOGY

Theory is assimilated into the humanities in two principal ways—by critical interpretation and by artistic experiment. "Heuretics," the latter approach, functions at the same level of generality as "hermeneutics." Theorists from Plato to Derrida have influenced the making of arts and letters as much as they have their analysis and interpretation (and often have been influenced in turn by the arts as much as by argument). Recognizing this fact opens an opportunity for a heuretic pedagogy. A review of the history of the arts indicates that the criticism that has been written and the art works that have been created are only a fraction of the kinds of things that *could* have been developed. Artists (and critics) in our century, for example, have favored Freud and Marx as generative resources, as in the well-known cases of the surrealist uses of Freud and the Soviet vanguard's adaptation of Marx to the arts, including manifestos by Dziga-Vertov and Eisenstein, among others. On the critical side, the products of psychoanalytic hermeneutics or ideological critique are well known.

Other equally substantial cases of theorists who have influenced art come to mind. Wittgenstein is as important to the conceptual or "language art" movement as to such critical developments as "ordinary language" philosophy. Structuralism was as important in the making of art as it was in the critical thinking of the human sciences. A heuretic curriculum teaches the different applications of a theory together, noting the *circulation* or dissemination of a cultural invention.

Roland Barthes's insight into structuralism as "an activity" may be generalized in this respect as a heuretic principle: "There exist certain writers, painters, musicians, in whose eyes a certain exercise of structure (and not only its thought) represents a distinctive experience, and both analysts and creators must be placed under the common sight of what we might call *structural man,* defined not by his ideas or his languages but by his imagination—by the way in which he mentally experiences structure" (Barthes, 1972b: 149). One implication of this statement (emended to read "men and women") is a challenge to the specialized divisions of knowledge presently organizing the university, which might be reformed by teaching as an *activity.* Heuretics contributes to what Barthes referred to as "the return of the poetician"—one who is concerned with how a work is *made.* This concern does not stop with analysis or comparative scholarship but conducts such scholarship in preparation for the design of a rhetoric/poetics leading to the production of new work.

Barthes characterized surrealism as an anticipation of structural literature in that it was experienced as an activity, specifically as "the controlled succession of a certain number of mental operations" (149). I read Breton as an example, as a relay, of how to appropriate a theory for the design of a method. The relevant question for heuretic reading is not the one guiding criticism (according to the theories of Freud, Marx, Wittgenstein, Derrida, and others: What might be the *meaning* of an existing work?) but one guiding a generative experiment: Based on a given theory, how might *another* text be composed?

To study Freud as an inventor, for example, is to observe the gradual dissemination of his ideas through a range of disciplines and institutions and into daily life (thus completing a cycle, since he drew upon these other institutions for many of his insights). To point out that a given theory lacks a politics (as has been said of deconstruction) or an aesthetics (as was said of Marxism) is not to refute that theory but to call for an invention. Nor is just one politics or aesthetics or pedagogy available in a theory but many, depending on who is doing the inventing and within the practices of what institution. Theory is only one ingredient in the formula of a cultural invention.

Surrealism

André Breton's invention of surrealism may be generalized as a sample of the generative approach to writing theory. Invention spreads by emulation (Hindle). To emulate Breton is to consider his "Surrealist Manifesto" as a discourse on method and take it as a model for my own project; its lesson is not limited to surrealism but extends to poetics as such. Another motive for starting with surrealism has to do with my interest in Derrida. As Elizabeth Roudinesco observes, "Within the history of psychoanalysis in France, the Derridian project was in part a renewal of the Surrealist gesture. . . . That problematic exists in Derrida, but in a different manner, and reemerged during a period when active Surrealism had disappeared from the French intellectual scene. . . . Nor did he draw on any Surrealist source. But it is as though his project, in the crisscrossings of its inquiries, came to occupy the place left vacant by Surrealist contestation" (387). One path to a Derridean discourse on method passes through the invention of surrealism.

How can an invention such as surrealism, rooted in a particular historical and cultural moment, be simulated in the heuretic experiment? The first step is to appropriate the manifesto format, which is not specific to surrealism, nor to the vanguard for that matter, since it is related to the entire tradition of discourses on method. The heuretic question addressed to the "Manifesto of Surrealism" is: How was it made? It is after all the story of an invention, a recounting of how surrealism was discovered, leading up to its formulation as a rhetoric/poetics. This story is perfectly familiar, almost a cliché by now, but since I want to use it as a map, it bears repeating.

This story of invention unfolds partly as a narrative and partly as an argumentative essay. To read it in terms of the classic model, the opening is the *exordium,* involving the reader emotively in the cause of the piece (Barthes, 1988: 78), seducing an interest by appealing to the *doxa* of the audience—its shared belief in childhood as a moment of freedom and the value of freedom as such. The problem is posed at once: everyday adult existence, organized by the demands of practicality, has suppressed all other modes of thought. The plan of the piece as a whole is anticipated in the general appeal to dreams as a resource for recovering a place for imagination in a world dominated by a narrowly defined logic. An inventive culture requires the broadest possible criterion of what is relevant.

In the *Narratio* — the account of the facts involved in the cause, supported by various kinds of descriptions (80)—Breton reviews a tradition in letters that supports his plan to base a problem-solving method on dreams. This tradition includes a variety of works from fairy tales to certain experiments by his contemporaries, such as the cubist poets. Also part of the facts of the situation is the existence of the theoretical work of Freud and the scientific legitimation of dreams in psychoanalysis. In the *Confirmatio* — the account of the arguments or "proofs"—Breton surveys the techniques invented to turn psychoanalytic theory into art, a practice countering the reign of logic, summarized as a formula or set of instructions. The *Epilogue* marks the conclusion of the performance with a summation of the feeling of the whole, declaring a "complete non-conformism."

Within this frame of argumentation, a story may also be discerned. One aspect of the story is the "eureka anecdote," marking the moment or flash of insight.

> One evening, therefore, before I fell asleep, I perceived, so clearly articulated that it was impossible to change a word, but nonetheless removed from the sound of any voice, a rather strange phrase which came to me without any apparent relationship to the events in which I was then involved, a phrase which seemed to me insistent, a phrase, if I may be so bold, *which was knocking at the window:* ... "There is a man cut in two by the window," but there could be no question of ambiguity, accompanied as it was by the faint visual image of a man walking cut halfway up by a window perpendicular to the axis of his body. Beyond the slightest shadow of a doubt, what I saw was the simple reconstruction in space of a man leaning out a window. (Breton, 21–22)

Part of the story, too, is Breton's reading of Freud, whose theories confirmed and directed Breton's project. The project is explicitly formulated in terms of several experiments, as in the section, "Secrets of the Art of Surrealist Magic," containing explicit directions or instructions for automatic writing. "Supply yourself with writing materials, after having settled yourself in a place as favorable as possible to the mind's concentration on itself. Attain the most passive or receptive state of mind possible.... Write quickly with no preconceived subject, so quickly that you retain nothing and are not tempted to re-read" (29). These directives could be joined with the instructions for "How to Write False Novels": "Here are some rather dissimilar characters: their names in your handwriting are a question of capital letters and they will behave with the same ease towards active verbs as the impersonal pronoun *it* towards words like *rains, is, must be,* etc.... Thus provided with a small number of physical and moral characteristics, these beings who in truth owe you so little will no longer swerve from a certain line of conduct to which you need only apply yourself." Breton adds that these instructions are equally useful for producing "false criticism."

Manifesto

"The Manifesto of Surrealism," and for that matter all of the manifestos of the avant-garde, belong to the tradition of the discourse on method. A comparison of Breton's manifesto with the various classics of method reveal that they tend to include a common set of elements, which are representable for mnemonic reference by the acronym *CATTt* (Ulmer, 1991b). The CATTt includes the following operations:

C = Contrast (opposition, inversion, differentiation)
A = Analogy (figuration, displacement)
T = Theory (repetition, literalization)
T = Target (application, purpose)
t = Tale (secondary elaboration, representability)

Consider how each of the operations is manifested in the first discourse explicitly devoted to the concept and procedure of method—Plato's *Phaedrus* (Gilbert, 3).

Contrast. The theorist (Plato in this case) begins by pushing away from an undesirable example or prototype, whose features provide an inventory of qualities for an alternative method. Plato defines his own position in opposition to that of the Sophists. The oppositional or marginalized stance of the avant-garde is the hyperbolic culmination of this opening move of method.

Analogy. Method becomes invention when it relies on analogy and chance (Buchler, 14). If methods tend to be *practiced* as algorithms, their *invention* is heuristic (heuretics is a heuristic approach to theory). To help invent the dialectic, Plato relies on an *analogy* between proper rhetoric and medicine. "In both cases there is a nature that we have to determine, the nature of the body in the one, and of soul in the other, if we mean to be scientific and not content with our empirical routine when we apply medicine and diet to induce health and strength, or words and rules of conduct to implant such convictions and virtues as we desire" (*Phaedrus*, 270b).

Theory. In each case the theorist generates a new theory based on the authority of another theory whose argument is accepted as a literal rather than a figurative analogy. The new theory will include in one register a literal repetition of a prior theory, modified, of course, by its interaction with the other elements of the CATTt. The analogy is drawn in this category from an abstract practice rather than a concrete one. Socrates obviously fulfills this function for Plato. The general theoretical position espoused by the Platonic Socrates concerns Pythagorean mathematics. In the Western tradition of method, mathematics has been the favorite authorizing theory for invention in other areas.

Target. The theorist has in mind an area of application that the new method is designed to address. The target is often identifiable in terms of an institution whose needs have motivated the search for the method. Thus *Target* supplies an inventory out of what is lacking or missing, or out of the excess of a new situation for which no practices yet exist. Plato's target is education. Indeed, method is the discourse of School as an institution, whose premise is that learning is transferable.

Tale. The "t" is the CATT's tail/tale, reminding me that the invention, the new method, must itself be represented in some form or genre. The tale conveying the method discovered by means of the CATT operations often turns out to be a dramatization of the theory of knowledge appropriate for the human subject envisioned by (or presumed by) the *Theory*. Plato's dialogues represented his premise that learning must be face-to-face conversation. His discourse on method did what it said (was a showing as well as a telling).

Phaedrus is the prototype for all subsequent "well-made" discourses on method. The implication is that, in principle, the other slots of the CATT could be generated by choosing the tale first and then imagining the learning experience appropriate to it. Breton's "tale," the style of his essay, is that of the "manifesto"— a polemical attack on the worldview of "realism"—dramatizing the learning style of the vanguard. This form inherits the aggression manifested first in the military vanguard, such as the spearheading and guerilla tactics typical of the French foreign legion, and then in the political vanguard, as in the polemics of Marx's *Communist Manifesto.*

The other features of the CATTt are easily identified in Breton.

Contrast: His aesthetic is first formulated in opposition to the conventions and logic of realist/naturalist literature. It is worth noting in this context that Breton's "eureka" anecdote, about the "man cut in half by a window," suggests that surrealism sides with the sophist Lysias against Socrates. Socrates' method (arrangement) aims for organic unity, "on the analogy of a single natural body with its pairs of like-named members, right arm or leg, as we say, and left," contrasted with the sophist's disarray: "We are not to attempt to hack off parts like a clumsy butcher" (Plato, 511).

Analogy. The new mode of thought is compared to dreaming and other "dreamlike" discourses such as that of the insane. But the more fundamental analogy (which is not merely parodistic) is with science or scientific experimentation (Carrouges, 313). Again, there is the reminder of Plato's analogy of rhetoric with medicine. Breton and Aragon had been medical students (they met at Val-de-Grâce Hospital), while Soupault, son of a renowned doctor, refused medicine as a career. The literary approach to Freud, that is, was self-consciously distinguished from the medical, clinical one (Roudinesco, 5) and led to a less favorable attitude toward the "organic."

Theory. The features of the new poetics are explicitly generated in relation to Freud's psychoanalysis in an operation that, according to Roudinesco, is more analogical than theoretical. But this analogical use of a prior theory is the norm in the tradition of method. Breton visited Freud to consult with him about his poetics, but the latter claimed not to understand what the Frenchman was talking about.

Target. Although the immediate domain of application is the arts, Breton also intended to change the status of art itself, constituting it rather as a practice of daily life better characterized as "politics" than "art." Surrealism, that is, represents a critique of bourgeois ideology by proposing and performing alternative attitudes and behaviors intended for the institutions of Family and Entertainment.

Counter-Cartesian

One of the best-known examples of the tradition of method is Descartes's *Discourse on Method.* To get a feel for how the CATTt may become generative (and for how to write "false criticism"— generated rather than "thought"), I want to undertake not a complete application of dream style but a simple transformation of Descartes. An exercise in "false criticism," using a simple reversal, could imitate a procedure that Socrates showed to be so obvious as to go without saying. After enumerating the qualities of the lover, Socrates breaks off his speech, much to the dismay of Phaedrus, who wants to hear what might be said for the "nonlover." "I tell you, in one short sentence, that to each evil for which I have abused the one party there is a corresponding good belonging to the other. So why waste words? All has been said that needs saying about them both" (489). Still, as the disappointment of his pupil indicates, it may be more productive to articulate a sheer contrary than Socrates is willing to admit in the context of his dialogue.

To begin this articulation, analyze the operation of the categories in Descartes's *Discourse,* and then revise it to say the opposite. Of course this revised *Discourse* will not yet be a new method, since *Contrast* is only one of the elements of the CATTt. I can imagine, in any case, that my revision is the one that Descartes's

"Evil Deceiver" might have written. Part of the interest of this exercise is that so many theorists of the contemporary paradigm have declared themselves to be anti-Cartesians. One caveat concerns the dialectical irony that opposites remain linked as a pair in a dualism; this is why *Contrast* does not suffice by itself to generate a new method. Indeed, no one of the elements alone suffices, not even theory itself. Still, the formula recognizes that it takes theory to make theory.

Descartes's CATTt may be summarized as follows: C = scholasticism; A = geometry; T = theology; T = natural science; t = autobiography. The strategy is to identify the central point of each of the six books of the *Discourse* and then accept its opposite as a principle of the new antimethod. The strategy is heuristic, employing several ad hoc rules that require continuous decisions and selections (there is no "algorithm" for this exercise). The chief such rule is to read the *Discourse* at the level of its particulars—its examples, analogies, and evidence—rather than at the level of its arguments. The antimethod will break the link between the exposition and the abstract arguments that provide the coherence of the piece. (This rule may be recognized as a "deconstructive" version of the commutation test). Accept Descartes's particulars, that is, but offer a different (for my exercise, an *opposite*) generalization at each point, to carry the examples elsewhere, to displace them. The idea is to strip off the level of argument and replace it with an opposite argument that should in turn be made similarly coherent (secondary elaboration). What follows is a sketch of one possible passage through the *Discourse,* juxtaposing an analysis of each book with its contrary.

"A Discourse against Method"

Book One. Problem: how to avoid being deceived, how to avoid error. Warning example: Don Quixote. "Thus it happens that those who regulate their behavior by the examples they find in books are apt to fall into the extravagances of the knights of romances and undertake projects beyond their ability to complete or hope for things beyond their destiny."

ANTI-ONE (contrary). *Problem: inhibiting effect of concern with error. Take Don Quixote as a positive emblem. Rely on fictional extravagances as sources of invention.*

Book Two. Rules of the method (architectural metaphor): Don't destroy your dwelling until you have someplace else to live. Unity of style is best. Steps: (1) Accept only that which is self-evident, clear, and distinct. (2) Analyze. Break issue into smallest parts. (3) Synthesize. Order items from simplest to most complex. (4) Check your work to be sure nothing is omitted.

ANTI-TWO. *Rules (building metaphor): strong version — raze the city: weak version — deface public buildings. Design of the architecture: many hands are better than one; plurality is better than unity; let the evolution of the city show, so that its history is manifest in the mixed styles of the buildings.*

Antimethod steps: (1) Any starting point is fine; no matter how absurd the idea, do not judge it. (2) Take the problem as a whole; treat it as a gestalt; cast it in the form of an image. (3) Juxtapose this gestalt with other images at random. (4) Assume that any given part suffices, that completeness is not necessary.

Book Three. Moral rules: (1) Obey the customs of one's country; reject all excess. (2) Act resolutely once a decision is made: "I patterned my behavior on that of travelers, who, finding themselves lost in a forest, must not wander about, now turning this way, now that, but should go as straight as they can in the direction they first select and not change the direction except for the strongest reasons." (3) Change one's desires rather than the established order. (4) Review all the known occupations in order to choose the best one.

ANTI-THREE. *Moral rules: (1) Mock and parody the customs of one's country. (2) Wander aimlessly (vagabondage). (3) Follow one's desire. (4) Do not look or seek anything in particular, but let things come or happen as they will.*

Book Four. Proof of God and the soul. "I think, therefore I am" is certain. Use geometry, formulate a version of the ontological proof to show that the existence of God is logical. Accept only reason, not imagination, in the proof.

ANTI-FOUR. [In this instance, it is too easy, too uninteresting, merely to propose atheism as the opposite. Therefore, pose an opposition to the category itself (religion)]. *Take entertainment as the primary dimension of experience. Cogito: I am without importance, therefore I play. Imagination and dream are more reliable than reason.*

Book Five. Applications to physics and the body. Fundamental distinction between man and machine (the superiority of the human over the animal, of the spiritual over the organic).

ANTI-FIVE. *The body is the source of value and the ground of action. There is no distinction between human and machine, between living and dead or artificial memory and mind. Take the machine as model for mind.*

Book Six. Withhold my insights; others seek only to make a reputation, but I am the one best suited to science. The purpose of science is to master nature.

ANTI-SIX. *Anyone could do this, could discover these things and write this discourse. Seek publicity rather than work. Abandon all attempts at mastery and renounce the ambition to master nature.*

It is perhaps worth considering that if this sketch for an anti-method were fleshed out into an essay, it could serve as a manifesto for much of what has gone on in the experimental arts and theory of the twentieth century. This correspondence may be read in several ways, as suggesting the predictive power of the CATTt or the lack of imagination of our century. Perhaps if the CATTt were applied to Descartes more self-consciously, more systematically—in the heuretics laboratory, for example, coordinating all the operations involved in the invention of a method—a student might generate a "false discourse on method" that would be not just contrary to Descartes but completely different.

There is a certain equivalence in "false criticism," in any case, between dreamwork and analysis, promising that inventions may be *written* — generated—without having to be "thought" first.

Freud explained that dreams could be translated into critical discourse, given an understanding of how the dreamwork distorted the latent dream by means of condensation, displacement, dramatization, putting into images, secondary elaboration. He observed further the dialectical nature of the relationship between critical and dream writing: "I shall describe the process which transforms the latent into manifest content of dreams as the 'dream-work.' The counterpart to this activity—one which brings about a transformation in the opposite direction—is already known to us as the work of analysis" (Freud, 1989: 148).

Here is an observation that has not found its practice. As a heuretic experiment, I might take any essay from the library of criticism and apply dreamwork to it to generate in this way its "dream." Every critique, every argument, every analysis, every theory carries this "false dream" within itself. The lesson is that any existing discourse on method may be analysed, and any new method generated, in terms of the CATTt.

My procedure now is to select the materials for these categories, assumed as an *inventio,* and emulating the tradition from Plato to Breton, to compose my own discourse on method. The experiment is meant to be generalizable to other materials, the procedures transferable, with the CATTt functioning consistently across different contexts. The CATTt is not itself "Derridean" anymore than it is Platonic or Cartesian. The modest proposal is: to invent an electronic academic writing the way Breton invented surrealism, or the way Plato invented dialectics: to do with "Jacques Derrida" (and this name marks a slot, a *passepartout* open to infinite substitution) what Breton did with Freud (or—why not?—what Plato did with Socrates).

2

HYPERMEDIA

The Logic of Cyberspace

Most of the resources for the CATTt that will guide the making of my discourse on method come from grammatology: *Theory* from Jacques Derrida; *Contrast* from book practices such as argumentative writing; *Target* from the electronic apparatus applied within the institutions of education. These items are predetermined by the program of grammatology, which is concerned with the history and theory of writing.

Writing as technology is a memory machine, with each apparatus finding different means to collect, store, and retrieve information outside of any one individual mind (in rituals, habits, libraries, or databases). Part of the contribution of hypermedia as

Target for my method is the models of memory developed for it, inasmuch as individuals and societies tend to internalize as forms of reasoning the operations of their tools. The current state of computer interface design, then, may hold some valuable lessons for a Derridean heuretics.

Taking up the design of hypermedia interface in terms of Derrida's theories requires specification of my assignment as it concerns the technologies of language. The technology that most interests me—because it represents an integration of most of the features of electronics—is the convergence of video and the computer in hypermedia (anticipating the eventual need for a grammatology of virtual reality). With this equipment it is possible to "write" in multimedia, combining in one composition all the resources of pictures, words, and sound (picto-ideo-phonographic writing).

For grammatology, hypermedia is the technological aspect of an electronic *apparatus* (referring to an interactive matrix of technology, institutional practices, and ideological subject formation). My interest is not only in the technology itself but also in the problem of inventing the practices that may institutionalize electronics in terms of schooling. These practices are not medium specific: rather, they entail a revision of the liberal arts *trivium* (grammar, rhetoric, logic) open to writing on a screen as well as on paper. It may be that eventually the screen will replace the page (and the database replace the library) as the support of all academic work. *Heuretics,* meanwhile, is intended as a means to achieve that transition in the most productive way, including using book strategies to help with the invention process and revising paper practices in the light of the new possibilities of thought manifested in electronic technology.

Part of working heuretically is to use the method that I am inventing while I am inventing it, hence to practice hyperrhetoric myself, which is assumed to have something in common with the dream logic of surrealism. For, as Jay Bolter noted, the practices of writing in a new technology are fundamentally different from the conventions of the treatise that presently dominate academic work. This difference in "logics" is the point of departure for imagining what a new rhetoric will do that does not argue but that replaces the logic governing argumentative writing with associational networks. Bolter notes that Derrida (along with a number of other critics, including Barthes in *S/Z,* as well as many authors of experimental literature) is already writing this way, simulating electronic effects in experimental books such as *Glas.* It is helpful in this context to recall that all the devices of the book apparatus, which are codified in the treatise (and enforced in practice from the five-part essay through the doctoral dissertation to the book that secures tenure), were themselves invented as the "interface" for print technology.

In this context of writing as a "social machine" it is easier to understand the opposition to Derrida—especially the insulting attacks upon him and some of his peers—when we recall that one of the men most credited with inventing some of the key features of the book interface (such as the spatial display of outlining)—Peter Ramus ("the first modern theorist of method" [Desan, 11])—was also in his day the target of extraordinary anger. As with Derrida, Ramus was guilty of tampering with the conventions of established logic. It has been suggested that his murder during the St. Bartholomew's Day Massacre of Protestants (despite a decree of protection from the king) was linked in some way to the extreme hatred his work aroused among his colleagues.

The death of Ramus—defenestrated, decapitated, and thrown into the Seine on the third day of the massacre—adds another dismemberment to the body count (recalling the sophists who butchered the organic body of a composition and Breton's man cut in half by a window) and suggests some relationship between discourses on method and murder. The death of Socrates has to be included in this dark formula of the fate of those who alter the reasoning practices of their age. Will Derrida, declared by a group of Cambridge University professors to be an enemy of science and the Enlightenment, escape assassination?

At one point Ramus's work was condemned by royal decree

for having "impudently and arrogantly" undermined the (Aristotelian) logic respected by all nations but "of which he himself was ignorant" (Desan, 79). This "impudence" is of the same sort embraced by the surrealists. As a result Ramus's books were suppressed and he was forbidden to teach or to write about philosophy. John M. Ellis's *Against Deconstruction* is not alone in taking a similar line against Derrida. Focusing his attack specifically on the claim that deconstruction is "a new and different logic," Ellis displays the full measure of that frustration Bolter mentioned. If he cannot refute a discourse that is alogical, Ellis wants at least to discredit the defenses made of this otherness.

> Why not examine it as well as use it? To this the answer tends to be that the alternative logic cannot be described and stated as can the old because to describe and state *is* to use the old logic. But we must draw some limits here: granted that standard propositional logic might be inadequate and some other kind might be needed, we still could not allow the claim that a different kind of logic could not be characterized in any way; that would be to exceed the boundaries of all possible logics. A logic must work in some way, and it must be possible to show how it operates and to characterize this operation. (Ellis, 4)

At what point does a style of reasoning cease to be "logical"? We have been aware for some time, after all, of the limitations of the finest institutional instantiations of logical and conceptual reasoning—of critique and hermeneutics in the human sciences, and of empiricism in the natural sciences—to the point that critique has become cynical. As Peter Sloterdijk explained, what was not foreseen in the invention of conceptual reason was the possibility of "enlightened false consciousness," which arose when the enlightened got into power. What these *Aufklärer* learned was that knowledge can be resisted; that knowing may leave people *unaffected;* that "people stick to their positions for anything but 'rational' reasons." Therefore critique developed, "besides the friendly invitation to a conversation—a second, combative stance" (Sloterdijk, 15). Critique became a "theory of struggle," a weapon against others, and an "instrument for gaining inner strength"; it thus "acquires a cruel aspect that, if it ever really admits to being cruel, claims to be nothing more than a reaction to the cruelties of 'ideology.'" The result or effect can be a dogma as oppressive or manipulative as that of the opponent whose mechanism of power was the object of the critique.

Most of the writers calling attention to the symptoms of the closure of conceptual reason do not want to abandon the principles of the Enlightenment. They retain a desire to act in the world, to make life better for all humanity, but they admit to an experience of impasse.

> How can intellectuals be *Aufklärer* at this precise moment in history: ... What forces do we have at hand against the power of instrumental reason and against the cynical reasoning of institutionalized power? ... How can one remain an *Aufklärer* if the Enlightenment project of disenchanting the world and freeing it from myth and superstition must indeed be turned against enlightened rationality itself? How can we reframe the problem of ideology critique and of subjectivity? (Huyssen, xiii)

What each one calls for at the same time, in different ways, is invention. It is time to craft some new means for thought and action. Sloterdijk lists as his primary motivation a veneration for philosophy, thinking of "the Greek dawn, when *theoria* was beginning and when, inconceivably and suddenly, like everything clear, understanding found its language. Are we really culturally too old to repeat such experiences?" (Sloterdijk, xxxviii). My project is to find an electronic *theoria*.

Poststructural Computing

Showing the process of a method in the making responds at least partially to an appeal for a characterization of a new reasoning (a logic of invention) that leads to the reinvention of *theoria* for an electronic apparatus. My claim is not that my discourse on method is Derridean but only that I am making it out of Derrida. Derrida himself, after all, has taken a great deal of trouble to reply to those who attacked deconstruction during the Paul de Man controversy, even calling for "an ethics of discussion" against the poison pens and nescience of those who display an attitude of 'I-do-not-want-to-read" (Derrida, 1989b: 823). So he, at least, is willing to argue, even if argument is displaced (but not eliminated) in hyperrhetoric.

Several influential commentators have observed that hypermedia "literalizes" or represents the material embodiment of poststructuralist (mostly French) theories of text. Many of the most controversial notions of textualism expressed by recent French critics (for example, the death of the author or the decentering of meaning), notions that seemed bizarre in the context of the book apparatus, are simply literal qualities of hypermedia. Here my situation could be described in terms of abduction as invention:

Some surprising phenomenon, P, has been observed. ($P =$ the features of hypermedia)
P would be explicable as a matter of course if H were true. ($H =$ Derrida's theories)
Hence, there is reason to think that H is true.

The most constructive attitude to this (unexpected) convergence of a theoretical school with a technology is the one stated by George Landow, that hypermedia now constitutes a laboratory for the testing of poststructuralist (or even more specifically, "deconstructive") theory (Delany and Landow, 6). Although these two phenomena evolved independently, it is reasonable to expect that each will or could influence the other as they come into communication, with deconstruction likely to be changed as much as it will in turn change the direction of computer applications. My assumption is that the theory is no more fixed or "arrested" than is the technology (or than is writing itself).

What role might a heuretic application of grammatological theory (based on Derrida's "poststructuralist" textuality) play in the appropriation of hypermedia for academic writing? This is the question that my method addresses. A preliminary issue related to my use of Derrida as theorist concerns the need to distinguish between Derrida and certain related practices of literary criticism (deconstruction). Jay Bolter, for example, identifies Derrida with a narrow concept of deconstruction, one characterized as "reducing texts to a play of signs that by its very nature can never end. Our reading of all texts becomes an endless transit from one passage to another, never out into a 'real' world beyond signs" (Bolter, 204). He takes notice mostly of a certain "critical" dimension of Derrida's theory, which he says is tied irrevocably to a critique of "the transcendental signified" that would finally delimit meaning. "While traditional humanists and deconstructionists have been battling over the arbitrary, self-referential character of writing, computer specialists, oblivious to this struggle, have been building a world of electronic signs in which the battle is over." Even if this battle were settled in favor of deconstruction, that movement itself, according to Bolter, may have little else to contribute to the next stage of development, since "it is incapable of acquiescing in the arbitrary and limited character of writing."

While my experiment supports Bolter's account in most other respects, his view that "the computer takes us beyond deconstruction" needs to be qualified. "Deconstruction tells what electronic writing is not. We still need a new literary theory to achieve a positive understanding of electronic writing" (166). Whatever the problems with "deconstruction" as literary criticism might be, my point is that the grammatological dimension of Derrida's theory (which Bolter neglects) is precisely the source for this positive account (it will be the burden of my method to generate out of Derridean grammatology the terms of an electronic academic writing).

The perception, shared by a number of critics interested in educational hypermedia, that hypermedia computing is inherently poststructuralist (postmodern, deconstructive, textual) raises several issues immediately. First is the fact that theorists of this technology have stressed that hypermedia as an apparatus need not and should not be driven entirely by the hardware and the technicians who design it. There is no inevitability, no technological determinism leading to some dystopian (or utopian) future social condition. Even if many of the applications still come from the side of the hardware, that need not be the case. As Ted Nelson has argued, the design process should and could begin with conceptual and psychological considerations and then work to the mechanics (the hardware is more flexible than most humanists might realize) (Nelson, 3). The design process in any case is carried out by interdisciplinary teams, and, at least in principle, the designers indicate a desire for new ideas that might come from other areas, including the liberal arts.

At the same time, the fact is that until very recently (with the development of "Storyspace," for example), poststructuralism has not informed the invention of the computer as equipment (even if its theories have anticipated the practices of an electronic apparatus). A considerable amount of theoretical activity has been associated with the computer—the whole field of cognitive science, for example—but the practical value of poststructuralism in this area was not appreciated. Part of the interest of including hypermedia in heuretics derives from the potential long-range importance of this alliance between a seemingly marginalized theory and a new technology.

The Frontier of Knowledge

Will the disciplinary organization of knowing (if not science itself) be different in an electronic apparatus? Francis Bacon's gesture at the beginnings of science, associating the scientific enlightenment with the discovery, exploration, and ultimately the colonization of the "new world," suggests one way to open up this question. This association continues today in the American exploration of "the final frontier," outer space, as in the flight of

Magellan, the unmanned spacecraft sent to investigate the planet Venus. The launching of the space shuttle *Atlantis* from Cape Canaveral with six astronauts and a military surveillance satellite on board in November 1991 makes explicit the passage from ancient to modern approaches to the "cosmos."

The question raised by this metaphor concerns the relationship of curiosity (the *desire* to know) in Discipline discourse to curiosity in the other institutions of culture. The protests led by the American Indian Movement (AIM) against the Columbus quincentenary have implications for science, in that the image of the ship carrying explorers to a "new world" has served as the chief metaphor of research in Western civilization. The metaphor of "the frontiers of knowledge" is ubiquitous, a reflex, a habit of mind that shapes much of our thinking about inquiry. As Hans Blumenberg noted, different epochs of the Western tradition (not to mention different civilizations) have had different attitudes to curiosity and set different restrictions on it, different limitations of relevance ranging from liberatory (encouraging a turning over of every rock just to see what might be under it) to censorious (condemning the vice of poking into matters that should not concern humankind). The attitude that Freud expressed in *Beyond the Pleasure Principle* should not be taken for granted nor assumed as "natural" or "obvious": "What follows is speculation, often far-fetched speculation," Freud wrote. "It is an attempt to follow out an idea consistently, out of curiosity to see where it will lead" (Freud, in Blumenberg, 448).

The modern age began with the rehabilitation of theoretical curiosity from the moral quarantine imposed on it during the Middle Ages (238). "Method," the "key word" of this beginning, was associated with the metaphor of the voyager, and the genealogy of seafaring was a "lasting theme in connection with the question of the legitimacy of man's curiosity" (267). "The self-consciousness of the modern age found in the image of the Pillars of Hercules and their order, *Nec plus ultra* [No further], which Dante's Odysseus still understood (and disregarded) as meaning 'Man may not venture further here,' the symbol of its new beginning and of its claim directed against what had been valid until then" (340). The "beyond" in Freud's title and in the titles of so many modern books marks the legacy of "beyond the Pillars of Hercules."

Columbus carried the epic of Odysseus into history as a figure of "curiosity rewarded," leading to Bacon's claim of a *right to knowledge.* In theorizing his method, Bacon had in mind the compass that made possible the voyages of discovery. With the compass, method is not a matter of having a predetermined goal, but of "holding to a path on which, in the field of the unknown, new land will eventually appear":

> The discovery of the compass enables one to imagine a net of coordinates laid over reality and independent of its structures, in which the unsuspected can be caught and arranged. . . . One may hope that nature conceals in its womb still more, of greater importance, which lies entirely outside the familiar paths of the power of imagination and which one can only be sure of finding through the systematization of accident. The tendency of Bacon's method is to set the human mind in controlled motion. (389)

The legacy of Bacon's method persists even in the work of theorists attempting to think "beyond" the modern episteme. Indeed, any attempt at a *post*modernist "method" is contradictory (an impossible possibility). Jean-François Lyotard's image of a search for the rules of a new discourse continues the seafaring scene, relayed from Kant's *Critique of Judgment*—the search for "passages" bridging the 'differend' (the lack of translatability between incommensurable genres of discourse), with cognition symbolized as an "archipelago": "Each genre of discourse would be like an island; the faculty of judgment would be, at least in part, like an admiral or like a provisioner of ships who would launch expeditions from one island to the next, intended to present to one island what was found (or invented, in the archaic sense of the word) in the other, and which might serve the former as an 'as-if intuition' with which to validate it" (Lyotard, 131).

The "differend" names an aspect of what is at stake in chorography (the name of the method I will have invented) as well: to write the paradigm, or to write the discourses of all the institutions of the popcycle, is to negotiate the passages among genres separated by differends. The very possibility of nationhood depends upon finding these passages. Chorography is designed to bring into invention the thought of "nation" as "place": "the Idea of a nation, the Idea of the creation of value. These situations are not the referents of knowledge phrases. There exist no procedures instituted to establish or refute their reality in the cognitive sense. That is why they give rise to differends" (27). And that is also why chorography is an impossible possibility.

Postcolonial Learning

The paradigm of adventure, of voyaging explorers, includes similar statements uttered in different contexts, different institutions, different discourses, concerning the "vehicle" or "diegesis" of the ancient metaphor of method, having to do with "travel." In the paradigm of this metaphor, a commander of the foreign legion, referring to the forts and roads the legion built in order to control North Africa, made a statement that resonates with the metaphor of method. Their mission, he said, was that of "pioneers who open a new country. We are the rugged, primitive laborers who do the hardest work. We are the visionaries who see wonderful possibilities in the future. . . . Every path we have [built] bears the pain of our men. It is they who have opened the way for civilization to come into the heart of this savage country" (Mercer, 255).

An electronic method cites this metaphor because the first theorists of hypermedia, the founders of educational computing, used terms associated with the frontier to characterize their invention. Vannevar Bush (who proposed the Memex library-in-a-desk before hypermedia technology existed) made such an allusion with his call for a "new profession of trailblazers, those who find delight in the task of establishing useful trails through the *indexing vs trains of associations.*

enormous mass of the common record" (Weyer, 89). These trails supplement the bookish mode of indexing by accessing information via "chains of associations." "The user could join any two items, including the user's own materials and notes." Douglas Engelbart thought of the "trailblazers" as working in small groups, constituted as "scouting parties sent ahead to map the pathways for the organization groups to follow.... You also need 'outposts' for these teams" (Engelbart, 29–30).

The inventors of hypermedia elaborated the metaphor of method as travel and settlement of an area into a model for the computer interface—the system of nodes linked into a network that a user negotiates in order to access information. Designers conceived of the "field" of cognition as a landscape, perhaps a "virtual town or amusement park" (Florin, 30). "Using a computer-based hypertext system, students and researchers can quickly follow *trails* of footnotes and related materials without losing their original context.... Explicit connections—links— allow readers to *travel* from one document to another, effectively automating the process of following references in an encyclopedia" (Yankelovich, 82).

The computer is responsible for the most recent "frontier of knowledge" then, bringing into existence a virtual if not a literal new world. Chorography, as a heuretic approach to inventing a "method" useful for this "world," takes into account the present state of imagination and curiosity. The "timing" of chorography is important because hypermedia still lacks a "rhetoric." "While the teaching of classical rhetoric may have waned over the years, an accepted set of conventions about style, syntax, and structure still exists.... No such 'rhetoric' exists for hypertext. To the contrary, it would seem that few of the notions of classical rhetoric can be used in constructing a hyperdocument" (Carlson, in Barrett, 96). But even if the classical rhetoric developed for alphabetic practices is inadequate for electronics, it is a good point of departure for imagining an electronic way of reading, writing, and reasoning.

A point often made in discussions of computers is that advances in technology have far outstripped software and interface design, not to mention social and institutional behaviors. "The only stumbling place for this onrushing brave new world," Alan Kay (often named as "father of the personal computer") observed, "is that all of its marvels will be very difficult to communicate with, because, as always, the user interface design that could make it all simple lags far behind" (Laurel, 204). "A major new direction that should be taken," Kay noted, "is towards a *rhetoric* for programs expressed as something more like essays— or in the hypermedia equivalent of an essay" (203).

Interface

Another name for "rhetoric" in a computer context is "interface"; the whole problem of interface design—giving an ordinary user access to the power of the machine (communication between a user and the tool)—is a fundamental difficulty for the new apparatus. "The way a user interacts with a computer is as important as the computation itself: in other words, the *human interface,* as it has come to be called, is as fundamental to computing as any processor configuration, operating system, or programming environment" ("Multimedia," 89). The invention of a new rhetoric or interface so far has been organized around the problem of finding an appropriate metaphor, something from the world familiar to users, that functions as a model of the system, mediating and giving the user an intuitive feel for how to interact with the equipment.

The first metaphor to reach application came from the book apparatus—the desktop (guiding the design of the Apple Macintosh interface, including index cards, files hidden in folders, a calculator, a phonebook, and so forth) (Laurel, 135). To take advantage of the convergence of media (sound, image, and writing) made possible by digitalization, Apple developed HyperCard (the first mass-distributed hypermedia system).

The model for HyperCard is the 3-by-5 card. A card is represented by a Macintosh screen. As you flip through screens (cards) you read them one after another, as if they were in a stack. Cards can hold any kind of information you want, in any format you want, including pictures. Rather than resting inertly, as on a Rolodex, information can be actively linked to any other point on any other card. Another way to imagine it would be to think of a book that had footnotes that appear only when you clicked on a passage you wanted to know more about. It would carry you to interesting details, which might themselves have footnotes which are footnoted and so on ("HyperCard Software," 102).

Walter Benjamin forsaw what a number of contemporary commentators have suggested—that hypermedia does for scholarship what photography did for portrait painting. "Today the book is already, as the present mode of scholarly production demonstrates, an outdated mediation between two different filing systems. For everything that matters is to be found in the card box of the researcher who wrote it, and the scholar studying it assimilates it into his own card index" (Benjamin, 78). Hypermedia "automates" scholarship (the finding and linking of information), thus making available to "amateurs" the resources once produced and consumed solely by small groups of specialists. Having available a databank or online archive of scholarship makes it possible for anyone to write "with the paradigm."

At the same time, it has been suggested that hypermedia frees scholars from the labor of compilation and indexing—as painters were freed from the primary task of representing the visible world—in order to invent new functions and styles for Discipline discourse. Benjamin's prediction that a "qualitative leap" in writing would emerge out of the new media of his day is even more reasonable in the context of hypermedia. This new writing, "advancing ever more deeply into the graphic regions of its new eccentric figurativeness, will take sudden possession of an adequate factual content" (78).

The technology, however, has already outgrown the interface metaphor of the book or library, a metaphor that was inadequate to begin with. Hypermedia is dynamic, not in the manner of pages to be turned, but in the manner of "a tutor to converse with or . . . as laboratory for conducting experiments. To prevent 'dusty-tome syndrome' electronic 'books' must become nonbooks in both function and name" (Weyer, in Ambron and Hooper, 1988:98). The new metaphor, which is replacing the book or desktop in recent interface design theory, is that of navigating an ocean of information—in short, Bacon's metaphor of Columbus voyaging beyond the Pillars of Hercules turned into a working model for traveling in an information environment.

In the modern (as opposed to archaic) tradition, beginning with Plato and his Academy, experience was posed in terms of problems to be solved. This tradition is associated with geometry as a "morality of motion"—everything in its *right* place, related to the doctrine of the *route* as a right way to proceed. "The Greek sense of *hodos* or 'route' expects rationalization. Our term 'method,' which means a *way* of proceeding but implies rational conduct, comes from the Greek words *meta* plus *hodos*" (Walter, 186). This notion influenced the manner of actual and figurative (theoretical) travel.

> To go the right way, one made a journey to a proper destination, and after the journey out, sought a return or homecoming. The traveler followed instructions, looked for tidings of the route, and depended on escorts, guides, and hosts to help him on his way. Advancing along the route, he was said to 'accomplish' the journey, which was usually understood as a round-trip back to his proper place. The opposite of going the right way was to wander or to go astray.

A "method of invention," however, deconstructs this opposition between returning home and wandering. Like many theorists of method before him, Derrida makes this point by referring to the legend of Odysseus. If *theoria* involves travel, there should be no attempt at "homecoming." "Evoking the same Ulysses, I would insist on that which distinguishes singularity from individuality, and from the totalizing circle.... Ulysses means the circle of return, nostalgia, dwelling, the oikoniomia. From this perspective, I would say that the architect of the next millenium—and of today already—will not be a Ulysses" (Derrida, 1991b:45). Instead, the feeling of method (in design or invention) will be close to that of the double bind or paradoxes of myth—a holding together of what does not "fit," enacted by an "anyone" (person or discipline) that is "a stranger to itself, foreign to itself. And that will be good."

Within the terms of grammatology and deconstruction, it is not possible simply to jump to a different metaphor for research. Such a jump would be easy enough intellectually. The electronic apparatus, however, is a *social machine:* the frontier metaphor is in our habits, our conduct, our emotions, in curiosity itself. My experiment, rather, is to deconstruct the metaphor associating method with colonial exploration, to put it under erasure in a certain way, "paleonymically," remaking "frontier" into *"chora."*

3

EXPERIMENT

Rhetoric

What will research be like in an electronic apparatus? Is it possible to imagine learning and invention that are not cast in the metaphor of a frontier explored by adventurers? The myth of adventure, as Martin Green reminds us, is a "masculinist" myth: "the idea that all human societies have a center where their laws are promulgated and revered, and a frontier where they are partially ignored, but where the law-making power fights life-or-death battles" (Green, 1991:36). This dichotomy, he adds, is imaged as "a campfire around which people cluster and a fringe of darkness where dangers lurk," or as capital cities versus national frontiers, or as "the city's daytime and official activities versus its criminal nightlife": "In all such cases, the frontier requires things of men (and of women) that are different from what the center requires." The electronic apparatus, however, is introducing, at every level of individual and institutional behavior, a *decentered* structuration in which maps designed in terms of centers and peripheries, of frontiers and adventure, no longer correspond to the territory. Choral work, that is, puts the "adventure of knowledge" under erasure, which is to say that it is only prelusive, a mere beginning, a proposal, an experiment.

The strategy of chorography for deconstructing the frontier metaphor of research is to consider this "place" and its "genre" in rhetorical terms—as a *topos*. The project is then to replace *topos* itself (not just one particular setting but *place* as such) with *chora* wherever the former is found in the *trivium*. In order to foreground the foundational function of location in thought, choral writing organizes any manner of information by means of the writer's specific position in the time and space of a culture. In the *inventio* of classical rhetoric, Roland Barthes noted, "place" logically speaking referred to "that in which a plurality of oratorical reasonings coincide" (Aristotle), or to "certain general heads to which can be attached all the proofs used in the various matters treated" (Port-Royal), or to "general opinions which remind those who consult them of all the sides by which a subject can be considered" (Lamy) (Barthes, 1988:64). The metaphors of location for invention, and of "heading," are the most relevant for now.

Why *place*? Because, says Aristotle, in order to remember things, it suffices to recognize the place where they happen to be (place is therefore the element of an association of ideas, of a conditioning, of a training, of a mnemonics); places then are not the arguments themselves but the compartments in which they are arranged. Hence every image conjoining the notion of a space with that of a storage, of a localization with an extraction: a region (where one can find arguments), a *vein of some mineral,* a *circle,* a *sphere,* a *spring,* a *well,* an *arsenal,* a *treasury,* and even a *pigeon-hole.* (65)

The method of invention was characterized analogically as a visit to such places to look for an appropriate statement.

The justification for inventing a method to be called "chorography" is that it is specifically an *electronic* rhetoric, one meant to exploit (but not limited to) the digital convergence of media in hypermedia. The five parts of traditional rhetoric—invention, arrangement, style, delivery, and memory—have operated differently in different historical periods, depending on which of the liberal arts was in ascendancy. "Rhetoric" names not only "persuasive discourse" but also one of the *trivium* of the liberal arts (along with logic and grammar).

As Barthes observed, with the coming of print education shifted from training the orator to training the essayist, causing two of the operations of rhetoric—delivery and memory—to be dropped because they were not relevant to print composition (Barthes, 1988:51). Academic writing, as Jay Bolter reminds us, is governed by a linear, cause-and-effect logic: it is fundamentally argumentative writing. Information is organized hierarchically (represented in the tree diagrams of outlining) and accessed by means of indexing. In contrast, hypermedia is organized as a network, and its "logic" is associational. "It is precisely the lack of a fixed order and commitment to a linear argument that will frustrated those used to working with and writing for the medium of print, just as it will liberate those willing to experiment with a new form of dialogue. For writers of the new dialogue, the task will be to build, in place of a single argument, a structure of possibilities" (Bolter, 1991:119).

In the struggle among the liberal arts for priority, Peter Ramus won the day for logic, for it was in his work that logic appropriated the operations of *inventio* and *dispositio* (the finding and arranging of arguments) and rhetoric was reduced simply to *elocutio* (style) (Barilli, 64). Ramus oversaw, that is, a change in the apparatus (from manuscript to print) that involved institutional practices as much as it did technology.

> The reduction of the elements of intelligibility to the spatial arrangements of printing of the topical logics suggests a further general theorem: the printer's font corresponds to the locus of the topical logics, and the printed page to methodized discourse. This theorem would express no more than a coincidence were it not for the fact that Ramus' notion of method is not only a product of the humanism which sponsors both printing and the topical logics, but also is thought of (by Ramus) as an arrangement of material *in a book*. In this context, "method" actually gains definition and final form as the interior of Ramus' own books become better spatially organized during the epoch when printers were freeing themselves from the manuscript tradition and were learning that the format of printing involves a radically different commitment to space than does the format of a manuscript. (Ong, 310–311)

The methodological innovation initiated by Ramus culminates in the five-paragraph theme that is a fixture of so many twentieth-century textbooks. "The model five-paragraph theme could be laid out on the page with the aid of colored lines, boxes, and arrows. Discourse had shape," due to structuralizing "concepts that were formerly means of invention" and dispersing them graphically within a theme as components of its arrangement (Crowley, 135). "The five-paragraph theme was the most thoroughgoing scheme for spatializing discourse that had appeared in rhetorical theory since Peter Ramus' method of dichotomizing division rendered all the world divisible by halves" (135). The point of Crowley's study of modern and contemporary composition theory is that rhetoric in general, and invention in particular, have disappeared almost completely from the Discipline of writing instruction.

Hypermedia, in the electronic apparatus, requires another radically different commitment to space from that of the book, a shift that chorography addresses in the substitution of *chora* for *topos* as the name for the places of invention. The symmetry within the elements of the apparatus connecting Ramus's logic with the space of the book page recurs in electronics in its own way. "Hypertext linking, reader control, and continual restructuring not only militate against modes of argumentation to which we have become accustomed, but they have other effects. The reader is now faced by a kind of textual randomness" (Delaney and Landow, 9).

The assumption is that changes in the equipment of memory involve changes in people and institutions as well. Chorography as a practice corresponds to recent developments in computing, such as connectionism. Opposed to the classical concept of memory as storing information in some specific locale from which it may be retrieved, connectionist designs of computer memory are based on a different characterization: "Information is not stored anywhere in particular. Rather, it is stored everywhere. Information is better thought of as 'evoked' than 'found.' Rather than imagining that particular neural units encode particular pieces of information, this view has it that information is stored in the relationships among the units and that each unit participates in the encoding of many many memories" (Rummelhart and Norman, 3). These "distributed" memories—which correspond to the qualities of *chora* as space—function by means of pattern making, pattern recognition, pattern generation. It is not that memory is no longer thought of as "place," but that the notion itself of spatiality has changed.

In the hardware of computers, connectionism or parallel processing (multiple low-level memory units linked in a network) is replacing (experimentally) the more standard serial processing (a central processor sequentially addressing large storage units). In short, the change in thinking from linear indexical to network associational—a shift often used to summarize the difference between alphabetic and electronic cognitive styles (or between masculinist and feminist styles, for that matter)—is happening at the level of the technology itself. Hardware and software design are both moving away from the alphabetic metaphors of knowledge within which they originally emerged.

The model of knowledge that dominated the Western tradition during the entire logocentric era—the idea that thinking as such is the logical manipulation of symbols according to a set of rules (Bechtel and Abrahamsen, 10)—is being transformed as part of the move into a new apparatus. The traditional logical mode of reasoning is now understood (deconstructively) to be a special subcase of the larger "illogic" of common sense. Computer hardware is being designed, perversely it seems to some, to perform in the style of commonsense reasoning, whose "irrationality" is based in the neurophysiology of the brain itself. Starting with a pragmatic definition that a "smart" computer is one that ordinary people can use, cognitive science and artificial intelligence are questioning the classic models of rationality, with revolutionary implications for all the institutions of society.

Jeremy Campbell summarized the implications of this "electronic" style as reasoning with memory rather than logic. Smart databases (supported by artificial intelligence systems), designed to operate in terms of commonsense reasoning (depending on how knowledge is organized in memory and how it is evoked) rather than in terms of formal, abstract logic, will have to possess a "culture," which is to say that they will not think in universal or objective terms but with the biases and prejudices of human thinking, including stereotypes. Campbell identifies this reasoning as "intuition," adding that "intuition is really a special case of Baker Street reasoning, where what a person comes to know greatly exceeds the meager evidence of which he is aware" (Campbell, 215).

An important aspect of chorography is learning how to *write* an intuition, and this writing is what distinguishes electronic logic (conduction) from the abductive (Baker Street) reasoning of the detective. In conjunction the intuitions are not left in the thinker's body but simulated in a machine, augmented by a prosthesis (whether electronic or paper). This (indispensable) augmentation of ideological categories in a machine is known in chorography as "artificial stupidity," which is the term used to indicate that a database includes a computerized unconscious.

The chorographer has a different relationship to language and discourse from the one operating in literacy; it is that neither of writer nor reader but of "active receiver." In the same way that the practice of reading privately and silently contributed to the formation of "self," so too will performing hyperrhetoric contribute to a new subjectivation in the electronic apparatus (in which one will have to find a new term of self-reference, neither "parrot" [to use Lacan's example] as in the clan identity of the oral apparatus nor "me" in the individualism of literacy).

In argumentative writing the reader deals with a product or end result of a reasoning process, whereas in hypermedia the process replaces the product—the user works directly with the topics, having access to all the commonplaces stored there, as if encountering what Benjamin called the composer's card box, that which is treated in the essay as "pre-writing." The user of a database, that is, encounters in principle the full paradigm of possibilities through which a multitude of paths may be traced. Argument provided one path and suppressed everything else (even if the oppositional position was presented in a show of objectivity, the goal of the enthymeme was to convince the reader that the solution offered to the problem was the only one possible). In hypermedia the composer constructs an information environment, and the user chooses the path or line through the place provided. The chorographer, then, writes with paradigms (sets), not arguments. One of the profound changes of a hyperrhetoric designed for organizing audiovisual as well as print practices will be the necessary return of delivery and memory and their adaptation to a new social machine.

Verification

The point to emphasize here is that the text that follows is an *experiment:* it is offered not as a proof or assertion of truth but as a trial or test. I offer it as a version of a practice whose value will be determined by those who choose to try it. The experiment might be replicated at any one of several levels.

The level of greatest generality is that of the CATTt. One way to use *Heuretics* would be to respond to this most general level, to test the CATTt itself by filling in the heuristic slots with one's own choices. These choices might be motivated by curiosity about a specific position (as in the case of grammatology), or they could be completely arbitrary, motivated by perversity, random selection, or brainstorming just to see what would happen. In any case, the result may be evaluated in at least two ways: what is learned while designing the method, and what sort of text the method generates. A method that was impossible to apply might still provide a powerful learning experience in the process of its construction. As the history of science shows, experiment teaches as much or more by failure as by success. And for every theory that happens to be taken up and translated into a poetics or rhetoric, many others are left undeveloped on the shelf.

A second level at which to test *Heuretics* would be to accept my CATTt (C = argumentative writing; A = Method acting; T = Derrida; T = hypermedia; t = cinema remake) but to use one's own particulars for some or all of the materials—a different popular work for the remake, different emotional memories for the rehearsal, a different aspect of Derrida's writings, and so on. If the general name for generating a method out of theory is *heuretics,* the particular name of the method I generated is *chorography,* named for the term *chora,* which Derrida borrows from Plato.

While *chorography* as a term is close to *choreography,* it duplicates a term that already exists in the discipline of geography, thus establishing a valuable resonance for a rhetoric of invention concerned with the history of "place" in relation to memory. Within geography "chorological analysis" produces a sense of place "that is similar to the sense of time that comes from the study of history" (Sack, 87), trying to capture a more subjective dimension of spatiality in specific rather than in generic terms.

These unexpected and different factors and associations affect the character of the places and make each generic place different, up to a point. . . . The incorporation of these "exceptional" factors and their interrelationships within a place, area or region is analysed through *chorological syntheses* and the result is a *specific* area, region or place. . . . We can think of a specific region or the specificity of place as coming about when the generic falls (88).

By definition, then, chorological syntheses "are not entirely subsumed within social science generalizations." Nor can there be a "generic" chorography in rhetoric.

The hyperrhetoric invented in *Heuretics* corresponds to the geographers' attempts to "capture the particular connections between people and places" that pose problems for conventional notions of science: "Geographers express this ambiguity by their constant reference to what might be described as the 'betweenness' of chorology (or chorography), the study of place and region. For example, chorology has been described as being located on an intellectual continuum *between* science and art, or as offering a form of understanding that is *between* description and explanation" (Entrikin, 15).

Derrida's interest in the generative potential of a specific geography is evident in a number of his most interesting essays. In a lecture at Cornell University, to take just one example of his approach, Derrida addressed the question of the foundation of education as an institution in topological (or rather, chorological) terms. The landscape of the Cornell campus itself provided the rhetorical organization for the discussion: "The administration proposed to erect protective railings on the Collegetown bridge and the Fall Creek suspension bridge to check thoughts of suicide inspired by the view of the gorge. . . . Beneath the bridges linking the university to its surroundings, connecting its inside to its outside, lies the abyss" (Derrida, 1983b:6). This scene is associated explicitly with the theoretical question: "The principle of reason says nothing about reason itself. The abyss, the hole, the *Abgrund,* the empty 'gorge' would be the impossibility for a principle of grounding to ground itself. This very grounding, then, like the university, would have to hold itself suspended above a most peculiar void" (9).

Derrida's chorography (using an actual place as the *inventio* of a discussion) recalls Plato's use of a landscape in the *Phaedrus*. Socrates goes with Phaedrus outside the walls of the city, in order to discuss the lessons in rhetoric that the latter has learned from the sophist Lysias. They find their way, as if by accident, to a significant spot along the stream Ilissus, choosing to stop near a place where, according to legend or myth, Boreas seized Oreithyia from the river. "Upon my word, a delightful resting place," Socrates exclaims, "with this tall, spreading plane, and a lovely shade from the highest branches of the *agnos*." The commentators assure us that it is no accident, however,

> that the landscape occupies a much more significant place in the *Phaedrus* than anywhere else in Plato. Nor is it accidental that the story of Boreas is told while Socrates and Phaedrus are taking a walk along the banks of the Ilissus, or the story about the metamorphosis of the crickets while both of them are lying under a plane tree lulled by their chirruping voices in the midday heat of a southern sky. All these things belong together. Hour and place, along with the mythical tales, form the actual and symbolic landscape of the work. (Friedlander, 190)

A third level of testing would be to accept the version of chorography offered here and try to use it, to *do* chorography. Again, there should be a variety of results, in the same way that other discourses on method have given rise to a diverse if recognizable body of work. *Heuretics* is not written as a complete example of its own poetics. It is not a recipe but an evocation of the attitudes and strategies of a specific practice. In fact, the method as such is related entirely by means of an analogy (the making of "Yellowstone Desert").

"Chorography" as a method is inscribed in other words within a tale—a remake of *Beau Geste*—the remake being the form that evokes the scene of learning appropriate to electronic invention, the same way that the dialogue evoked Plato's model of learning or the autobiography (the genre of the *Discourse on Method*) modeled Descartes's rationalist commitment to introspection. The remake serves as a "place" within which the theory of method may be displayed. The remake itself ("Yellowstone Desert") was never completed. Nor has the architectural *folie* that inspired it ever been built.

PART TWO

CHOROGRAPHY

When suddenly you know that the geographical history of America has something to do with everything.

Gertrude Stein

4

FOLIE

Premises

I have been designing a method for writing and thinking electronically, imagining a time when learning is done in cyberspace. One of the features of the method, chorography, is that it does not lend itself to direct communication, at least not yet. It has no algorithm, but it may be reconstructed through inference. There is no general version of chorography but only individual practices of it. I know what it is *for*—learning electronic writing (regardless of medium). Even if I cannot define chorography, however, I can show something of what it is *like*. To use this analogy, one must substitute one's own materials for the examples I provide, and extrapolate.

Figure 1. Method

Chorography is like commemorating the Columbus quincentenary. The value of this analogy might seem to be qualified by
the fact that few people were sure what to do about this anniversary of America. In fact, this uncertainty, the hesitation and controversy surrounding the date 1992, make it a stimulus for invention. There is no central, dominating event to point to—nothing
like the Chicago Columbian Exposition of 1893. For my purposes, a good example of the 1992 quincentenary celebration is
Robert Abel's multimedia production, *Columbus: Encounter, Discovery and Beyond (a multicultural experience)*. IBM's first multimedia package, run on an IBM PS/2 Model 57 platform, distributed as a set of three videodiscs and one CD-ROM, the *Columbus*
database includes 4,400 articles, 900,000 links, 3,800 key concepts
used to link all possible combinations of data, media and tools, 7
hours of audio, 5 hours of video, 1,800 still images and graphics,
and over 200 maps. "The project is not just about Columbus and
the discovery of America. It is a tool for navigation through a
storehouse of information. The images, text, music and ideas are
accessible from any number of directions. You can meander
down a path of your own choosing, simply taking in the sights,
or you can actively pursue a line of sociological importance. You
decide" (Abel, 30–31).

What am I supposed to do with this Columbus collection?
The "you decide" coming at the end of the description seems so
attractive, so simple, yet it turns out to be the name of a problem
and an appeal for an invention. How to move "electronically"
through a storehouse of information (whether its memory is paper or disc)? This movement, this method, is like commemorating the Columbus quincentenary. Electronic logic is commemorative. My decision was to test Jacques Derrida's *inventio* as the
source for this method by using it to create my own *Columbus,*
or at least one passage, through a virtual database by that name.
"You do not know where you are going to get by way of thinking, writing, or speaking until you get there," J. Hillis Miller says,
describing Derrida's procedure. "For [Derrida] these activities
are acts of extrapolation reaching out into the void to create the

goal they will attain rather than acts of interpolation filling in the path between an origin and a predetermined goal. Nevertheless, by a strange kind of magic, it appears when you reach the goal that it has been there all along waiting to be discovered. The act of invention creates the field within which the thought already exists" (J. H. Miller).

That is how I am going to invent chorography—by creating the field within which the insight I seek already exists. Compose a "diegesis"—an imaginary space and time, as in a setting for a film—that functions as the "places of invention," using this phrase in the sense associated with it in the history of rhetoric. The *topics* store the "treasures of tested and approved ways of investigating a chosen subject, ways both of conducting an argument and of analysing a theme or subject prior to discussing it" (Dixon, 26). In order for rhetoric to become electronic, the term and concept of *topic* or *topos* must be replaced by *chora* (the notion of "place" found in Plato's *Timaeus*). That is what I learned from Derrida. For now a dictionary definition must suffice: *chora* is "an area in which genesis takes place" (F. E. Peters, 197).

Chora is not thinkable on its own but only within a field, a diegesis, considered as my *premises*. "Premises" in logic are propositions that support a conclusion, explicit or implicit assumptions, or a setting forth beforehand by way of introduction or explanation. "Premises" may also refer to a tract of land—a building together with its grounds and other appurtenances. The creation of a field (out of received, extant materials, drawing on a database such as *Columbus,* which could include potentially every document produced in the West in the past five hundred years) within which might emerge the surplus value of a revelation or an innovation that has not been thought as such, has something to do with the luck of these two *premises*—one logical, the other architectural, combined in the phrase the "grounds of reason" (the need to reason from certain established or provisional assumptions). Here is a principle of chorography: do not choose between the different meanings of key terms, but compose by using all the meanings (write the paradigm). In my study, these premises are themselves the object. What guides my passage through the database *Columbus* is the desire to discover this place or *chora* of my own premises, the diegesis within which I have been thinking, presuming, the setting that has gone without saying but that has provided the logic of all my work. I want to write the diegesis within which my own grounding presuppositions might come into appearance. Then I will be able to *write* judgment rather than only feel it or think it.

The idea of learning chorography by contributing something to the quincentenary occurred to me in 1989 when my mother sent me some clippings from my hometown newspaper about preparations for the centennial celebration of Montana's statehood. The Montanans planned a cattle drive described as "the largest contingent of horsemen and wagons gathered in one place in Montana during the past century." It was likely that the place in which I grew up would form part of the diegesis of my *premises*. The coincidence of the year with the bicentennial of the French Revolution (and of the American Constitution) set me thinking about my francophilia. Was there any link between growing up in Miles City and my attraction to everything French—especially to French theory? I asked Mom to contact some of my old classmates still living in Miles City, to see what they were doing for the centennial, and to inquire about how I might be included. Word came back that I should make a proposal to the local organizing committee. In the process of developing that proposal I discovered chorography.

Parc de la Villette

I was committed in principle to using Jacques Derrida's theories to generate my plan for the centennial committee. The coincidence of the two *premises* suggested anyway that an architectural invention might also serve as a guide to the invention of a logic, or a rhetoric. I was reading about the Parc de la Villette in Paris, announced as a "park for the twenty-first century" that was intended to promote a spirit of creativity in its visitors. The park reminded me of the tradition of international exhibitions and world's fairs, of which the Columbian Exposition was one of the most important examples. "Imagine an area the size of a small city center, bristling with dozens of vast buildings set in beautiful gardens; fill the buildings with every conceivable type of commodity and activity known; surround them with miraculous pieces of engineering technology, with tribes of primitive peoples, reconstructions of ancient and exotic streets, restaurants, theaters, sports stadiums and band-stands" (Greenhalgh, 1). Disney World, along with the Epcot Center, keys to the economy of Florida (and hence to the success of the University of Florida), amounts to a museum of this tradition.

Bernard Tschumi, the chief architect of the Villette project, invited a number of other architects to design a series of *folies* within the park. The American architect, Peter Eisenman, asked Jacques Derrida to collaborate with him on the design of one of these follies. The follies are, in Tschumi's plans, a series of red steel cubic cages that may be submitted to any possible "deviation" of design through a process of permutation and combination of a restricted set of parts. Resisting requests from bureaucrats to change the name of the cages from folie to *fabrique* (factory), Tschumi stressed the deliberately hybrid significance of his term, mixing allusions to a seventeenth-century "extravagant house of entertainment" (as in the *Folies-Bergère* or the Ziegfield Follies) and to "contemporary psychoanalytic discoveries" (*folie* = "madness") (Tschumi, 1987:5). In short, he was applying the choral principle of writing with the "paradigm" or "set" of a term, and in so doing he provided a specific content for my hybrid *premises*: the architectural premises could be this "house of entertainment," and the logic would come from psychoanalysis.

The first part of the hybrid definition has to do with the derivation of *folies* from the Latin, *foliae,* or *feuilles* (leaves) in French, denoting "a house that stands hidden beneath the leaves" (Castle, 16). "The term *folies* had developed into an expression used for many years to describe a 'field' where clandestine lovers spent their romantic evenings." It was later extended to denote a place for dancing, drinking, and watching entertainments. The allusion to music in "choral works"—the title adopted for the Derrida-Eisenman collaboration—evokes the history of the music hall that informs Tschumi's sense of *folie*.

Here was the first lead—the follies in the music hall. The electronic rhetoric I sought would operate in the mode of *folie*.

Saloon

"Miles City" is "anywhere" (it is where I happened to be, and "I" am "anyone"). In the diegesis I am constructing, Miles City forms a network with Parisian follies and the 1893 Columbian Exposition. The first premises of this choral place concern a saloon (a fandango house). Miles City was founded by sutlers in 1876, who came to sell whiskey to the soldiers building Fort Keogh (named after the owner of the horse, Commanche, the only creature to survive the Custer massacre), commanded by General Nelson Miles. Here is an architectural fact: the first building in Miles City, as in many new settlements on the Western frontier, was a saloon—in this case, John Carter's saloon (Goff, et al., 56). When I learned that *saloon* is an Americanized misspelling of the French *salon* (Erdoes, 3), I knew I was on the right track.

When the railroad came to Miles City in the early 1880s, the follies came with it. Many of the forty saloons in town by that time included music halls. "After the railroad put Miles City on the theatrical map, touring companies stopped regularly in town," featuring many acts with *follies* in their titles (Goff, et al., 26). The saloon after all was a multipurpose place:

> Besides being a drinking place, it was an eatery, a hotel, a bath and comfort station, a livery stable, gambling den, dance hall, bordello, barbershop, courtroom, church, social club, political center, dueling ground, post office, sports arena, undertaker's parlor, library, news exchange, theater, opera, city hall, employment agency, museum, trading post, grocery, ice cream parlor,

even a forerunner of the movie house in which entranced cow-
hands cranked the handles of ornate kinetoscopes to watch the
jerky movements of alluring cancan dancers. (Erdoes, 9)

Burlesque tours were scheduled into Bill Reece's Cottage Saloon.
While I was growing up I knew about this aspect of the town's
history only through oral culture, through scandal and rumor.
Miles City was notorious for its red-light district located at the
end of Pleasant Street, in continuous operation from the founding of the town until the 1960s (it was closed down by an ambi-
tious district attorney about the time I left to go to college).
Unacknowledged in the booster accounts (despite a certain
pride of distinction) was the founding role played by the madams
of the houses.

> "The red light district had been a main attraction since the town's
> beginnings, and it grew with the town after 1881. Frequent refer-
> ences in the *Yellowstone Journal* attest to the role 'ladies of easy
> virtue' played in Miles City life. Wealthy madames even bank-
> rolled respectable business ventures and were reputed to have
> subsidized major constructions, such as the Bullard Block at
> Main and Sixth Streets. Many prostitutes assumed French names
> and even advertised in the city directories, as did 'Belle' Brown,
> near Fourth and Pleasant." (Goff, 26)

Here is a grafting point, a button linking Paris to Miles City—
this prestige of French names with the women of the *maisons de
joie,* as they are called in the local history. Cowboys are attracted
to French names.
This link between Montana and France gave me the idea for
my commemoration proposal—to perform a piece on the program of a burlesque show in the reconstructed setting of one of
the original concert saloons of the town. The saloon as a place
would allow me to explore a number of issues important to de-
fining my premises, premises that led inevitably to thinking
about America in a post-Columbian era. For what I had learned

from my discipline long since was that my thinking was American—that "America" is a material discourse, a mode of thought, a logic that I used no matter what medium I worked in, no matter what problem I set for myself.

"It has been jokingly said that, with the exception of the Battle of the Little Bighorn, all western history was made inside the saloons, and there is a grain of truth in this" (Erdoes, 9). The stereotyped saloons of Hollywood films refer to a real place, one of whose social functions was to serve as a setting for a puberty rite for boys, whose first visit was part of becoming a man (10). The saloon of legend was "the fortress of Anglo machismo where masculinity extends its hide, the castle of male chauvinism with hair on its chest, the 'rooster crow of democracy'" (4). Such would be the setting for my performance—a typical example of the dance hall saloon: wooden boardwalk in front, a few horses tied to the hitching rack, wooden posts (whittled perilously thin in places by idlers with big knives) holding up the awning, swinging doors, sawdust on the floor, spittoons by the brass rail running along the base of the bar (when brawls started, men stuck their fists into these "goboons" and used them as metal boxing gloves), a giant reproduction on the back wall of "Custer's Last Stand" by Cassily Adams, which was distributed by the thousands during the 1880s to advertise Budweiser beer (45–50).

The "professor" is at the piano, the term referring to a certain type employed in most establishments, "usually an elderly man, who, in addition to soliciting patrons, presided at the piano. However, just how or where the title 'professor' originated is a bit of a mystery" (Brown and Felton, 145). Miles City boasted an academic professor, J. H. Price, who "always wore a monocle, was dignified in bearing, and never used an obscene expression" (151). In response to questioning under oath, during a trial in which he was called as a witness, Price stated that he had taught at Oxford University and that Cecil Rhodes had been one of his students. The women in saloons were called "painted cats," among other things (194).

I had not realized how varied the programs were for the

shows staged in the concert saloons. They might include any-thing from "the head of a Sioux Indian kept in a barrel of rye whiskey" to an academic professor lecturing on Plato's *Timaeus* (167). There is no record of whether or not Oscar Wilde made it to Miles City during his tour on the circuit. If he did, his topic might have been the same one offered to the miners of Leadville, Colorado: "The Practical Application of the Aesthetic Theory to Exterior and Interior House Decoration, with Observations on Dress and Personal Ornament" (Erdoes, 173). With such ex-amples in mind, I thought it might not be unreasonable to try to introduce some French theory into the program—to explain "there is *chora,* and here it is (for me)."

Having settled on the idea of being part of a follies perfor-mance in a simulated saloon of the 1880s, I still had to decide on a specific presentation. Burlesques of Shakespeare were popular at that time, so it could be a version of *Hamlet*:

HAMLET: Zounds! here's a pretty rig! O Lord, defend us!
Pr'ythee no more such frightful spectres send us!
Be thou a jovial sprite or goblin damn'd;
Be thou or aether-puff'd or sulphur-cramm'd;
Be thy intents indiff'rent, good, or bad,
I'll speak to thee, thou look'st so like my dad. (Poole, 11)

Considering my ethnic background, I might do one of the "Dutch" bits that were so popular on the circuit, such as the scene at Peter Schlanginhauffen's house: "(*Knock door*) Who dos vot, I wonder? Gome in. (*Knock again*) Gome in, I say! Dot peoples must be deaf. (*A series of very loud knocks*) Donner und blitzen! vos you want to knock de door in? (*Knock repeated*) Hol euch der stock schwere noth! Dot vos too much. (*Rushes to door*)" (McNamara, 129).

The term that best fits the process of composition operating in burlesque, as Allen described it, is "hybrid"—from "the mon-strous hybrid gender that both aroused and repulsed William Dean Howells" to the formal hybrids, crossing the minstrel show, vaudeville, musicalized travesty, and feminine spectacle (Allen, 163). In a burlesque performance "the drive toward narrative resolution was constantly suspended for songs, dances, bits of visual business," unmotivated by the logic of plot, and altered "to work in local and topical allusions" (168). The variety acts of the "olio" or middle part came to be "interspersed within a larger dramatic vehicle rather than separated into its own segment." To participate in this hybrid style is to begin to get a feel for the nature of *folie,* and hence of electronic thinking.

Boosters

The 1893 Columbian Exposition affected Miles City in two ways and helped me decide on at least the form of my follies performance. The decision about what to include in my diegesis or database, or what links to follow in my passage through *Columbus*, is guided by the pattern that is emerging gradually. Beginning by looking for signs of France in Miles City, I also found signs of "Columbus." The first such sign concerns architecture. The town had two periods of growth when it actively promoted itself, participating in a tradition whose American version has been attributed to the special circumstances of the frontier. "Such fantastic growth itself fostered a naive pride in community, for men literally grew up with their towns. From this simple fact came a much maligned but peculiarly American product: the Booster Spirit" (Boorstin, 1987: 200).

To commemorate the quincentenary I thought I should evoke this boosterism (the term was invented in 1900). The writings of boosters continue, if only in a "degraded" way, the ancient tradition of the urban panegyric that "helped to shape the ideal of a city and the way we still grasp the qualities of a place": "They describe in exalted language the location of the city, the topography and visual impression; the tale of its origin with special attention to founding myths; the illustrious deeds of its inhabitants; the unique beauty or impressive size of the city; the look of its sacred and secular buildings; the characteristics of its principal rivers" (Walter, 202).

A. "Buck" Buchanan, one of Miles City's most influential boosters, promoted our town in his *Seeing Miles City* (1911 and 1915, during the second booster period, the first being in the 1880s, after the arrival of the railroad), which featured photographs of most of the landmarks of the place and offered a euphoric view of the city's future (Goff, et al., 47–49). Among the landmarks was the significant series of buildings designed by the Helena architects Haire and Link—the Ursuline Convent, the Carnegie Library, the third Post Office Building, the hospital, the First National Bank—all reflecting the influence on American architecture of the 1893 Columbian Exposition: "These buildings changed the course of architectural history in the development of downtown Miles City, for they stimulated a demand for new, light colored, formal and symmetric compositions" (36). Haire also designed private residences, "including the George Ulmer House (1902)" [no relation], which "inspired a new style of domestic architecture." In other words, the buildings I looked at every day with complete indifference, and whose images I can recall at once simply by closing my eyes, were "Columbian." That this fact was news to me marks a principle of choral research: to collect what I find into a set, unified by a pattern of repetitions, rather than by a concept. Electronic learning is more like discovery than proof.

Tableau

A link between the Columbian Exposition and the follies actually gave me the idea for the form to use—the "living tableau." The first theatrical performance in Miles City—*Uncle Tom's Cabin*—took place in Charlie Brown's Saloon. The stage was improvised, "made of planks supported by beer and whiskey barrels. As Elizah fled from the bloodhounds she stumbled, dislodged a board, and fell amid rolling kegs" (Erdoes, 175). A device for presenting melodramas and patriotic plays that would have avoided this mischance was the living tableau. A favorite scene was "the apotheosis of little Eva" in this same *Uncle Tom's Cabin*: "Gorgeous clouds, tinted with sunlight. Eva, robed in white, is discovered on the back of a milk-white dove, with expanded wings as if just soaring upward. Her hands are extended in benediction over St. Clare and Uncle Tom, who are kneeling and gazing up to her. Impressive music.—Slow curtain" (Allen, 94).

The tableau form in fact originated in lower-class venues as an excuse for viewing undraped women and was adapted in middle-class settings to shift interest from the erotic to other, more ennobling emotions. As Robert Allen noted, the first thing that usually comes to mind when someone thinks of burlesque (the American equivalent of French follies), is "striptease." "Striptease" is an invention associated with the Columbian Exposition, and hence part of my diegesis (the one I am composing so that "chorography" may become intelligible). The display of the body as spectacle actually began in modern America in the context of "education" in a "dime museum" (exhibiting all manner of freaks) that made its lecture hall available to Lydia Thompson and the "British Blondes," initiating burlesque in 1868 (the Folies-Bergère opened in Paris in 1869, and closed in 1992). These women, wearing pink tights that revealed their bodies, played men's roles in such high-culture works as Byron's "Mazeppa." The innovation of adding theater to a museum is credited to P. T. Barnum, who later served as official advisor to the Columbian Explosion (Greenhalgh, 43, 91).

The British Blondes elaborated on a practice dating back to the 1830s in which theaters and museums presented "tableaux vivants": "By the late 1840s, some enterprising showman realized that interest in their exhibitions might be increased through the representation of paintings and statues of nude or partially revealed subjects." Favorite themes were "Venus Rising from the Sea," "Suzanna in the Bath," and "The Three Graces." The beginnings of striptease proper are traced to the Columbian Exposition, where the "cooch" dance was introduced. "Within months, practically every burlesque troupe in America had added a Fatima, Little Egypt, or Zora to do her version of the famous *danse du ventre*" (225). The exposition, that is, included international exhibits organized to mix education with entertainment (Barnum's contribution). The villages (from Persia, India, Japan, Egypt, Algeria, Sweden, Ireland, Lapland, Java, Turkey, and Germany) were ordered in a sequence (designed by consultants from the newly formed science of anthropology) to show the "progress" from primitive to civilized (from African and Native American to European).

At the "semi-civilized midpoint along the avenue, visitors to the 'Streets of Cairo' and Algerian village exhibits witnessed the belly dance being performed publicly for the first time in the United States" (227). The performance attracted huge lines to see the "ethnological exhibit" of a dance that came to be called the "cooch" or "hootchy-kootchy." Associated with the Arabian "dance of the seven veils," the cooch evolved eventually into the stripping that dominated burlesque in the 1920s.

Stereotypes

What is the cooch dance doing in my program, in the diegesis of my premises (it turned up in the field I am constructing, following the emerging pattern)? It represents, perhaps, the link between invention and stereotype. I am inventing chorography not only with the theories of Discipline, but also with the common sense of everyday life (with judgment and intuition). Another name for reasoning intuitively by means of stereotypes, Roland Barthes suggests in his description of the "cultural code," is *ideology:*

> The locus of an epoch's codes forms a kind of scientific vulgate which it will eventually be valuable to describe: what do we know 'naturally' about art?—'it is a constraint'; about youth?— 'it is turbulent,' etc. If we collect all such knowledge, all such vulgarisms, we create a monster, and this monster is ideology. As

a fragment of ideology, the cultural code *inverts* its class origin (scholastic and social) into a natural reference, into a proverbial statement. (Barthes, 1974:98)

The weakness of "truth," the reason that its "secrets" always seem to be just out of reach in a way that makes even torture seem justified as a way to get accurate information, has something to do with the operation of stereotypes in knowledge. Truth in science (in Discipline discourse) suffers from a version of what Barthes observed in the invention of striptease in Entertainment.

Here, as in any mystifying spectacle, the decor, the props and the stereotypes intervene to contradict the initially provocative intention and eventually bury it in insignificance: evil is *advertised* the better to impede and exorcise it.... There will therefore be in striptease a whole series of coverings placed upon the body of the woman in proportion as she pretends to strip it bare. Exoticism is the first of these barriers. The classic props of the music-hall, which are invariably rounded up here, constantly make the unveiled body more remote, and force it back into the all-pervading ease of a well-known rite. (Barthes, 1972a:85)

In adopting the living tableau form for my appearance in the follies, I will try to learn from Barthes's example, his attempt to write *with* stereotypes and thus to take into account his own "stupidity": "the writer's only control over stereotypic vertigo (this vertigo is also that of 'stupidity,' 'vulgarity') is to participate in it without quotation marks, producing a text, not a parody" (Barthes, 1974:98). This "stupidity" informs my premises. But I am compensated for this discovery by a repetition forming the pattern of the diegesis (which is turning out to be a history of cultural inventions), a pattern without which I cannot hope to think chorography.

The mark appears in relation to the French invention of the striptease, assigned to the same year as striptease appeared in

America (1893) but with a different genealogy. The innovation is credited to a showman who hired a woman to repeat on stage what she had done at a student party, the *Bal des Quat'z Arts,* held at the Moulin Rouge, midnight on February 9, 1893. In the midst of a drunken celebration, a debate about the attractiveness of two women ended with the winner standing on a table completely naked. Dramatized as "Yvette Goes to Bed," the strip became an instant vogue throughout Paris (Castle, 95–97).

The *Quat'z Arts* was one of the early cabarets of Paris. The cabaret, like everything else cultural, had to be invented (by one Rodolphe Salis, in this case).

> A black cat placing a disdainful paw on an obliterated goose— such was the emblem of the first cabaret, and its originators were quick to suggest to us that this graceful, magical cat born from the pages of Edgar Allan Poe, represents art; its unworthy prey, the sullen, squawking, silly bourgeois. The first cabaretists gave birth to an eclectic cat. A cat who could sing, recite, dance, show shadow plays, write music, lyrics, farce, and above all, perform. (Appignanesi, 15)

This legendary black cat, then, became the emblem of my own heuretic heuristic—the CATTt of discourses on method. Perhaps the link between the saloons that founded my hometown and the cabarets that harbored the artists and intellectuals of the European avant-garde that I admired so much was not as arbitrary as I first thought. Because of the Chat Noir's location in Montmartre, the "treacherous" outlying district of Paris, inhabited by the "worst" elements of the population, the bohemian artists and intellectuals who patronized the cabaret irrevocably associated with the whole variety of social outcasts of the city, the *canaille,* known as the *"apaches* of the Parisian frontier" (16). I had forgotten that the French romanticized the Western frontier as much as I romanticized Paris.

5

CHORA

Design

To guide my choice of work to perform in the commemorative follies I looked closely at the scene of instruction displayed in the discourse of my discipline, in which Jacques Derrida responds to Eisenman's invitation to help design a *folie* for Villette Park by providing the architect with a reading of Plato's *Timaeus*. The reading is entitled *"Chora."*

Jeffry Kipnis documented (and participated in) the six sessions during which Peter Eisenman's design team met with Derrida to develop a plan for the *folie* at Villette Park. The record of these brainstorming meetings provides an example of invention in the institution of Discipline, an example to be translated in chorogra-

Figure 2. Atlantis

phy to rhetorical invention. Derrida's initial contribution—the essay on the *Timaeus*—conforms to the strategy of encounter or "confrontation" informing Tschumi's general plan. Derrida's participation does not require "competence" in architecture. On the contrary, the invention strategy is to bring foreign competencies to bear on the target area, to bring in this case philosophy to bear on architecture; to superimpose a reading of the *Timaeus* on Villette Park, without ever claiming that one has anything intrinsically to do with the other.

It is important to note not only the choice of text to offer to Eisenman as the basis for his program but also Derrida's tactic of cutting out of the dialogue as if in collage style one notion and the images associated with it to supply the visualization required by the design. Within Timaeus's account of how God or the Demiurge fashioned (in the manner of a craftsman) the world and human beings, Derrida focuses on the discussion of the three kinds of natures at the origins of the world: "the uncreated, indestructible kind of being (the eternal Ideas); the sensible copies of the eternal (the objects of opinion and sense); and space, the 'home of all created things'" (Magill, 129). One of the special contributions of *Timeaus* to Platonic philosophy was to add between being and becoming this third kind of nature, identified as "space" or the "receptacle" (Cornford). The name for this space from the Greek is "*chora*," whose character, Derrida adds, is one of the least understood, most puzzling, most resistant to interpretation (hermeneutics) of any element in Plato's works. He calls attention to a passage from the dialogue:

> My verdict is that being and space and generation, these three, existed in their three ways before the heaven, and that the nurse of generation, moistened by water and inflamed by fire, and receiving the forms of earth and air, and experiencing all the affections which accompany these, presented a strange variety of appearances. And being full of powers which were neither similar nor equally balanced, was never in any part in a state of equipoise, but swaying unevenly hither and thither, was shaken by them, and by its motion again shook them, and the elements when moved were separated and carried continually, some one way, some another. As, when grain is shaken and winnowed by fans and other instruments used in the threshing of corn, the close and heavy particles are borne away and settle in one direction, and the loose and light particles in another. In this manner, the four kinds of elements were then shaken by the receiving vessel, which, moving like a winnowing machine, scattered far away from one another the elements most unlike, and forced the most similar elements into close contact. (*Timaeus* 52d–53a)

Part of Derrida's contribution to the design is to propose to Eisenman the Platonic notion of space, as embodied in the several metaphors given to it in the dialogue, not so much for their own sake but as a model for an invention strategy. *Chora* evokes an image of cosmological creation for a park of creativity. One of Plato's metaphors for the relationship among the three natures in the creation of the universe is that of the family: the eternal forms are in the position of father, the created copies of becoming are the offspring, and the receptacle of space is the mother or nurse. Another image concerns the crafting of gold into jewelry. In still another analogy, *chora* is in the cosmos what the liver is in the body: "The liver mimics *chora*. The liver persuades the lower passions into rational order by spreading bitterness throughout itself when desires drive away the reflections of thinking, and by saturating itself with sweetness when the reflections of thought are present" (Ashbaugh, 78).

At Eisenman's insistence, Derrida produced a drawing and a descriptive concept of this *chora* image, specifically addressing the *folie* design.

I propose therefore the following "materialisation": in one or three exemplars (with different scalings) a gilded metallic object will be planted *obliquely* in the ground. Neither vertical nor horizontal, a most solid frame will resemble at once a mesh, sieve, or grid and a stringed musical instrument. An interpretive and selective filter which will have permitted a reading and sifting of the three sites [at the Park] and the three embeddings." (Derrida, in Kipnis)

The Impossible

Besides the images or metaphors of *chora* excerpted from *Timaeus* as the basis for the visual design of the Villette folly, Derrida also contributed to the invention process in another way. In his reading of *Timaeus*, Derrida mimed the unusual strategy of Socrates in this dialogue. Rather than leading the discussion as he normally did, here Socrates placed himself in the position of listener, of active receiver or receptacle, of the discourse. The staging or *mis-en-scène* of the dialogue as drama, that is, with Socrates in the position of addressee, repeated or displayed the theory of *chora* developed later. "Socrates is not *chora* but he would look a lot like it/her if it/she were someone or something. In any case he puts himself in its/her place, which is not just a place among others, but perhaps *place itself,* the irreplaceable, the unplaceable place from which he receives the word(s) of those before whom he effaces himself but who receive them from him for he it is who makes them talk like this" (Derrida, 1987b:281).

In the six planning sessions leading to the design of the folly, Derrida performs *Timaeus* and places himself in the same relationship to Peter Eisenman and his collaborators that Socrates held in relation to Timaeus and his companions. Derrida mimes Socrates, then, but it is not the interrogating Socrates of Platonism. In the first session, Derrida explains that he comes to the project with one idea that he wants to introduce into the process. He describes *chora* in Plato's terms and comments on his own interest in it.

> What interests me is that since *chora* is irreducible to the two positions, the sensible and the intelligible, which have dominated the entire tradition of Western thought, it is irreducible to all the values to which we are accustomed—values of origin, anthropomorphism, and so on. . . . *Chora* receives everything or gives place to everything, but Plato insists that in fact it has to be a virgin place, and that it has to be totally foreign, totally exterior to anything that it receives. Since it is absolutely blank, everything that is printed on it is automatically effaced. It remains foreign to the imprint it receives; so in a sense, it does not receive anything—it does not receive what it receives nor does it give what it gives. Everything inscribed in it erases itself immediately, while remaining in it. It is thus an impossible surface—it is not even a surface, because it has no depth." (Derrida, in Kipnis)

Although *chora* in Plato's familial analogy is in the position of nurse or mother, the traditional roles of kinship are inadequate for evoking it. "*Chora* does not pair off with the father, in other words with the paradigmatic model. She is a third gender/genus. . . . *Chora* marks a place apart, the spacing which keeps a dissymetrical relation with all that which, 'in herself,' beside or in addition to herself, seems to make a couple with her" (Derrida,

1987b:291). It is not that *chora*-as-woman does not function according to a "logic," only that this logic is a hybrid, neither mythos nor logos. The philosophical tradition can speak directly only of stories of fathers and sons. The rest has to be figured indirectly: "These remarks permit us perhaps to glimpse the silhouette of a 'logic' which seems virtually impossible to formalize" (266). This "logic" provides the Theory for the CATTt of chorography.

Chora, then, evokes together the thought of a different kind of writing (without representation) and a different mode of value. The participants agree that the seeming impossibility of "representing" *chora* could make their project exemplary: the goal is not just to design a folly but to explore the invention process itself by means of this problem: What would a writing be that produces understanding without representation? After all, as the book *No Way: The Nature of the Impossible* (ed. Davis and Park) indicates, the challenge of "impossibility" has been a major factor in the history of invention and discovery. With essays on "impossible" inventions covering disciplines in all three divisions of knowledge as well as in the professions, *No Way* takes as its guiding image the conquest of Mount Everest, reiterating the formula: physical adventure = cultural invention.

The impossibility of chorography is analogous to Eisenman's difficulty when he accepted *chora* as the program for his folly. He had to give architectural form to that which is unrepresentable. My problem, in inventing an electronic rhetoric by replacing *topos* with *chora* in the practice of invention, is to devise a "discourse on method" for that which, similarly, is the other of method. Responding to a question about the possibility of a deconstructive architecture, Derrida states: "I think that if there were a definition of such a thing, with a concept, rules, techniques, methods, it would be of no interest, it would be over, so to speak. . . . Precisely due to the issues of idiom and singularity, one cannot extract a technique, method or system or architectural rules from deconstruction" (Derrida, in Kipnis). There are not deconstructive objects, he adds, but only deconstructive processes.

That chorography is more grammatological than deconstructive does not reduce the impossibility of the program: the method of no method (the possible impossible). How to practice choral writing then? It must be in the order neither of the sensible nor the intelligible but in the order of making, of generating. And it must be transferable, exchangable, without generalization, conducted from one particular to another.

Metaphor

Derrida's drawing (used to illustrate the cover of *Teletheory*) evokes the paradigm of *chora*, whose nature has been named in a series of images or metaphors. What I have been calling the "field" and the "premises" of chorography may be recognized as attempts to translate this theoretical *chora* into a method. One of the difficulties in grasping the nature of *chora* as *genos* or genesis is that, being neither intelligible nor sensible, it has to be approached indirectly, by extended analogies. Analogy is inherently ambiguous, since it is never certain which aspects of the vehicle domain are to be mapped onto the tenor domain, and which aspects ignored.

Francis Cornford, for example, stressed that the winnowing basket in Plato's simile for *chora* is woven as in basketwork and not perforated as in a sieve.

> It is the *liknon* or *vannus* described and figured by Jane Harrison, a wide, shovel-shaped basket, high at one end and flattened out at the other, held by two handles projecting from the upper rim at the sides. "The winnower takes as much of grain and chaff mixed as he can conveniently hold and supports the basket against the knee. He then jerks and shakes the basket so as to propel the chaff towards the shallow open end and gradually

drives it all out, leaving the grain quite clean. The wind plays no part whatever in this process." (Cornford, 201).

The discussion is based on a photograph of Mr. Wilson, Sir Francis Darwin's gardener, using a *liknon*. Cornford wondered if an ancient reference to "the Phrygian Earth Mother, Hipta," placing a *liknon* on her head in which she receives and carries the infant god Dionysus, might have suggested to Plato his simile.

Richard Mohr argues that Cornford's concern about the differences between winnowing baskets and sieves and different sifting motions (back and forth versus twirling) is misplaced, that he has misread the relevant details of the analogy, whose point has less to do with shaking and more with sorting out (the emphasis being not on chaotic motion but on ordering) (Mohr, 122). Mohr notes that a common feature of all the uses of *chora* is its positioning *between*, in the middle. The point of the analogies with such everyday materials as a mixing bowl, a base for perfumes, or gold that is malleable into many different shapes is best conveyed in the simile of the *mirror*: "space" (*chora*) makes the intelligible order (being) visible by receiving or containing the copies of the ideas (becoming) just as a mirror contains reflections or images of actual things. The functional meaning of all the similes, Mohr observes, is that of *medium*. An important aspect of Plato's meaning is that this receptacle/medium is active, participating in terms of its own nature as much as do the other two orders: in the interaction of being and becoming in the medium of space, the intelligible is made sensible.

Mohr makes a comment that is of special interest: "If Plato had lived in our century, he might very well have chosen, not gold, but a movie screen or television screen as his analogue to a field across which ceaselessly changing non-substantial images may flicker" (Mohr, 94). Not that this modernizing of the analogy is a new insight. Modern commentators commonly compare the scene of the cave in the *Republic,* where prisoners are able to observe only shadows cast by effigies paraded before a fire behind their backs, to a movie theater. As Anne Ashbaugh noted in her survey of the metaphor throughout all Plato's dialogues (the usage proving to be consistent), *chora* appears in the analogy of the cave to name that bright place outside the cave where one is able to see truly by the light of the sun. In other words, the analogy of the cave and the analogy of the sorting basket treat the same question. Plato obviously is not thinking television, or the computer monitor, but he is saying it, writing it, the awkwardness and obscurity of his language owing, it has been said, to his anticipation of a technology that would not be invented for another two millenia.

Chora thus evokes electronic media, keeping in mind that the spirit of the analogy concerns not this or that machine, not a winnowing basket or a convex mirror, not a computer monitor, but machinery or technology as such. Not that this substitution of figures explains anything; on the contrary, everything having to do with media may be rethought within the perspective of *chora.*

From Topos to Chora

Derrida, although he explicitly discouraged thinking of *chora* in terms of the chiché of "Plato's Cave," nonetheless did make the electronic analogy. In the third meeting, for example, during his summary of the points made in his reading of the *Timaeus,* Derrida suggests that the folly might include the use of video monitors. The main motives of his essay were, he adds, "first, the inclusion of narrative in narrative, boxes within boxes. Then, Socrates as *chora,* as the receptacle of the dialogue, a universal receiver. Finally, in Plato, *chora* is thought as in a dream—a hybrid, dreamed of. The idea of the dream is very important here. That is why I thought of the video. It has to do with light, but also with dreams, phantasms" (Derrida, in Kipnis).

The terms for a reconsideration of electronics in the context of *chora,* relevant to my discourse on method, should be distinguished from Ashbaugh's analysis, which argues that the "dialectical other" of *chora* is *topos,* that space and place relate to one another in a way similar to the other pairs in Plato's system, governed by the distinction between the philosopher and the sophist. "The dark region of nonbeing is called *topos,* an individual region in which images cannot be reflected, a place suited for hiding. Being, on the other hand, reflects itself in a bright space, a *chora* that reflects many images, a place suited for showing" (Ashbaugh, 109). Derrida would agree that the place he is talking about is not *topos,* but as he insisted at the first meeting, he wants to avoid dialectical oppositions.

Derrida's effort to extract *chora* from the tradition of Platonism is shared by E. V. Walter, who distinguishes it from *topos* by noting that the former term names a "grounded" mode of thought that was available in Plato but that has been buried, forgotten in the idealism of the conventional interpretation. Calling this buried alternative "topistics," Walter anticipates the possibility of a hyperrhetoric in which the places of invention are figured not as *topoi* but as *chora.* Or rather, the task is to rethink the association of invention with place before "place" was split into *topos* and *chora.* Because of this split, "place"—emptied of personal and social feeling—came to be associated with a neutral container, as in Aristotle's understanding of *topos* as the seat of arguments, and a collection of commonplaces to serve as the focus of discussion (Walter, 126). "The older word, *chora,* retained subjective meanings in the classical period. It appeared in emotional statements about places, and writers were inclined to call a sacred place a *chora* instead of a *topos*" (120).

Grounded Platonism, according to Walter, would rely less on mathematical rationalizations and more on the topistics of expressive intuitions: a haptic rather than analytical mode of thought. Topistics replaces problems, arguments, solutions with a choral "dream reasoning" of riddles. A place is experienced wholistically as a riddle understood in terms of the *ker,* ghost, or bogey associated with the energy of space as an active receptacle, as dramatized in the haunting of Thebes by a Sphinx (68). Its best manifestation in the contemporary world, Walter says, is in the ecology or environmental movements (208). Chorography attempts to translate this "dream reasoning" into a method.

Geschlecht

Derrida also distinguishes *chora* from *topos* in terms of the question of "spirit," which is related to the ancient notion of a spirit of place invoked by Walter's topistics.

> It is something which cannot be assimilated by Plato himself, by what we call Platonic ontology, nor by the inheritance of Plato. Further, it has nothing to do with *topos,* though Plato sometimes uses the word *topos*—a determined place—instead of *chora. Chora* is the spacing which is the condition for everything to take place, for everything to be inscribed. The metaphor of impression or printing is very strong and recognized in this text. It is the place where everything is received as an imprint. (Derrida, in Kipnis)

The notion of *chora* as imprint concerns Derrida's association of *chora* as "genesis" with the concept of *Geschlecht,* referring to the complex of "sex, race, family, generation, lineage, species, genre/genus" (Derrida, 1983a:65). Derrida uses *Geschlecht* to open up the complexity of the third kind of order (*genos*).

Geschlecht evokes the problematic of multiculturalism and diversity, concerning what Cornel West described as "the New Cultural Politics of Difference"—a "new vocation of critic and artists to trash the monolithic and homogeneous in the name of diversity, multiplicity and heterogeneity; to reject the abstract, general and universal in light of the concrete, specific and particular; and to historicize, contextualize and pluralize by highlighting the contingent, provisional, variable, tentative, shifting and changing" (West, 19). The "new" element in this approach, West says, "is how and what constitutes difference, the weight and gravity it is given in representation and the way in which highlighting issues like exterminism, empire, class, race, gender, sexual orientation, age, nation, nature, and region at this historical moment acknowledges some discontinuity and disruption from previous forms of cultural critique." The theme of *Geschlecht,* in other words, addresses the problematic of 1992: what will be the mark or trait of identity of "America" after the age of Columbus? How does "America" *gather* after 1992?

The "imprint" that Derrida associates with *chora* is also the common denominator in all the multiple significations of *Geschlecht*: "My most constant concern is evidently the 'mark' *'Geschlecht'* and what in that mark *remarks* the mark, the striking, the impression, a certain writing as *Schlag, Pragung"*; in short, "a matter of the inscription of *Geschlecht* and of *Geschlecht* as inscription, stamp, and imprint" (Derrida, 1983a:82). This imagery of the "stamp" helps locate the tradition Derrida is renewing.

"The faculty of imagination that is 'grasped' by the evidence of the object gains currency in the Stoic system of metaphor," Hans Blumenberg observed, "both in the imprint metaphor of the "stamp" and also in Chrysippus's simile of the idea that grabs a man by the hair and forces him down to assent" (Blumenberg 260). This view of cognition is to be distinguished from that of "the 'naturalness' of truth, which was characterized with the help of the metaphor of light." Here is the feature that distinguishes Derrida's metaphor from Plato's cave, and from the enlightenment heritage in general. *Folie* is a logic of touch (feeling) more than of vision.

Derrida is questioning also the humanistic tradition of *Geschlecht* in which the human hand has served as the fundamental mark of distinction separating humankind from the rest of creation. The search for a new gesture of invention—asking what is to be done *today* (in America)—is conducted in the context of the Stoic argument for self-restriction of the pretension to knowledge. When must theoretical curiosity be capped, suspended, according to this tradition (associated with truth as mark rather than as light)? There must be a criterion for action mediating between the idea and *judgment:* "The precipitancy of judgment, which is (so to speak) seduced by the cognitive drive, is theory's original sin" (Blumenberg, 258).

Zeno is said to have illustrated the definition of this truth criterion as *katalepsis* (a grasping) with gestures of the hand:

After exhibiting the inner surface of his hand, with the fingers spread, he said, "Such is an idea [*visum*]." Then, with his fingers somewhat bent, "Such is assent." Then when he had drawn them together entirely and made a fist, he said that that was katalepsis . . . ; but when finally he used his left hand as well and tightly and forcibly squeezed the first together with it, he explained that this was the knowledge that no one but the wise man possesses. (259–260)

The skeptic axiom is, "When in doubt, refuse to act."

Derrida has something else in mind with his survey of the paradigm of philosophical uses of the hand, as in his reading of Heidegger.

"If there is a thought of the hand or a hand of thought, as Heidegger gives us to think, it is not of the order of conceptual grasping. Rather this thought of the hand belongs to the essence of the *gift,* of a giving that would give, if this is possible, without taking hold of anything. If the hand is also, no one can deny this, an organ for gripping, that is not its essence, is not the hand's essence in the human being. (Derrida, 1987a:428; translation by John Leavey, University of Florida)

No wonder, then, that it is difficult to "grasp" *chora,* even if it is to be thought in haptic terms. But this difficulty is to be expected of a method designed as an alternative to conceptual thinking. The aspect of this complication of the "gesture of knowing" important for chorography is that the differences among nationalities, genders, ages, and so on are a matter of "writing." The writer using chorography as a rhetoric of invention will store and retrieve information from premises or places formulated not as abstract containers, as in the tradition of *topos,* but by means of *Geschlecht.* Chora, in other words, as a figure of spacing, is another name for what has concerned Derrida in nearly every text he has ever written: *differance.* The premises of my judgments are to be retrieved from the pattern stored in what is named by *Geschlecht*.

Atlantis

Ashbaugh's survey of Plato's dialogues calls attention to the domains associated with *chora*. The common denominator of the usages concerns "how scattered things can be rounded up into a single class that exhibits how each thing is both one and many" (111). Chorography gathers information into a set in ways different from the category formation of conceptual thinking. This new manner of electronic classification affects every manner of sorting, of determining borders. *Chora* as active medium is also mediator, and one of its important domains has to do with "motherland," a land or country, "a demarcated region shared by many individuals who must live harmoniously as one *polis*" (103). Plato extrapolates his technical meanings from the ordinary, literal usage of his time, Ashbaugh notes, inflecting the term with his specialized concerns.

Ashbaugh summarizes her findings in terms that are relevant to how America might commemorate 1992.

> The ordinary sense of *chora,* meaning land or country, in turn presents a coherent picture of how the many things may be organized by nature or by law, into a unity which does not abolish the individual differences of the things it embraces. Given some common measure, the composite deserves a name that shows the bond joining its component parts. Household, city, land, country, and singular term naming a gathered plurality instantiates what spatiality effects. (111)

The link between the monologues by Timaeus and Critias in Plato's dialogue, that is, is this sense of *chora* as containment, referring to a country, and of introducing intelligibility into any multiple, dispersed condition, and there is more than one way to perform this operation. Indeed, chorography suggests the possibility of a method that is never practiced the same way twice.

Since the *Timaeus* is one of the central documents in the history of method, it offers a useful point of departure for reorienting method in an electronic apparatus. As a cosmogony and cosmology, it is a story of invention. Most of the talking in this dialogue is done not by Socrates but by Timaeus, a Pythagorean astronomer. Socrates brought together several persons with practical experience in the art of politics—Timaeus, Critias, and Hermocrates—"to tell something of their adventures so that the portrait of the ideal state [as set forth in *The Republic*] can begin to take on living character" (Magill, 126). The question concerns application: how to turn abstract principles into action.

My analogy of chorography as a commemoration of the Columbus quincentenary alludes to a scene in *Timaeus*, the report by Critias about the origins of ancient Athens. Critias heard the story he tells when he was ten years old. The story of the great empire of Atlantis defeated by the ancient Athenians when it attempted to conquer and enslave the Greeks had been forgotten in the official memory of the state. Solon, during his travels in Egypt, heard the story from a priest, but it survived only in the private memory of Critias's family, passed along from grandfather to grandson. His grandfather told Critias the story of Atlantis on the day of a state celebration—"the Registration of Youth, at which, according to custom, our parents gave prizes for recitations, and the poems of several poets were recited by us boys, and many of us sang the poems of Solon" (Plato, 1156). Critias offered the tale in turn to Socrates as "a fitting monument of our gratitude to you, and a hymn of praise true and worthy of the goddess, on this her day of festival."

The *Geschlecht* marking the identity of Athens might hold a lesson for America in 1992. Who are "we" in this story? The first thing to note is that any interpretation of the legend as an allegory is as likely to associate "America" with Atlantis as with Athens. One of the inventors of the modern scientific method, Francis

Atlantis

Bacon, associated Columbus's discovery of America with the legend of Atlantis, and by extension, he associated the whole scientific enlightenment with the discovery, exploration, and ultimately the colonization of the "new world."

A consensus arose in some quarters in the sixteenth century that Columbus may have found Atlantis. "Francesco Lopez de Gomara first made the suggestion in 1553 and the idea was popular for the next three centuries. Quite a number of maps of the seventeenth and eighteenth centuries make the identification, and Sir Francis Bacon adopted it in his utopian novel *The New Atlantis*" (Ramage, 30). One modern writer "credited the 'enigma of Atlantis' with doing more toward motivating the conquest of the New World than the 'politics of princes'" (Speck, 13). Perhaps my *folie* in the saloon could evoke this secret identity of "the United States of Atlantis."

Curiosity

What sort of "place" does "Atlantis" name in my diegesis, the field of my premises? The moral point of the tale is at least ambiguous. Atlantis was an evil empire that *deserved* its legendary fate due to the moral decay of its once virtuous population. It was only the heroism of the prehistoric Athenians that prevented the empire from conquering all of the known world, yet this mythical Athens also perished in the cataclysm that sank Atlantis.

The real lesson of Atlantis might have less to do with evil and heroism than with memory, and the memorial quality of catastrophe. There is something in the image of a drowned city of treasures, "of a city beneath the sea," Evan Connell observed, that motivates curiosity. "We can't stop looking for it: Atlantis ranks with buried treasure, monsters, ghosts, derelict ships, inexplicable footprints, and luminous objects streaking through the sky as topics that never fail to excite us" (Connell, 47, 57). The choral quality of "Atlantis" concerns this power of fascination, this capacity to motivate the practice of *search*.

Atlantis and Lemuria (the civilization that preceded Atlantis) are afforded their own chapter in a book on pseudoscience, along with topics covering everything from Bridey Murphey and dowsing rods to the anthropology of Aryan superiority (Gardner). So many people looked for Atlantis or specialized in the lore of this search that there is a name for this branch of knowledge: Atlantology (Ramage, 3). The inventors of the "white magic" of theosophy and anthroposophy thought the heirs of Atlantis were living in southern California. Nazi theorists claimed that the Nordic race had its origin in Atlantis (Gardner, 167).

Those who speculated on the actual location of Atlantis offered evidence for its existence in such places as "Ceylon, Malta, Iceland, Palestine, the Canary Islands, Spitsbergen, and at least a dozen more places":

> In 1952 a German pastor announced that the Atlantean capital lay six miles east of Heligoland on the floor of the North Sea—not far from the pastor's home. More recently a British investigator suggested Bronze-Age Wessex. At first this predilection for situating Atlantis in one's own neighborhood seems strange, just as it seems strange that devout Christians always expect the Second Coming to take place somewhere nearby—perhaps in the backyard between the birdbath and the azaleas. (Connell, 52–53)

In our commonsense or folk psychology "Atlantis" names an expectation similar to the possibility of visitors from outer space (Curran). Such forms simulate in modern cultural literacy the experience of the Aztec wisdom that prophesied the return of the god Quetzalcoatl, who, according to legend, had gone by sea to join the sun god in the East. "In a sense, Montezuma had known the conquering strangers all his life. They bore a remarkable resemblance to some of the extraordinary creatures that inhabited the Aztecs' elaborate legends and myths" (Wilson, 16).

Chorography has to learn from "Atlantis" something about curiosity, about how to motivate a search. The database of *Columbus,* with its 900,000 links, is already available, as a hint of what an online learning environment might be (cyberspace). But what are the *premises* of electronic memory? What will motivate a passage through an infinite archive? At this point the psychoanalytic dimension of *folie* becomes relevant regarding the question Jacques Lacan posed to science: "What is this passion of knowledge in modern man? Science is prompted by an obscure desire, but it doesn't know what this desire means. . . . The desire of a better understanding of the world has itself to be justified and explained" (Leupin, 19).

Now the striptease in my diegesis is clarified as another indicator of the nature of curiosity. Nietzsche, in Discipline discourse, suggested that "one should have more respect for the bashfulness with which nature has hidden behind riddles and irridescent uncertainties. Perhaps truth is a woman who has reasons for not letting us see her reasons? Perhaps her name is—to speak Greek—*Baubo*?" (Nietzsche, 38). In the discourse of Entertainment, however, Nietzsche's caveat was ignored. The burlesque show gradually became the "girlie show" on the carnival circuit, at which "a strip might end with a gynecological anatomy lesson" catering to "the insatiable male curiosity about the exact nature and geographic disposition of 'women's part'" (Allen, 236). The regulars at such shows were allowed to bring flashlights, a scene that offers a glimpse of the nature of "truth," regardless of the institution within which it is practiced.

6

BEAU GESTE

1939

Although I was committed to present a living tableau on the program of a follies show commemorating the Columbus quincentenary, I had not yet selected which text I would perform. Again, I consulted Derrida. In *L'Autre Cap* (1991a) (*The Other Heading*, recording his comments at a conference on the question of European cultural identity) Derrida provided another context for 1992, the year in which European economic unification was supposed to take place. The issue concerns what relationship—if any—there might be among economic, geographic, and symbolic unification. Fearing that economic unification would lead eventually to cultural unification, Denmark in 1992 refused to ratify

Figure 3. Francophilia

the pan-European charter and hence put the whole process in doubt.

Still thinking about my francophilia, I was curious about Derrida's explanation of European cultural identity, especially of the national identity of France. Why do I respond so favorably to anything French? What was it about my own formation or acculturation—the identification with European letters—that motivated me to seek a degree in comparative literature in the first place? With what did I identify, exactly?

Europe projects an image whose nature, Derrida suggests, may be recognized by a glance at the map, at the land mass projecting out of Asia like the head of some creature. This "head," in the idiom of *cap*, organizes the whole essay, which is written as a kind of exercise generated out of the word image of the map: collect all the senses of *cap* and its related terms (*capital, capitale, capitain,* and the like), find some relationship among these meanings, and apply it to *Europe.* Such is the assignment Derrida set for himself, using the *inventio* of writing with the paradigm.

One of the senses of *cap* is "bow or prow of a ship." This prow or advanced position on the ship, to which is often affixed some figure, some sculpted body or head, is the very image of European identity and of identification as such. "Perhaps identification in general, the formation and affirmation of an identity, a self-presentation, the presence to oneself of identity (national or not, cultural or not—but identification is always cultural, it is never natural, it is the exit outside of the self in the self, the difference *with itself* of nature) always has had a capital form, the figure of the prow, of the advanced point, and of the capitalizing reserve" (Derrida, 1991a:31).

Here is a gesture that typifies theoretical writing: the image opens a connection between the particular and the general. This generalizing movement is not done arbitrarily, however; Derrida justifies his interpretation of the image by citing a disciplinary precedent. Taking the year 1992 as a moment of supreme *imminence,* full of potential and portents for the future, Derrida turns to an essay by Valéry written in 1939, the most recent previous moment of supreme crisis, representing the self-consciousness of European intellectuals on the verge of World War II (the moment of such groups as the Frankfurt School and of the College of Sociology, asking, "How is fascism possible *today,* here and now?").

Racism, after all, Derrida observes, is one way to construct the other, the dominant construction since 1492 (and before). The complexity of overcoming such habits of mind should not be underestimated. They are entangled, that is, with the modernist gesture of "the universal rights of man." What is the paradox of modern European ideology? The French essence, Valéry explained, is just that *feeling* and judgment of the universal relevance of its national idioms.

The modernist gesture was to mistake for universal something that was particular, local, idiomatic. "Abstract or 'pure' thought, like technical thought, works to efface what comes to the thinker from his/her nation or race, because it aims at creating values independent of place and persons" (Derrida, 1991a:99). France invented the "Rights of Man" and took as its mission to impose them on its neighbors and colonies in the name of "universal value." The projecting head that Europe forms on the map represents its self-image as the "advanced guard," the vanguard or avant-garde ahead of everyone else, guiding, leading the way into a progressive future of universal identification with these "Rights of Man." "No cultural identity ever presents itself as the opaque body of an untranslatable idiom but always, on the contrary, as the irreplaceable *inscription* of the universal in the singular, the unique witnessing of human essence and of what is proper to mankind" (72).

The invention of "America" may be reconsidered in this context. Derrida observed (in a bicentennial celebration address at the University of Virginia) that the American "Declaration of Independence" reflected a "fabulous retroactivity":

There was no signer, by right, before the text of the Declaration which itself remains the producer and guarantor of its own signature. By this fabulous event, by this fable which implies the structure of the trace and is only in truth possible thanks to the inadequation to itself of a present, a signature gives itself a name. It opens *for itself* a line of credit.... The *self* surges up here in all cases (nominative, dative, accusative) as soon as a signature gives or extends credit to itself, in a single coup of force, which is also a coup of writing, as the right to writing. The coup of force makes right, founds right or the law, gives right, *brings the law to the light of day.* (Derrida, 1986b:10)

Here is explained the relationship of enlightenment to *Geschlecht,* of reasoning according to vision and by means of the mark (the *coup* of force). The *mark* provides the *premises* for the light. The "fabulous event" refers to the foundational act of the revolution creating "America," an act that may be generalized to all acts of invention, demonstrating the foundational—and idiomatic—nature of invention. My own *premises* and the invention of chorography are part of this process. Derrida isolates a pure example of this temporality in Francis Ponge's "Fable," "the essence of the fabulous about which it will claim to be stating the truth, will also be its general subject," as if, he adds, one were to make an invention named "invention":

Fable
By the word *by* commences then this text
Of which the first line states the truth
But this silvering under the one and other
Can it be tolerated?
Dear reader already you judge
There as to our difficulties ...

(AFTER seven years of misfortune
She broke her mirror.)
                    (Derrida, 1989a:30)

The projection of Europe as the vanguard head on the prow of a ship is part of the modern tradition, now reaching its closure, for which Derrida proposes finding *another heading,* an alternative, postmodern direction (Derrida, 1991a:32). What might such a gesture be? It requires an invention out of an "experience of the possibility of impossibility: the proof of the aporia out of which to invent the only invention possible, the impossible invention" (43).

Chorography is a response to this appeal for invention, however impossible, based on the assumption that invention may not be undertaken "in general," solely by means of abstractions that leave out the foundation of thought in the practices constituting the cultural identity and ideology of the inventor. At the same time, keeping in mind the timing of invention, the inventor's ideological *premises* do not determine in advance the outcome of the process but constitute the field, place, diegesis, or *chora* of its genesis. "The relation between the order of invention and the order of presentation," Roland Barthes observed, "and notably the gap in the orientation (contradiction, inversion) of the two parallel orders, always has a theoretical bearing: it is a whole conception of literature which is at stake each time" (Barthes, 1988:50).

With these questions of heuretic timing in mind, I was able to decide on the work to perform in the follies by asking, regarding Derrida's talk on Europe in 1992, "What is that for me?" I am an American in the same way that Derrida is a European (although he is from French Algeria, he says he *feels* European, "among other things"). Derrida poses the problem of inventing *today,* repeating Valéry's demand from 1939, "What are you going to do? What are you going to do TODAY?" (18). What is *imminent* in our moment, dated post-1992? I need to think about 1992 in America by means of 1939 *in America,* with a text that is to American cultural identity what Valéry's essay on the crisis of spirit in Europe is to the French. That text, for me (anachronism and all) is *Beau Geste.*

The Golden Year

My father was twenty-three years old in 1939, the year he met my mother and began "courting," as it was still called. The only thing they could afford to do was to go to the movies, in what turned out to be perhaps the single greatest year in the history of Hollywood, according to Ted Sennett's *Hollywood's Golden Year, 1939: A Fiftieth Anniversary Celebration.* The "eureka story" of invention has been associated with "gold" at least since Archimedes. Sennett's celebration of this "golden year" is a good place to look for a clue to the spirit of America in 1939, since it places his reviews of the films in the context of the moment.

In January/February of that year, the release of *Gunga Din,* starring Douglas Fairbanks, Jr., and Cary Grant, coincides with the opening of the Golden Gate International Exposition in San Francisco. "Singer Marian Anderson is denied permission to perform in Washington's Constitution Hall by the Daughters of the American Revolution. . . . 22,000 members of the German-American Bund rally in New York City. . . . In Germany, Jews are forbidden to practice as dentists, veterinarians, or chemists. . . . Neville Chamberlain meets Benito Mussolini in Rome" (Sennett, 1). Among the films foregrounded as the best of the best year are *Stagecoach, Wuthering Heights, Dark Victory, Goodbye, Mr. Chips, Young Mr. Lincoln, The Wizard of Oz, Mr. Smith Goes to Washington, Ninotchka, Gone with the Wind.*

"Other Notable Films" are described, and the volume concludes with a list of honorable mentions, which is where I found the text for my memory of 1939: *Beau Geste,* "a novel about honor, treachery, and brotherly devotion in the French Foreign Legion," directed by William Wellman for Paramount from the novel by Percival Christopher Wren (whose ancestor was the greatest architect in the history of England), starring Gary Cooper, Ray Milland, Robert Preston, Susan Hayward, Brian Donlevy, Albert Dekker, Broderick Crawford, J. Darroll Naish, and Donald O'Conner. Gary Cooper was my father's favorite actor.

Responding to the considerable popularity of *Beau Geste* when it first appeared in print, Paramount immediately produced a silent version of the story in 1926, starring Ronald Colman. Three remakes followed: in 1939 (the favorite), in 1966 (a disaster, featuring Tele Sevalas), and in 1977, a parody by Marty Feldman,

The Last Remake of Beau Geste. The remake is a specifically American practice (Protopopoff, 13), marking the peculiarities of our cinema as an institution (distinct from other national cinemas, such as that of France, where *ciné-clubs* keep original versions in circulation). The motive for a remake goes beyond the market system to the dynamics of collective memory, having to do with the way a story ages, becomes dated, or is revived, depending on the mentality of a society at a given historical moment. "If we can discount *Gunga Din's* racist attitude and historical distortions," Sennett says, "we can enjoy the film for its spectacular action, its boisterous if sometimes juvenile humor, and the broad strokes of the performance" (Sennett, 11). But this "discounting" is just what does not happen in chorography, tuned to *Geschlecht.*

With its three versions and a parody, *Beau Geste* is about average for the phenomenon of the remake, being neither in the category of *The Blue Angel,* whose status depends largely on the aesthetic qualities of one specific film and is therefore nearly impossible to repeat (at least successfully) (Protopopoff, 72), nor, at the other extreme, of a "myth" such as that of Tarzan, which separates from its original version, whether book or film or both, to take on a life of its own in general culture. The most filmed of such myths, Tarzan was played by seventeen actors in forty-four versions between 1918 and 1984, not including the television series (50).

Why another *Beau Geste* in 1939? It is one of those films using the formula of European empires, Richard Slotkin observes, to convey the secret history of America's own experience of imperialism in fulfilling its Manifest Destiny on the frontier, a "genre" that includes *The Charge of the Light Brigade, The Lives of a Bengal Lancer,* and *Gunga Din,* among others. Such works use the mythological reasoning of Entertainment discourse, casting historical events into ideological categories: the "secret history" of a film such as *Beau Geste* concerns its hidden political or propaganda function, which is disguised by formulating public, historical events in terms of private or personal conflicts.

The popularity of any genre is relative to its appropriateness for "representing the public concerns" of its moment. In *Beau Geste* the formula mythologizes "a major ideological shift in American politics, away from isolation and toward preparedness for engagement in the conflicts of Europe and the Far East" (Slotkin, 19), essentially preparing America to be the "successor of British and French colonialism in the Third World." Many films of the period carried this same secret history, as Robert Ray has shown in his discussion of *Casablanca* (Ray).

And why another remake of *Beau Geste* in 1992? Have the conditions of 1939 come around again (as our behavior in the Gulf war might suggest)? If not, then what has changed? What is different about being "American," *today*? *Beau Geste* serves in chorography as an example of how the discourse of Entertainment works. In Discipline discourse Derrida sent Plato's *Timaeus* to Peter Eisenman as a sign in the context of a problem to be solved. In the case of the institution of Entertainment, *Beau Geste* is the message received by my parents, sitting in a movie theater in Chicago at a time of world crisis. Sent by whom? The American nation.

The Vanguard

I *recognize* myself in Derrida's interpretation of the *cap* or heading of Europe's image—the prow of the ship—as showing Europe's association with the "avant-garde" among world nations. That is the gesture I identified with, no doubt. In my case, at least, my francophilia is equaled by my enthusiasm for the avant-garde in the arts. The challenge and difficulty of Derrida's strategy for inventing another gesture for Western identity after 1992 carries the name *deconstruction,* concerning how to produce the new out of the old, how to break a habit of thought.

Perhaps I can get a better perspective on my vanguard *premises* by using the choral strategy of writing with the paradigm—to include the "set" of possible terms collected under the heading of a given concept or category, rather than to select one part and suppress the remainder. Writing with the paradigm is a practice related to (but not identical with) the structuralist insight into meaning as "value," referring to the position of a term in a system of signification: "the relationship between the sign and other signs that it could conceivably be, but is not" (Fiske, 48). Chorography adds to the notion of "value" the sense of the "remainder" to suggest that the absent terms have been suppressed because their availability as substitutes seemed "impossible."

Consider the three primary senses of "vanguard" (military, political, artistic). "Avant-garde" is originally a military term referring to the foremost division or front part of an army—the shock troops, the probes—which was the position and function most often assigned to troops of the foreign legion throughout many wars. If I want to draw upon the practices and example of the experimental avant-garde in chorography, I cannot ignore its shadow, the military vanguard. The premise of writing with the whole paradigm in chorography, mobilizing the whole set of "vanguards," is that a new gesture or unforeseen "heading" (in every sense of the term—geographic and symbolic) is most likely to emerge when categorically distinct elements are brought into contact. I am composing, then, with the "heading" (topic becoming *chora*) of "vanguard."

Consider the relationship between the French surrealists (model for my heuretic CATTt) and the foreign legion. One of the most important political events of the early 1920s, when André Breton and company were inventing surrealism, was the war in Morocco fought by the legion against Arab rebels led by Abd-el-Krim, whose stronghold was the Rif Mountains. Eventually regular French troops joined the legion, due to the successes of the Arabs against the Spanish. Abd-el-Krim's popularity among all the Moors established him historically as "a forerunner of a nationalist spirit that had not yet quite been born" (Mercer, 235).

The surrealists, totally opposed to the Rif war, decided to engage in a politics of scandal. To express their opposition to French nationalism and colonialism, to all racism, anti-Semitism, and xenophobia, they published an insulting pamphlet (entitled

"A Cadaver"), which was their obituary for Anatole France. France, as a national hero and "epitome of the bourgeois literary establishment," represented everything the surrealists despised (Lewis, 23–24). Led by Breton, the group responded to "the spectacle of a country in mourning for a national hero," one whose very name was *France,* by engaging in a kind of "sounding" or "slashing," addressing to the memory of "France" every insult they could think of: "With France, a bit of human servility leaves the world" (Breton); "I think it's a remarkable idea to waste any time addressing farewells to a corpse from which the brain has been removed!" (Soupault, referring to the fact that France's brain was dissected "for the benefit of science" and declared to be "the finest brain that can be imagined") (24). In a related demonstration at a banquet, the surrealists yelled, "Long live Germany! Down with France! Long live China! Long live the Riff!" which resulted in a brawl (25). With a huge French army fighting in North Africa, the surrealists were widely regarded as traitors.

The aggression of the experimental artists is a figurative equivalent of the other vanguard, the legion: the tactic is the same, whether military, political, or cultural—attack the enemy. As spearhead of many expeditions, the foreign legion performed the spirit of Europe, as for example in 1883 when Colonel François de Negrier took a batallion of legionnaires with him to Indochina. The Americans confirmed the French self-image by following this lead.

In chorography this "spearhead" may be thought differently, perhaps by exploring the German as well as the French translation of the term. In his discussion of the crisis in the spirit of Europe, Derrida refers to Heidegger's term for Europe as "place"—*Ort,* signifying in the Germanic idiom "the point of a lance, where all the forces join and assemble at the limit": this point concerns a *telos,* the beginning and end of Europe, like "that which conducts or guides the avant-garde of a battle" (Derrida, 1991a:29). Heidegger speculated on this *Ort* in terms of *chora,* not as a "point" but as a place of convergence, figured in the X or *Chi* crossed through "Being," putting it "under erasure."

The X was not negative but signified the *Quadriparti* or the *Geviert,* the place gathering the four elements of Heidegger's cosmology: earth, heaven, mortals, and gods (Derrida, 1987a:589). What is this *pas* or step, Derrida wondered, this crossing-out that is not negative? "The form of the chiasmus, the X, interests me greatly, not as the symbol of the unknown but because there is here a sort of fork (the series *crossroads, quadrifurcum,* grid, grill, key, etc.) which is moreover unequal, one of its points extending its scope further than the other: a figure of the double gesture and the crossing" (Derrida, 1987c:166). This X is the mark and point of *chora* in Discipline discourse. As for the good timing of chorography, one need only observe the magical appearance of the X everywhere in America in 1992, whose vehicle was Spike Lee's *Malcolm X,* the X announcing that "America" is under erasure.

To put "America" or *Beau Geste* under erasure is not a negative act but a call for the invention process to continue. In his article on Adami's "Study for a Drawing after *Glas,"* Derrida discusses the X as a sign: "X, the chiasmus letter, is *Chi,* in its normal transcription. This is what I call the other scene, following, if you like, the anagrammatical inversion of *Ich,* or of *Isch* (Hebrew man)" (165). In trying to write my own *premises,* my "other scene," I am this *Ich* that is *Chi* (and so is every chorographer). The X "describes the demiurgic operation in the *Timaeus:* 'Having thus obtained the systasis, he split it in two from one end to the other with a lengthwise slit; he fixed these two bands across one another at the center, in the form of a X; then he plied them to make a circle of each one and joined up all the ends opposite the crossing point.... He adjudged the movement of the outside circle to the nature of the Same, and that of the inside circle to the nature of the Other'" (166). Adami's drawing of the operation figures a fish being hooked, like the invention I want to catch in the crossed network of my *premises.*

Meanwhile, in the Entertainment institution, the time of the Rif war and of the invention of surrealism coincided with the publication of *Beau Geste,* which was not welcomed in France, whatever its popularity might be in the English-speaking world.

Official France did not appreciate representations of the legion, including the Gary Cooper remake, which was banned in France until 1977 (Weber, 4). Although in America and other parts of the world there was considerable sympathy for the Riff cause, with Abd-el-Krim perceived as a kind of Robin Hood of the Moors (Mercer, 235), in Hollywood the tendency was to cast the Riffians as the stereotyped villains, as in the case of the producer whose idea for a film consisted of three star actors in a desert; whenever a writer proposed a setting or situation for the story, he would ask, "Where are the Riffs?" or "Who are the heavies?" (Cameron, 33).

To write with the paradigm, chorography might take as a point of departure the series beginning with the term *Rif* (a mountainous coastal region in northern Morocco); *Riff* (a member of a group of Berber-speaking tribes living in northern Morocco); *riff* (in jazz, a melodic phrase, often constantly repeated, forming an accompaniment for a soloist). The project is to learn to write with patterns that function more like music than like concepts.

Justice

My question, then, concerns the relation of the history of writing to the evolution of national identity. Eric Havelock, reviewing his career in relation to the disciplinary emergence of what I call grammatology, mentions his monograph, "The Linguistic Task of the Pre-Socratics," which, "by restricting itself to an examination of all actual Pre-Socratic quotations, has been able to draw the conclusion that this 'task' should be conceived not as offering rival systems of thought, but as the invention of a conceptual language in which all future systems of philosophic thought could be expressed; this same language, however, being extracted from Homer and Hesiod and given a new non-oralist syntax" (Havelock, 2).

Associated with this new language practice was the invention of the concept and behaviors (ideology) of *self*. "The 'self' was a

Socratic discovery or, perhaps we should say, an invention of the Socratic vocabulary. . . . The person who used the language but was now separated from it became the 'personality' who could now discover its existence. The language so discovered became that level of theoretic discourse denoted by *logos*" (114). Subject formation—subjectivation—is itself subject to invention.

The abstracting power of philosophic and ultimately of scientific discourse was born out of a long struggle, of which one of the earliest examples is Hesiod's treatment of *dike* or "justice."

> Hesiod cannot conjure the required discourse out of thin air. We could easily manage it today, because we inherit two thousand years of literate habit. He, on the contrary, must resort to the oral word as already known—the only preserved word that is known. He must build his own semi-connected discourse out of disconnected bits and pieces contained in oral discourse. . . . He still will not be able to tell us what justice is, but only what it does or suffers. He has taken one decisive step toward the formation of a new mentality by inventing the topic to take the place of the person. But he cannot take the second step of giving his topic a syntax of descriptive definition. It will still behave rather than be. (102)

This hard-won abstracting capacity, of which academic writing is a "normalization," a routinization, as powerful as it is must be reinvented if it is to function in an electronic apparatus. The questioning of abstract disciplinary discourse is possible in part because of the advent of a new technology. Electronics introduces a new dimension into the relationship between the oral and written registers of language, requiring and making possible nothing less than another round of inventiveness of the sort that produced philosophy in ancient Greece and science in Renaissance Europe. What was achieved in the logocentric era of philosophy and science, at the level of discourse, was that "static 'facts of the case' began to replace dynamic 'goings on.' In the language of Philoso-

phy, 'being' (as a form of syntax) began to replace 'becoming'"
(104).

What is under way in the electronic apparatus is the collective
invention of a new mode of reason (based on a new relationship
among technology, institutions, and the human subject) whose
symptoms it has been one task of grammatology to describe. One
symptom, for example, is the pervasive dissatisfaction precisely
with abstraction itself—a concern with the remainder that is lost
or excluded in abstractive reasoning. The primary symptom of
the closure of the invention and development of conceptual
thinking is named "Auschwitz."

"Auschwitz" may be included in an analytical regime of
phrases, as in this example: "That referent is real which is declared to be the same in these three situations: signified, named,
shown. Thus, respectively: in an internment camp, there was
mass extermination by chambers full of Zyklon B; that camp is
called Auschwitz; here it is. A fourth phrase states that the signified referent, the named referent, and the shown referent are the
same" (Lyotard, 43). Despite following all the rules of proof and
representation, however, the effect of *verification* fails, the reality
is not *proven* (it functions only on paper, or only in hypermedia).
Rather, "the 'Auschwitz' model would designate an 'experience'
of language that brings speculative discourse to a halt.... It
would be a name without a speculative 'name,' not sublatable
into a concept" (88). If "justice" (*dike*) was the experience that
motivated one of the first concepts, an experience of the greatest
"injustice" has shown the limitations of conceptual reason.

"Auschwitz" marks the limitations of the organization of the
human subject within the alphabetic apparatus—the practices of
"self." It is the question of how individuals are formed into
groups—into "nations," for example. The dilemma of German
nationhood after the Holocaust is instructive for thinking about
theoria in America, which is related to the description of the German dilemmas as "the inability to mourn" the death of Hitler
(the denial of a collective identification with Hitler as an ego ideal
and hence his centrality to the formation of "selfhood" for a gen-

eration of Germans). Hamlet is said to be the "negative patron saint" of the second generation of postwar Germans, who are haunted by their fathers' biographies (Santner, 36). At the same time, the "culture industry," including the "auratic gaze" of Hollywood film stars and the consumerism of American tourists, is accused of being a continuation of fascism by other means.

In an effort to repair their sense of national identity, German conservatives complain that only the "victor's" side of World War II has been told. They want to retell the story of the Holocaust in a way that will make it possible to repair the rupture in the history of the nation caused by the Nazi period, to assimilate the "final solution" by relativizing it as one more genocide among others in a perennial saga of migrating peoples seeking living space (including the destruction of the American Indians).

German liberals respond that the lesson to be learned from World War II rather is that a new sort of national identity should be sought, replacing the sense of unity, the "we" created by excluding the "other," and altering the very nature of "selfhood" that is the foundation assumed in a declaration beginning "We the People." What is needed, as Jürgen Habermas argued, is a "postconventional" identity, open to difference and diversity. In this context, the inability to mourn is rather "an inability to celebrate" (Elsaesser, 248), that is, an inability to invent this other style of group formation. Comparing national defense to ego psychology, Sloterdijk argued similarly that "the well-behaved sociopsychological enlightenment thought the problem lay in the 'incapacity to mourn.' But it is even more the incapacity to have the right rage at the right time, the incapacity to express, the incapacity to explode the climate of care, the incapacity to celebrate, the incapacity to let go" (Sloterdijk, 127).

America has its own version of blocked mourning, or its own need to learn how to celebrate—how to invent a postconventional identity at both the individual and collective levels. The symptom of this dilemma is the controversy surrounding the celebration of the Columbus quincentenary, exemplified by the different uses of the "Holocaust argument." Indian activists compare the destruction of Native Americans to the Jewish Holocaust and point out that only the victor's version of the history has been told. As the German situation shows, it is difficult to control the effects of such arguments, since all parties to the debate have recourse to the same accusation. Russell Means (American Indian Movement) used it against the enemies of Native Americans by comparing "Columbus Day" in America to celebrating a "Hitler Day" in Germany; Bob Wiemer, an editorial writer for *Newsday*, used it against the friends of AIM by drawing an analogy between "PC [politically correct] speech" and "German Nazi euphemisms," such as Goebbels's effort to expunge "alien" words from pure German.

There might be something to learn in this context from Jürgen Syberberg's *Our Hitler.* "First of all, Hitler is not conceivable without us," Syberberg stated about his film. "If one looks and hates but is forced to recognize human features there, how can we justly picture ourselves and this guilt and this common will and these intermediate tones of hope without harming ourselves through lies, self-deception" (Syberberg, 13). The American situation is different, of course, involving a different kind of forgetting or blocked mourning—not that of repression but of "taking for granted." Syberberg's statement could apply to America, nonetheless, if the name "Columbus" is substituted for "Hitler."

A possible subtitle for my remake, then, could be "Our Columbus" or "Columbus: A Method Made in America." It has to do with the mystery Freud said was "beyond pleasure," involving the most secret secret—the one that is kept from oneself. Hyperrhetoric may bring this secret into visibility by marking the trace through the associative structure of "Columbus," as Syberberg tried to do with the associative structure (memory) of "Hitler" when he followed the genealogy of the poetic line, *"Üb' immer Treu und Redlichkeit":* "It was the glockenspiel tune in Potsdam until its destruction, the melody by Mozart and verses from Germany's pietistic eighteenth century. Then it was taken over by the Freemasons and engraved on Frederick II's church as the hallmark of Prussia." Then it was taken up "as the signal of the

Deutschland Radio Network," to be understood in the film as "the dismal, macabre, tragic ending of a Hitler-history of Germany: 'Be ever loyal and honest until the cool grave'" (18). Let this German story be a cautionary tale of invention.

7

MYTHOLOGY

Diegesis

My proposal is to perform a living tableau (a still life) from *Beau Geste* in the Miles City follies. I still need to choose a specific scene as the basis for the act. It so happens that the story of *Beau Geste* is itself composed around a tableau. "Everyone recalls the fort 'defended' by dead soldiers," Ted Sennett commented in his brief note on the film in his anniversary volume on Hollywood's Golden Year, indicating the mnemonic capacity of the scene.

The story begins with the arrival of a legion column at Fort Zinderneuf, where the soldiers discover the aftermath of a great battle in which a large force of Touareg tribesmen attacked the small legion garrison. Arriving too late, the relief column perceived the massacre (according to Wren's book) as a "silent, frozen tableau." At first everything had seemed normal: the flag was flying over the fort, and soldiers could be seen positioned at every firing slot of the parapet. The men stood like stone statues, as if "in a dream or nightmare." All were dead at their posts, still holding their rifles. It was as if a ghost army had repulsed the Arabs. What could have happened? My piece in the follies can take advantage of this formal coincidence between *Beau Geste* and the music hall.

The "field" or network I must construct, within which an invention, or the premises of inventive thinking, might appear has all the qualities of a diegesis in a film. Where *is* Fort Zinderneuf located, exactly? Referentially, Zinderneuf is associated with an actual place in Algeria, one of the many outposts scattered throughout North Africa (if not the headquarters itself) of the French foreign legion. "The fort in *Beau Geste,* P. C. Wren's 1924 novelized paean to the French Foreign Legion, might be the 300-year-old Turkish outpost at Bou Saada," Mort Rosenblum stated, recounting how legionnaires had painted on its walls in three-foot-high letters, "This is France, forever" (Rosenblum, 260). The actual headquarters was established in 1843 in Algeria, south of Oran, "on the site of the grave of a religious hermit named Sidi-bel-Abbes" (Mercer, 35).

This real legion has a link with the Parc de la Villette. The site of the park is far from the historic center of Paris but not in the suburbs; rather, it is in "the urban fringe." The location included two existing structures—a museum of science and industry, and the *Grande Halle,* formerly a slaughterhouse but now transformed into "an exhibition–cum–concert center." On this site in 1871 the foreign legion fought one of the fiercest battles of its history. Brought into France to help fight the Germans in the Franco-Prussian War, the legion became the "spearhead" of the government's counterattack to retake Paris from the rebels of the commune in the civil war that followed the French defeat (Mercer, 105). Among the warehouses and slaughterhouses of the Villette barge basin "dockers and carriers fought from building to building to the last man," fought as fiercely, it was said, as any Arabs (108).

My premises, like the diegesis of *Beau Geste,* are a hybrid (exactly the term Wren used to describe Sidi-bel-Abbes in his novel):

> Entering the town itself, through a great gate in the huge ramparts, we were in a curiously hybrid Oriental-European atmosphere in which moved stately Arabs, smart French ladies, omnibuses, camels.... No less hybrid was the architecture, and the eye passed from white gleaming mosque with glorious minaret to gaudy cafe with garish lights.... Hybridism insisted through other senses too, for the ear caught now the 'Allah Akbar! Lah illah il Allah!' of the muezzin on the minaret; the shouting of an angry Spanish woman; the warning cries in *sabir* of a negro driver." (Wren, 216)

The 1939 film version of *Beau Geste* was shot not in the desert of Algeria but in Arizona, near Yuma, and on the sets at the studio in Hollywood. Not until the 1950s was it common to shoot on location. The setting of Zinderneuf, then, is an "arbitrary construction" of a "geographical limbo" to which the name "Algeria" has been grafted. "Hollywood's particular brand of isolationism was propelling it towards a picture of the world made up of two countries, the United States, and the Other Place" (Cameron, 30). In the era before *Beau Geste,* if a desert were labeled "America," one expected cowboys and Indians; if "Africa," one expected legionnaires and Arabs. The diegesis of my premises is composed in this verisimilar way.

In short, to construct my premises in the style of a film diegesis means that I am working with the logic of the Hollywood "dream factory." "In the movies you can do almost anything: when a wheel comes off Bob Hope's car in the climactic chase of Frank Tashlin's *Son of Paleface* (1952), he uses a rope to support the axle as he drives on. 'Hurry up,' he yells to Roy Rogers, who has ridden off in pursuit of the wheel, 'I've just realized that this is impossible'" (Cameron, 19). Such a setting is just right for inventing an impossible method.

Enigma

A diegesis involves time as well as space, and my plan is to represent not just a place but an event. The diegesis I borrow from *Beau Geste* (as the field within which an invention might appear) comes, as do most narratives, with the temporality of a puzzle, riddle, or enigma in need of resolution. Wren shows Major Beaujolais describing his puzzlement over the scene at Zinderneuf in terms of "Holmes and Watson" to make clear that the tale is a mystery—the enigma of what happened at Fort Zinderneuf. My tableau involves, then, not only a certain place, but also a direction or "heading," a dynamic undertow of time carrying me toward a certain end. The transformation of this temporality from the mode of mystery (interpretation, truth) into the feeling of eureka (invention) is an important goal of chorography.

Jacques Lacan experimented with this temporality when he introduced a description of Poe's "The Purloined Letter" into his yearlong seminar, "The Ego," in order to illustrate his theory of the unconscious. The context of the whole seminar is important for chorography (associated with that part of the paradigm of *folie* having to do with "madness" and its theory in psychoanalysis) because it clarifies the *specific* analogy Lacan wanted to make. The individual subject (whose consciousness, ego, or self-image is organized by the imaginary order) is inscribed in the symbolic order of society. The unfolding of events that was characterized as "fate" or "fortune" in an earlier episteme, and that Freud described as the Death Drive, Lacan defined in terms of a combinatorial machine—a computer. In chorography Lacan's analogy is assimilated to the series of metaphors naming *chora*. In fact, Lacan used one of the Platonic metaphors for *chora* to describe the mediating function the analyst plays for the analysand: "Throughout the course of the analysis, on the sole condition that the ego of the analyst does agree not to be there, on the sole condition that the analyst is not a living mirror, but an empty mirror, what happens between the ego of the subject and the Others? . . . The analysis consists in getting [the subject] to become conscious of his relations with all these Others who are his true interlocutors, whom he hasn't recognized" (Lacan, 1988:246). These Others, who are my superego, dictate the premises of my judgments.

The narrative of *Beau Geste* is structured by a mystery quite similar to the one organizing Poe's story (it turns out, in any case, that almost all narratives share this structuration). The Poe mystery is initiated when the minister purloins the compromising letter that he observed being delivered to the queen while the king was away. The story then turns on the circulation of the stolen letter from one owner to another until it is returned to the queen by the detective, Dupin. In his apologue, Lacan takes advantage of a basic principle of storytelling to make his point about the workings of the unconscious as the symbolic order of our institutional life. One of the devices operating in most narratives, that is, is the circulation of some significant "prop," whose movement in the plot signals the relationships and modalities among the characters.

Beau Geste is ordered by the circulation of a purloined jewel, the famous "Blue Water" sapphire. The enigma guiding the practical details of the plot concerns who stole the jewel. In the story, one of Sir Hector's ancestors originally confiscated the jewel in India, as "booty" of colonial conquest. While the no-good Sir Hector is away, wasting the resources of the estate, Lady Brandon secretly sells the stone to a man from India in order to raise capital needed to keep things going and replaces it with a fake. Beau Geste happens to witness the sale, but says nothing. Some years later, word comes that Sir Hector is returning in order to sell the jewel. The lights suddenly go out while the family is admiring the (fake) sapphire, and when they come on again the stone is gone. Beau stole it not to blackmail his beloved "Aunt Patricia" but to cover for her. He flees to the foreign legion (which he has been thinking of doing since he was a boy).

Michael "Beau" Geste is well named, the motivated quality of his signature being the punch line of the novel. The *inventio* or generator of the plot, in other words, is an antonomasia (exchange between proper and common noun)—how "Beau" performs his name. At the end of the novel, Beau's brother John returns from Zinderneuf (the only survivor of the massacre) bringing a letter. Lady Brandon reads the letter, in which Beau explains his sacrifice (thus resolving the narrative enigma). The letter is signed "'Beau' Geste." "'A *beau geste*, indeed,' said Aunt Patricia, and for the only time in my life, I saw her put her handkerchief to her eyes" (Wren, 411).

The Hermeneutic Code

One purpose of my tableau remake is to learn how to drop the use of enigma to guide curiosity and replace it with the "gest" of invention. Chorography in this context could be considered the symmetrical complement of Brecht's non-Aristotelian epic theater. In the same way that Brecht used the alienation effect to introduce critical distance into popular theatrical entertainments, the chorographer introduces empathy, projection, and identification effects into critical theory, as in the reading together of Derrida and Wren. The gap separating the discourses of Discipline and Entertainment has to be crossed in both directions. The point is not to reduce one to the other but to open a circuit between them.

Brecht used the term *Gestus* to mean something similar to the old English *gest* — "bearing, carriage, mien, a mixture of gesture and gist, attitude and point" (Bullock and Stallybrass, 265). The basic gest of a Brechtian play communicated "not merely the meaning but also the speaker's attitude to his listeners and to what he is saying." Wren manages to compress in Beau's story nearly all the dictionary meanings of *gest* as a tale, a deed or exploit, deportment or conduct, gesture, and even "the stages of a journey."

The paradigm of *gest* includes as well Derrida's concern for assuming responsibility for the heritage of modern Europe even while changing its heading: "To be faithfully responsible *for* this memory, and thus to respond rigorously to this double injunction: will this have to consist in repeating or in breaking with, in continuing or in opposing: Or indeed in attempting to *invent another gesture,* an epic *gesture* [*geste*] in truth, that presupposes memory precisely in order to assign identity from alterity?" (Derrida, 1992c:29–30). Such is the "gesture" I seek in my remake.

To select the scene for my tableau, and to locate a site for grafting a Heuretic code to the story, I had to review the operations of narrative. Roland Barthes's description of the five codes constituting the "field" (or score) of narrative offers useful guidance. Two codes govern temporality, the syntax (arrangement, *dispositio*) of the release of information over time. One is the code of Action—the event units, such as enlisting in the foreign legion, boarding the ship for North Africa. The Action code is subordinate to, and organized in turn by, the Hermeneutic code, the code of enigmas or of "truth" that groups the actions into sequences of questions or puzzles and their eventual resolution (What happened at Zinderneuf? Who stole the family jewel?).

Peter Wollen explained the Hermeneutic code by extending Lacan's reading of "The Purloined Letter" to narrative in general. Wollen noted that there are three times or positions organizing the drive to discover truth: (1) seeing but being blind, merely looking; (2) interpreting or misinterpreting—the time it takes to (mis)understand; (3) knowing or denying knowledge (conclusion) (Wollen, 41). The protagonist passes through all three positions, rotating through each role: as victim, criminal, and detective (investigator) (43). In the rotation or "revolution" the third position is the one of power, although the discovery of a secret tends to instigate violence (as was the case with Beau, who was killed at Zinderneuf) (45). Depending on the spectator's awareness of the secret, three different effects are associated with the timing: suspense (spectator knows and character does not); mystery (spectator knows there is a secret but doesn't know what it is); shock (secret suddenly revealed unannounced (47).

The researcher working with the unknown as mystery to be

solved may expect to work through at least these three times. Chorography, however, keeping in mind Lacan's point that a *fourth* discursive position is available (his own position retelling the tale) adds a further register to this circulation. Meanwhile, this rotation of times and positions has been stated in classic Freudian terms as a displacement of the child's discovery of sexuality (the problematic of *Geschlecht,* the discovery of a mark of difference), dramatized as the satisfaction of curiosity in witnessing the "primal scene." Oedipus, of course, is the prototype (along with Hamlet) of all detectives in this scenario of a "looker" or "seeker" implicated in a "crime" (Pederson-Krag). The guilt associated with the "crime" is a fundamental part of the experience of rotation in timing, with the time of knowledge constituting a recognition of one's own responsibility for the process of meaning or making sense. In his study of Leonardo, Freud generalized this Oedipal experience as the ground of all scientific curiosity.

In psychoanalytic theory the Oedipal story is an apologue for the entry into language that puts one in one's place (as son, for example, with an opportunity to take one's turn at the other available positions). The theory is made memorable in our cultural literacy by being told as a story about "castration." Roland Barthes has demonstrated that most narratives are about castration in this theoretical sense. Barthes used a Balzac story, "Sarrasine," to demonstrate his theory of codes, a story in which the narrator strikes a bargain with his object of affection. The telling is part of a seduction scene, with the narrator appealing to the curiosity of a woman by offering to tell her what he knows about the mysterious Zambinella in exchange for a night of love. But the tale he tells is too disturbing, and the beloved breaks the contract. *Beau Geste* is a "Victorian" version of the same contract, with George Lawrence retelling the tale he heard from Major Beaujolais to Lady Brandon, the woman he idolizes, in the hope that it might be exchanged for some sign of favor from her.

Barthes's admiration of the Balzac story may be appreciated in the light of the rest of the narrative codes. As in the case of the syntagmatic axis, a hierarchy of two codes organizes the "paradigmatic" axis (governing *inventio* or selection of materials): the code of Semes involves all the "props" of setting and person, signaling the nature of the characters associated with them; the Cultural code organizes the Semes into the stereotypes and commonplaces informing the cultural literacy of a given historical period. The fifth code, the Symbolic code, is at the top of the other two hierarchies, and orders and coordinates in turn the axes of selection and combination. The Symbolic code translates into narrative theory the insights of Lacan's symbolic order.

Barthes selected "Sarrasine" for his theoretical demonstration because Balzac's "structural artifice" of having the hero mistakenly fall in love with a castrato opera star made the story itself nearly a theory. Barthes describes this plot device (the enigma of Zambinella's—the castrato's—identity) as the identification of the Hermeneutic and Symbolic codes:

> making the search for truth (hermeneutic structure) into the search for castration (symbolic structure), making the truth be *anecdotally* (and no longer symbolically) the absent phallus. . . . Aphasia concerning the word *castrato* has a double value, whose duplicity is insoluble: on the symbolic level, there is a taboo; on the operative level, the disclosure is delayed: the truth is suspended *both* by censorship and by machination. The *readerly* structure of the text is thereby raised to the level of an analytical investigation (Barthes, 1974:164).

It is the structure to be discussed later as the *mise en abyme.*

A similar crossing of the Symbolic and Hermeneutic codes occurs in *Beau Geste,* albeit in a more allusive way, displacing the threat of castration into the environment, in a few dark allusions to "unspeakable torture and mutilation at the hands of the Arabs" (Wren, 236). A history of the legion describes the Riffian as a fanatical, ferocious fighter, whose "wish to emasculate his enemy before he killed him" makes the threat explicit. The Riff women were said to be even more cruel than the men:

When a prisoner fell into women's hands, they customarily stripped him and staked him spread-eagled to the ground. After pulling out his fingernails and toenails, they often roasted the soles of his feet with burning brands. Throughout their fiendish ritual they took pains to revive him each time he fainted. As a climax they castrated him. Sometimes, too, they disembowled him, blinded him, cut off his ears and nose. If he did not die immediately, they poured honey on his wounds to attract ants and flies which swarmed into his still-living body. (Mercer, 237)

The analytical benefit of merging the Symbolic and Hermeneutic codes is that it shows something about the nature of the search for truth—no curiosity without castration. One of the fundamental resources for the discovery of truth, practiced in the legal system of the ancient Greeks and in more than one-third of the world's modern states, is torture. "The very idea of truth we receive from the Greeks, is inextricably linked with the practice of torture, which has almost always been the ultimate attempt to discover a secret 'always out of reach'" (duBois, 7). The ancient Greek word for torture, duBois explains, is *basanos*. "It means first of all the touchstone used to test gold for purity." In a practice that turned out to be typical of the policy of most colonial powers, the "putting of the question" by torture was routinely used by the French against the Arabs in Algeria (E. Peters, 134).

Chorography is designed to introduce into the narratives and arguments of the print apparatus a Heuretic code, to supplement and replace the Hermeneutic code and its drive to reduce enigmas to truth. The rationale for disengaging curiosity from "truth" in this way derives from the transformation of literacy underway in the electronic apparatus. In selecting the scene for my tableau I need to show how to graft the Heuretic code onto the Hermeneutic code at the point of greatest enigma, thus transforming the X from the mark of the unknown to the chiasmus of invention.

The Left Hand of Wood

The Symbolic code (translating the psychoanalytic theory of castration into rhetoric) uses the structure of myth to organize the other codes of narrative and argument, as may be seen in the story of the "foreign legion." The question of how to stimulate and manage curiosity in writing may be explored by considering the appeal of the foreign legion to boys (as depicted in *Beau Geste*). Why would someone want to join the foreign legion (considering this "want" as the same force that education and science depend upon)? Paul Rollet, a famous legion general known for his bad temper, was said to have been most irritated by "the factual inaccuracies" of Wren's "romance about the Legion" (Mercer, 247). He failed to understand the value of Wren's books as recruiting devices, as demonstrated by the case of Simon Murray, an Englishman who joined the legion in 1960, and who disagreed with the general:

> I had read Wren's *Beau Geste,* as every Englishman has, and I held the traditional English view that service in foreign armies in foreign lands was an acceptable way to begin life—crusading it used to be called! What I did not know at the time was that Wren had painted a picture of the Legion that was not all that inaccurate and I was about to step into a very hard way of life indeed for which I was totally unprepared. It could not have been less romantic. (Murray, 10)

The legion had a reputation as the most glamorous military organization in the world and is known to cultivate its own mystique, legend, and traditions. *Glamour* (a term whose invention is credited to Walter Scott), a corrupt form of *grammar,* as Walter Ong noted, is defined as "a delusive or alluring charm; a magical or fictitious beauty attaching to any object or person." That *beau geste* is a glamorous term is shown in the ad placed by Intimate Treasures in various adult magazines; it offers a "natural sex attractant"—something to do with "pheromones" speaking the "silent language of love." The one for women is named "Bare Essence," and the one for men "Beau Geste." To use it is "dangerous but worth the risk ($19.95)."

What is the attraction of an organization that promises, "You, Legionnaires, are soldiers to die. And I will send you to where death is" (Rosenblum, 247)? With its slogan, "March or Die," its battle cry, *"A moi, la Légion!"* (shouted by a soldier standing in a breached wall, facing a hail of bullets), it is a kind of *liknon,* a social machine for sorting men according to two values: good (courage and death), and evil (cowardice and life). "Better to die well than to live badly." "I will be somebody, or dead!" The reason most commonly given for joining is "to forget a woman." Part of the mystique concerns the possibility of a new start in life, escaping the past, taking a new name, and carrying a secret to the grave. Once in the legion, any man might be mistaken for Private Sobieski, whose secret was disclosed by a comrade after Sobieski was killed. He was the last descendant of King Sobieski of Poland, who had saved Vienna from the Turks (Mercer, 79).

The legion itself, then, is another metaphor for *chora,* and for *Geschlecht,* another figure of the sorting machine, having to do with all manner of identity and identification. That the shape (*Eidos*) of this memory machine is "square" may be anticipated in the name of a famous infantry formation—in practice actually a rectangular arrangement of two lines of soldiers, one kneeling and one standing—the same one the English used to break Napoleon's cavalry at Waterloo. The infantry square figures prominently in the story of the most glorious death of all the heroes of the legion—that of Captain Danjou at Camerone, Mexico, April 30, 1863. In Mexico to support the establishment of a French empire—known as "Napoleon's folly" (Napoleon III)—the legion assigned Danjou and his sixty-two men to escort a large shipment of gold. Ambushed by an army of two thousand juaristas, the troop formed a square and thus was able (despite incredible odds) to hold off the attacking cavalry while retreating to the abandoned village of Camerone. The legion troop fought to nearly the last man in a defense that saved the caravan. Danjou's body was never found, but only his wooden left hand (a prosthesis for the hand he lost at the battle of Sebastopol). This left hand (but why was it left?) is now the most sacred relic of the legion, kept on display in the trophy museum at the headquarters and paraded every year on Camerone Day (Mercer, 84–92). One of the greatest honors for a legionnaire is to be asked to carry Danjou's hand during the ceremony. This amputated, prosthetic hand embodies the spirit of the foreign legion, a spirit of manliness, suggesting that the hand is to the theory of *Geschlecht* what the phallus is to the Oedipal theory in psychoanalysis.

Mourning

Beau Geste identified with the "beautiful death" of Captain Danjou. As a boy, Michael and his brothers rehearsed the "Viking's Funeral" in their games (dead Vikings were cremated, burned in their ships with their dogs at their feet), each promising to provide the honor for the others should the opportunity arise. The mysterious fire at Zinderneuf that so puzzled Major Beaujolais is Beau's funeral, provided by the lone survivor of the battle, John Geste. The "dog" placed at Beau's feet is the corpse of the evil sergeant. Gary Cooper was almost killed in the filming of this scene. Notorious for being able to fall asleep anywhere, Cooper nodded off during the lengthy preparations for the shoot, lying in the bunk in his legion uniform. "After the fire was started and the cameras were rolling, [Robert] Preston looked around for Cooper, didn't see him and realized where he was. Rushing into the burning set, Preston woke Cooper and led him out through the smoke" (Kaminsky, 96).

The Viking's Funeral manifests the myth of the beautiful death that informs the Symbolic code of *Beau Geste*.

> One escapes death by the only means known—the perpetuation of the proper name. This proper name must be proper not only to the interested party, but also to the collectivity (through patronym, eponym, or nationality), since the collective name is what assures the perenniality within itself of individual proper names.

> Such is the Athenian "beautiful death," the exchange of the finite
> for the infinite: the *Die in order not to die.* (Lyotard, 100)

The legion, in which men bearing assumed names die for a foreign nation, demonstrates the full power of this myth, whose operation may be deconstructed, however, by putting the narrative under erasure.

Beau Geste typifies the mythical appeal of adventure books. *Myth* is used in this context in structuralist terms (defined by Claude Levi-Strauss) as a contradiction within the morality of a culture that is mediated and resolved illusorily through the course of a narrative (Green, 1979, 55). According to this theory, narrative is arranged by a double bind that the characters, with whom we identify, struggle to resolve. Keeping in mind that double binds literally drive people crazy, the value of mythology as a social machine for resolving contradictions may be appreciated.

The double bind or contradiction informing adventure is that between the promotion of the official values of the middle class, which are associated with the business life of merchants and trade, on the one hand, and on the other hand, an unofficial admiration for the aristomilitary virtues (19). The merchant class, devoted to a conservative practicality, condemned as "murderous and vile" the values of chivalry and honor motivating the aristocratic caste. Yet in practice the virtues merchants admired in their sons were not duty, obedience, and piety (the domestic virtues) but dash, pluck, and a lion-heart (220). The businessmen had a horror of "milksops" and an imperative requiring "manliness," an imperative that put their sons in a double bind. In my experience, this is still how men are gendered in America. This gendering, like the other practices inscribing individuals into communities—practices of class, race, or nationality for example—*happens* to people prior to the age of consent; for this reason, the superego is (partly) unconscious. The experience of participation in the collectivity of the symbolic order has been described as the paradox of the "forced choice": "The situation of the forced choice consists in the fact that the subject must freely choose the community to which he already belongs, independent of his choice—*he must choose what is already given to him*" (Zizek, 165). To write one's own *premises* is to recover the moment (that never *happens*) of this choice.

As Green observed, the myth of adventure is not just a matter of composing books but of authoring a cultural identity through the "invention" of a tradition (as in cultural literacy). The psychological agency of these traditions is the superego (the agency that administers "castration"). How is the myth of the beautiful death enforced? At a collective level a feeling may arise, one associated also with pathological states of mourning (melancholia), "where the subject feels that he is the brunt of criticism and denigration: 'we see how one part of the ego sets itself over against the other, judges it critically, and takes it as its object'" (Laplanche and Pontalis, 436).

> It may be that some aspects of super-ego functioning are manifestations of the conventional conceptual structures embodied in internalized language. It would then make sense that the voices expressing the criticisms in verbal idle thoughts are less a matter of a personal voice directed against a personal enemy, than a public voice, a voice which is "not mine," directed against an enemy which is also "not mine," but which represents a threat to the cultural conventions found in the culture as a whole and in the language which codes them. (Aylwin, 54)

The conscience is this hortatory inner voice "calling its person to order" (53): Do your duty!

The beautiful death is a foundational myth marking the trace of the premises of a national identity. Nations, that is, are inventions, formed by means of epideictic events, in which the "people," the living citizens, listening to the traditional story about a war, perhaps the war of Athens against Atlantis, assimilate the dead heroes in a foundational recognition of themselves as "Athenians" (or "Americans" or "Germans" and so forth).

"The time of the narrations is not distinguished from the time of the diegeses: to tell or to hear is already 'to die well.' . . . Whoever is not of this people cannot hear, cannot tell, and cannot die well" (Lyotard, 105).

Nations are invented out of the memorial or mourning conducted by their citizens. This "mourning" for those who died well is associated with psychoanalytic "castration," referring to any sense of loss and separation, a lack compensated for by the acquisition of language, community, culture. "The oedipal resolution also governs the creation of a superego; and here too we find an important relation to the work of mourning and the elegy. At the most obvious level, we recall Freud's suggestion that the superego is made up of the 'illustrious dead,' a sort of cultural reservoir, or rather cemetery, in which one may also inter one's renounced love-objects, and in which the ruling monument is the internalized figure of the father" (Peter Sacks, in Santner, 169).

After Auschwitz, after the Holocaust, Lyotard argues, the beautiful death is no longer available in the same way, having been appropriated by the Nazis, who extended the funeral oration to every dimension of life. The "we" founded by sacrifice is denied the Jews of the Holocaust (or the victims of any genocide), who are not addressed by their death decree, not a party to the legitimating contract of the nation (the law) whose action intends to kill even the victims' death itself (to deny the event).

Perhaps the Holocaust is the difference between 1939 and 1992, the watershed, the divide requiring a new phase of national invention. How can I convey this feeling in *Beau Geste* to show both feelings, the double bind (1992 in 1939)? Freud's critics thought his topography (which has to be renamed *chorography*), including the introjection of parental figures in identification, was too anthropomorphic and the superego too tied to a "realist" mode (Laplanche and Pontalis, 438), even though Freud clarified that the judges were not people but "agencies": "Thus a child's superego is in fact constructed on the model not of its parents but of its parents' superego; the contents which fill it are the same and it becomes the vehicle of tradition and of all the time-resisting judgments of value which have propagated themselves in this manner from generation to generation" (Laplanche and Pontalis, 437). Or, as Lacan put it in his discussion of transference, "It is a matter of the subject progressively discovering which Other he is truly addressing, without knowing it, and of him progressively assuming the relations of transference at the place where he is, and where at first he didn't know he was" (Lacan, 1988:246).

To perform *Beau Geste* — the scene of the beautiful death, of the Viking's Funeral—is to enact this identification, to bring into appearance the *premises* of my superego, made accessible through this displaced location, the diegesis of my remake.

8

ACTING LESSONS

The Method

I am developing an analogy for chorography, saying that electronic writing is like performing a tableau vivant from *Beau Geste* as part of a follies show at a frontier saloon commemorating the Columbus quincentenary. Once I had the idea for the scene to use as the basis for the tableau—Beau's "Viking's Funeral" at Fort Zinderneuf—I still had to learn how to act the part. I decided to try Method acting.

A practical reason for using the Method (as it is called in the business) for my analogy is its familiarity in contemporary culture; even those who are not familiar with the theory are familiar with the product, Hollywood acting. It thus meets the requirements of an interface metaphor (to gain access to the unfamiliar by means of the familiar). The Method was derived from the "system" of Konstantin Stanislavski (whose nickname was "the camel"), which was in its day an avant-garde innovation. When the French foreign legion was fighting the Rif war in Morocco, and Percival Christopher Wren was writing *Beau Geste,* and Freud was working out the theory of the superego, and Breton was inventing surrealism, Stanislavski was invited by a man named Morris Gest (Gordon, 185) to bring his ensemble from Russia to America (1923–1924).

The "reality effect" produced by actors trained in Stanislavski's system was an immediate sensation in America, a success that led eventually to the migration of the style from the Russian avant-garde to the American mainstream by way of the Actor's Studio, headed by Lee Strasberg. Some of the performers associated with the Actor's Studio include Marlon Brando, James Dean, Paul Newman, Jack Nicholson, Dustin Hoffman, Al Pacino, Robert De Niro, and Robert Duvall. Women using the Method include Marilyn Monroe, Julie Harris, Geraldine Page, Shelly Winters, Anne Bancroft, Lee Grant, Kim Stanley, Ellen Burstyn, Estelle Parsons, and Sandy Dennis, among others (F. Hirsch, 293).

Stanislavski's system was never meant to be a performing technique but was instead a technique for rehearsal. The practice began with "table work," in which the actors took over some of the director's analytical function by learning to read the play in a certain way, reorganizing it as a character's Objectives and Actions: a Through-Action or larger goal of the play is identified and then broken down into a series or sequence of specific Aims, Goals, and Problems in each scene (what the character wants propels the actor to execute an Action, which in turn consists of both physical and psychological elements—for example, to open a door "as if" in search of a corpse (Gordon, 239).

Elia Kazan, director of *On the Waterfront,* believed that the most important lesson of the system for film acting could be stated as "to want": "We used to say in the theater: 'What are you on stage *for?* What do you walk on stage to get? What do you want?'" (Blum, 63). This motivation of actions in terms of desires reflects the most controversial aspect of Lee Strasberg's transformation of the system into the Method—his heavy reliance on psychoanalysis. The Method actor could be described as reproducing in performance the "lack of being" of Lacan's theory of the subject: "The child is born into the experience of lack, what Lacan terms the 'want to be'; and the subject's subsequent history consists of a series of attempts to figure and overcome this lack, a project that is doomed to failure. Though the form and experience of lack may alter, the basic reality of it persists and defies representation" (Lapsley and Westlake, 67).

The essence of the Method, in this context, could be defined as an identification of the actor's "want to be" with that of the character's. The value of the Method as analogy for chorography concerns the way it requires the actors to merge their personal culture with that of the play, whose themes and scenes are translated in rehearsal, using the technique of Affective memory, into the actors' own experiences, cultural backgrounds, and memories. During rehearsal a series of improvisational exercises, often far removed from the words of the script, remake the play in terms of the actors' autobiographies, finding equivalents and analogies in their life stories for the Idea, Objectives, and Actions that emerged from the table work. At the same time, the actor learns as much as possible about the world of the play, exploring its setting both informationally and experientially.

Through the "magic As-If," the actors identify with the role, not just giving the outward signs of emotions (as in earlier approaches to acting) but actually feeling the emotions "on stage." One key to acting by the Method is "the psychological gesture": "a physical movement that awakens the actor's inner life. It serves as a guide to the essential or hidden features of his character, and, equally important, as the key to memorizing the part. Psychological Gestures may be large or diminutive in size, abstract or natural, but they are always simply executed. A character may have as few as one Psychological Gesture. In performance, the actor need only think of the Gesture to feed his internal characterization" (Gordon, 173). According to Michael Chekhov, one of Stanislavski's most successful disciples, "the movement that forms the basis of the Psychological Gesture may be as abstract and fantastic as an arm stretching endlessly through an imaginary prison window (Chekhov's Gesture for Hamlet); or as concrete and realistic as the stroking of a cat while softly speaking of the heartless destruction of Russia's gentry (a gesture traditionally associated with Lenin)" (Gordon, 164).

Examples of the Method in practice often refer to Marlon Brando, who is said to be to the Method what Picasso is to cubism (an inventor). There is the moment in *On the Waterfront* in which Brando talks with Eva Marie Saint in a bar. "Frustrated, he raises a hand to his chin, holding the thumb stiffly, almost as if he were going to suck it; then he pinches the chin between thumb and forefinger, pulling at it like a goatee. The gesture is more important than anything he says, expressing in one fluid movement the anguish of a child trying to be 'manly'" (Naremore, 206). This bodily detail, registered in close-up, could be the Psychological Gesture of the whole film, given James Naremore's assessment of the Brando character as "a sort of child, in appealing contrast to the stereotypical and sententious 'adults' who surround him" (205).

To translate his system from a rehearsal technique to something more practical for play production, the later Stanislavski reduced the time devoted to table work and deemphasized Affective Memory (the psychoanalysis-like search through the actor's childhood memories). A more efficient access to the emotions could be had through specific physical gestures associated in memory with specific emotions. "The key to Emotional Recall can be found first in Sense Memory. Instead of recollecting his memories directly, or in story form, the actor recalls the individual sensory details, or the experience's imprints. This allows the actor to control or direct the remembered emotion and bring the feeling into the present tense" (Gordon, 232).

The actors found the gestural trigger of the emotion (anger, love, envy, hate) by reconstructing the physical setting of a memory from childhood, or of a close observation of life. The formula for building a "subtext" supplementing the words of the play is "Go from yourself," asking "What do I want in this scene?" The differences and conflicts between the script and the actor's subtext create a dramatic effect. Most if not all of the "inner work" or "work on the self" the actors do to prepare for the role in rehearsal is hidden or suppressed in the public performance, in which the carefully constructed Psychological Gestures are received by the audience as if they were natural or spontaneous; they thus produce the familiar "reality effect" that so facilitates audience identification with Hollywood actors.

The part of the Method appropriated in chorography as the analogy for the purpose of electronic rhetoric is not the public performance but the rehearsal, not the realistic effects of a finished performance but the "work around the margins" of the play, the improvisational exercises conducted in response to the play, parallel to the play and different from it, in which an autobiography and a work of art are brought into a fragmented correspondence. A chorographer reads disciplinary texts the way a Method actor reads a (screen)play.

Triggering Towns

To write as a Method actor I need to compose a subtext out of my own experience for what I want in *Beau Geste* (and for what I want in Derrida's "*Chora*"). What is Beau fighting for? He desires a "beautiful death," the paradox of dying so as not to die, to be remembered in his home place. To rehearse this scene I think of my own place, my hometown, Miles City. But I should not move too quickly to that place, according to the poetry professor I had at the University of Montana, Richard Hugo, who used a version of the Method to teach writers how to turn intuitions into language.

The emotion of the poem might be generated by a memory from childhood: "The poem is always in your hometown, but you have a better chance of finding it in another" (Hugo, 12). Why? Because the key to the craft is to "switch your allegiance from the triggering subject to the words." To make this transference easier, Hugo suggested picking a substitute town, at least for a time. "Take someone you emotionally trust, a friend or a lover, to a town you like the looks of but know little about, and show your companion around the town in the poem" (13). Be a tour guide, but what the guide says is motivated not by the scene but by the sounds of words.

Following Hugo's lead, I will mix my metaphors temporarily, to get a feel for the Method analogy. Hugo's tourist metaphor is helpful in learning how to extrapolate from the principles of Method acting to a method of electronic rhetoric, in that it appears again in Timothy Corrigan's discussion of how fans read a cult film. The fan liberates individual images and moments from a narrative—a style of reading and writing that is like the video of a city made by a tourist. The fan *remakes* the cult film the way a tourist's video "misreads" Paris, using the bits and pieces of images and clichés to "reread the self." The surrealist "taste for the tawdry exoticism of despised film genres" resonates in Corrigan's analogy with what is usually considered a "degraded" cultural practice (tourism). The analogy of a tourist visit to a place with the purpose of taking in the scene of an invention can be a useful way of understanding how to apply the memory exercises of the Method to hyperrhetoric.

The analogy rests on the ancient comparison of "method" to a "way" or journey. "Cult movies are always after a fashion foreign films: the images are especially exotic; the viewer uniquely touristic; and within that relationship viewers get to go places, see things, and manipulate customs in a way that no indigenous member of that culture or mainstream filmgoer normally could" (Corrigan, 27).

Twin Peaks, the television series by David Lynch and Mark Frost, turned the cult attitude into a poetics, by bringing its "paratext" (all the materials generated around and about a text) explicitly into the production process. The series was supplemented by various publications—*The Autobiography of F.B.I. Special Agent Dale Cooper;* Cooper's audio tapes to Diane; *The Secret Diary of Laura Palmer;* a "Twin Peaks" newspaper. The advertisement for the "Twin Peaks Collectible CardArt" reads: "David Lynch and Mark Frost invite you to take a revealing, self-guided tour of the town. Snoop around. Find out that Dr. Jacoby is an Aquarius, that Cooper has a middle name. Visit the Great Northern Hotel. . . ."

The ad is on the back of *Welcome to Twin Peaks: Access Guide to the Town,* a book that resembles the famous Michelin green tourist guides. The combination of these paratexts with the series narrative creates the effect of a hypermedia "annotated movie." The guide merges the fictional lives of the characters with factual information about the region, the flora, fauna, geography, history, geology, weather, and so on. And when a *Peaks* boom hit Japan, groups of Japanese tourists began visiting Snoqualmie, Washington, the town thirty miles east of Seattle where the series was shot.

The link between tourist travel and methodology in the cult fan analogy returns me to the *Timaeus* and Solon (who brought the tale of Atlantis back from Egypt). Solon is credited with being at once the first tourist and the first theorist. E. V. Walter noted that Herodotus described Solon's visit to the ruler of Lydia as being for reasons that included *theoria:* "Originally *theoria* meant seeing the sights, seeing for yourself, and getting a worldview. The first theorists were 'tourists'—the wise men who traveled to inspect the obvious world. Solon, the Greek sage whose political reforms around 590 B.C. renewed the city of Athens, is the first 'theorist' in Western history" (Walter, 18).

"The Greeks," Wlad Godzich explained, "designated certain individuals to act as legates on certain formal occasions in other city states or in matters of considerable political importance. These individuals bore the title of *theoros,* and collectively constituted a *theoria.* They were summoned on special occasions to attest the occurrence of some event, to witness its happenstance, and to then verbally certify its having taken place" (Godzich,

1986 xiv). Others could see and make claims, but their reports would have merely the status of "perceptions"; only the *theoria* (the institutionally authorized witnesses) could certify the attested event so that it could be treated as fact. "What is certified as having been seen could become the object of public discourse." In its original sense, *theoria* "did not mean the kind of vision that is restricted to the sense of sight. The term implied a complex but organic mode of active observation—a perceptual system that included asking questions, listening to stories and local myths, and feeling as well as hearing and seeing. It encouraged an open reception to every kind of emotional, cognitive, symbolic, imaginative, and sensory experience" (Burnet, 18).

Solon's travels model the possibility of a "method" or way of thinking that does not segregate the styles of theory and tourism, *topos* and *chora*. The best English term for naming what Solon was doing in Lydia, according to one commentator, is *curiosity:* "And it was just this great gift of curiosity, and the desire to see all the wonderful things—pyramids, inundations, and so forth—that were to be seen that enabled the Ionians to pick up and turn to their own use such scraps of knowledge as they could come by among the barbarians" (Burnet, 25).

My rehearsal of *Beau Geste*—improvising by means of Affective Memory a visit to Miles City, Montana, in the 1880s—is made in the spirit of Solon, or (after David Lynch) as a fan of Gary Cooper.

The Fan

Fans of soap operas and cult films have anticipated the hypermedia capacity of writing the paradigm in their viewing practices. Their attention to the entire context of a film or series, extending its range through anecdotes and legends, reviewing all its paratexts, collectibles, the star in and out of character, is a symptom of this shift from plot to paradigm. "*Casablanca* became a cult movie because it is not *one* movie," Eco says. "It is 'movies.'

And this is the reason it works, in defiance of any aesthetic theory" (Eco, 208). *Beau Geste* shares something of this same quality.

I may conduct my "table work" on *Beau Geste* by reading it as a *fan*. In the cult relation of the audience to the screen the Oedipal positioning of the subject, fixing the subject in a "social machine," is weakened: "The notion of a presiding, determining, or patriarchal relationship comes apart" (Corrigan, 28). Rather than being satisfied with internalizing a fantasy, the fan disregards textual authority and systematic coherence (29). Umberto Eco proposed that the fans' viewing practices were an effect of the film's structure itself. "I think that in order to transform a work into a cult object one must be able to break, dislocate, unhinge it so that one can remember only parts of it, irrespective of their original relationship with the whole. In the case of a book one can unhinge it, so to speak, physically, reducing it to a series of excerpts. A movie, on the contrary, must be already ramshackle, rickety, unhinged in itself" (Eco, 198).

For texts that are not already unhinged, there is "deconstruction," defined as "simply a way of breaking up texts" (202). *Casablanca*'s status as the prototype for all classical cult films is based not only on its loose organization but on the richness and multiplicity of clichés, stereotypes, and archetypes compressed into its narrative. "Two clichés make us laugh but a hundred clichés move us because we sense dimly that the clichés are talking among themselves, celebrating a reunion" (209). Hoberman and Rosenbaum traced the practice of fragmentation in fan experience to surrealist "research" into "synthetic criticism," parodying the fetish effect of the film image—watching a film through their fingers, entering after a film started and leaving as soon as the plot line became clear, the "irrational enlargement" of certain details. A prototype at the level of production is Joseph Cornell's remake of *East of Borneo* into *Rose Hobart*—distilling a studio adventure movie into twenty-four nonlinear minutes and projecting it at silent speed through a piece of blue glass accompanied by excerpts from the album *Holiday in Brazil*—"as though it were a documentary about the leading lady of the original footage" (Hoberman and Rosenbaum, 34). Television, they add, now places this "dilapidation" in the machine itself.

In my rehearsal of *Beau Geste,* then, I will treat the clichés as points of articulation, places where the narrative comes apart, falls into pieces, creating a repertoire for a remake.

Erasure

To take up another aspect of Richard Hugo's tactic, I will not rehearse Fort Zinderneuf as "Miles City," not at first, but as "Philadelphia," the city in which was invented the United States of America, the city of the Founding Fathers. For the purposes of my analogy, however, it will be better not to recall the Philadelphia of 1787, scene of what George Washington and James Madison referred to as "the miracle at Philadelphia," which is represented in the Constitution that launched the "grand national experiment" (Bowen, xi). Or rather, to get a feeling for the dream reasoning of *chora,* I will let David Lynch's Philadelphia, a city of dreams as depicted in *Eraserhead,* stand in for the Philadelphia of political miracles.

Lynch's film provides a kind of fable for an exercise in Affective Memory, showing that the Method systematizes an *inventio* that poets have long exploited. "Our triggering subjects, like our words," Richard Hugo observed, "come from obsessions we must submit to, whatever the social cost. It can be hard. . . . It is narcissistic, vain, egotistical, unrealistic, selfish, and hateful to assume emotional ownership of a town or a word. It is also essential" (Hugo, 14).

Asked to name the single greatest influence on his work, Lynch replied without hesitation, "Philadelphia." "There were places there that had been allowed to decay, where there was so much fear and crime that just for a moment there was an opening to another world. It was fear, but it was so strong, and so magical, like a magnet, that your imagination was always sparking in Philadelphia. I just have to think of Philadelphia now, and I get ideas. I hear the wind, and I'm off into the darkness somewhere" (Lynch, 20).

Several aspects of *Eraserhead* recommend it in my context, not least of which is its status as a cult film and its positioning in the market as "that impossibility, an avant-garde hit" (Hoberman and Rosenbaum, 214). It is a lesson in innovation and dissemination—the penetration of the mainstream by a "czar of the bizarre," evolving from a $20,000 "underground classic" through a series of Hollywood films and into television. The peculiar mode of identification that *Eraserhead* provokes in its fans resembles the "booster spirit" of the city fathers.

An added motive for my purposes comes from Rosenbaum's explicit association of this film with Derrida as a way to characterize a style of writing "under erasure."

> For French philosopher Jacques Derrida, the act of writing "under erasure" is, according to Derrida translator Gayatri Spivak, "the strategy of using the only available language while not subscribing to its premises"; a comparable conundrum seems to haunt Lynch. Spivak describes the process as follows: "Since the word is inaccurate, it is crossed out. Since it is necessary, it remains legible." (If one substitutes "forbidden" for "inaccurate" and "unavoidable" for "necessary" in Lynch's case, the application may be closer.) (Hoberman and Rosenbaum, 228)

For me, the key word in the citation from Spivak is "premises."

Rosenbaum describes Lynch as "purely American" (219) in that his film is "about a situation in which people are back to living in bomb shelters—which is like the fortress mentality of the fifties" (302). Naremore similarly explained the success of Method acting as due to "a stylistic or ideological leaning within fifties culture": the tone of that era, which persists into the present, suited the Method as a style (as opposed to a rehearsal technique), in that the expressive inarticulateness conveyed by actors trained in the Method evoked the tension between surface conformity and disguised alienation—a tension of repressed sexuality—that characterized that period. This fortress mentality recalls the mentality of Fort Zinderneuf in *Beau Geste.*

The instructions provided by *Eraserhead* are to generate a composition out of the elements of a "mechanical" invention, understood as displacements of the story about a cultural invention ("America"). Lynch's eureka anecdote, for example, arises out of the history of the pencil, which makes it a grammatological fable. The setting of *Eraserhead* is an urban landscape associated with but not imitative of the city of Philadelphia, which inspired it: "a mosaic of muddy streets, smoky alleyways, the factory where a severed head is pronounced made of the finest rubber and processed into pencil erasers, dingy apartment buildings where a man's bed is transformed into a bottomless pool of milky liquid and the radiator is the doorway to a dimension in which a woman sings of heaven while squashing fetal worms beneath her shoes" (McDonagh, 73). Lynch explained that the film sprang fully formed out of a single intuitive impression of this place. "My original image was of a man's head bouncing on the ground, being picked up by a boy and taken to a pencil factory. I don't know where it came from" (Corliss, 87). This dream factory recalls the term *fabrique* (the rejected synonym for *folie*).

For my purposes it is even better if the invention is French, as in the case of the graphite-clay pencil, a technology invented by Nicolas-Jacques Conté in France in 1792 (marking the three hundredth anniversary of "first encounters"). Petroski, who mentions Lynch in his history of the pencil, discounts the claims to simultaneous independent invention made on behalf of an Austrian of the period (Petroski). Lynch never mentions whether or not he knew that the idea to attach an eraser to the head, tip, or end of a graphite-clay pencil, accomplished in 1858, is credited to Hyman Lipman of Philadelphia. Where did Lynch's idea come from? From Philadelphia itself, perhaps, where Lynch's noted sensitivity to the effects of "place"—to the ghost, spirit, or *ker* of place—caused him to reanimate Lipman's original insight as nightmare.

If Lipman's idea for the eraser had come from a dream, it might have had much in common with the image that Lynch turned into *Eraserhead.*

Strange Attractors

Having intuited the *inventio* or text generator of find-the-invention in *Eraserhead,* David Lynch repeated it in *Twin Peaks.* On what does the mise-en-scène of the Lynch-Frost series insist? The coffee and doughnuts consumed in excessive quantities by Agent Cooper, Sheriff Truman, and the others display Lynch's stylized use of clichéd schemas, as in the opening scene of *Blue Velvet* with the firetruck parading by the house with the white picket fence. Participating thus in a technique associated with postmodernism, Lynch-Frost neither simply use the cliché in a naive or nostalgic way nor simply "mention" it in a knowing parody but appropriate the stereotype as a schema of discourse with which to construct further meanings.

A similar situation exists in *Twin Peaks.* The coffee and doughnuts, that is, cue a structuration derived from topological geometry, "often described as rubber-sheet or plasticene geometry. In the strange world of topology, where distances have little meaning, a single-handled mug and a doughnut are indistinguishable" (Peterson, 50). The rubberiness of the eraser is present, carried to the level of the principles of plasticity itself. "A doughnut and a coffee cup are topologically equivalent because it's possible to imagine expanding the coffee cup's handle while shrinking its cup until all that's left is a ring" (51). Given Lacan's extensive use of topology (especially the torus) to figure his theory of the subject (personhood constructed around a lack), it is easy to find in this mathematical invention the generative principle of the narrative of *Twin Peaks.* One purpose of my method is to move this topological *inventio* into a choral (electronic) dimension.

An intertextual link exists, for example, between *Peaks* and the café scene in Godard's *Two or Three Things I Know about*

Her—a meditative sequence cutting between shots of the characters (Juliette and the young man) and close-ups of the coffee in the cup:

> [Low actual sound, including clinking of spoon, but no room ambience or noise of pinball machine.]
>> (The coffee is stirred and the spoon is put down on the saucer.)
>> COMMENTARY 11
>> *Maybe an object is what permits us to relink . . .*
> [Silence.]
>> *to pass from one subject to the other, therefore to live in society.*
>> (The young man looks at Juliette. She returns his gaze.)
>> *to be together. But then.*
>
> (in Guzzetti, 132)

If it is true that in commodity or consumer culture human relationships have been displaced into things, then these same things, taken up into the details of a diegesis, become the places of passage linking otherwise unrelated discourses (D. Miller). Conductive (electronic) logic, that is, supplements the established movements of inference between things and ideas (abduction, deduction, induction) with a movement directly between things (unconscious thought).

The extreme close-up of the swirling cream in the stirred coffee suggests the turbulence referred to in discussions of the invention of chaos theory. "An astonishing variety of systems can be modeled as strange attractors," Katherine Hayles reported. "The group of graduate students at Santa Cruz who became pioneers in the chaos theory played a coffeehouse game of guessing where the nearest strange attractor was: in the din of dishes coming from the kitchen? in the swirl of cream in coffee? in the clouds of cigarette smoke coming from the next table?" (Hayles, 150). In the same vein, the phase-space appearing in chaotic processes is described as being "squeezed and then folded over itself again and again, much as croissant dough is rolled out and folded over itself again and again" (150). It would not be difficult to imagine that this passage from one strange attractor to another, from one object-process to another, could provide a "plot map" for *Two or Three Things* (which in any case is *about* commodity fetishism).

Twin Peaks is classified as a (hybrid) soap opera, and much topological research has been stimulated by "soap-film" experiments (research into minimal surfaces). One consequence of the coming convergence in the home of television, telephone, and computer, resulting in "the nexus of a new social machinery," according to Jonathan Crary, is the need (and possibility) for a reasoning that collapses the distinction between the concrete and the abstract, between stereotype and concept, at least in the cultural practices essential to an electronic national identity. The soap opera seems capable of supporting just this sort of reasoning.

> Consider *General Hospital,* allegedly the most widely watched afternoon soap opera. It is consumed essentially as strings of representations that never surpass their functioning as an abstract code. In its construction and effects, *General Hospital* announces the disappearance of the visual and narrative space that seemed to have authorized it and points toward a fully programmable calculus of continually switching syntheses of figural and narrative units. The consistent repetitions of "formulas" is no longer even a possibility. In *General Hospital* any character, relationship, identity, or situation is reversible, exchangeable, convertible into its opposite.... Discontinuities, substitutions, and duplications shatter the illusion which once would have been called bourgeois verisimilitude. (Crary, 289)

The "realism" of dominant culture is developing a new dimension in the same way that philosophy once emerged out of the narratives of mythology, becoming a mode of calculation rather than a "content" referring to "life." It is a set of "abstract, manipulable elements ready to be harmonized with a plethora of other electronic flows" that could come from any area of information, a language for the hypermedia equipment that Entertainment discourse is making available and Family discourse is internalizing. In the final scene of the concluding broadcast episode of *Twin Peaks,* agent Cooper transforms into the evil spirit "Bob," a metamorphosis predicted by the relationship between the coffee cup and doughnut he made such a show of praising throughout the series.

I can learn something about "Gary Cooper," about his electronic capabilities, from his offspring in Lynch-Frost. The lesson is: for a database (no matter how extensive) to become a place of invention, it must be *formatted* by means of the Method.

PART THREE

REHEARSAL

Instead of sounding himself as to his "being," he does so concerning his place: "Where am I?" instead of "Who am I?" For the space that engrosses the deject, the excluded, is never one, nor homogeneous, nor totalizable, but essentially divisible, foldable, and catastrophic.

Julia Kristeva

9

JUDGMENT

A Eureka Story

When I remember Miles City, wanting to write a rehearsal of *Beau Geste,* I think of a man named Red Cryer. I did not think about him much while I lived there, yet I find that he is one of the most vivid memories I have of that time and place. I am rehearsing not just the scene of Beau's beautiful death, but the larger scene of instruction—of my father receiving that myth—to learn how to write (send) from the position of *receiver.*

It was one of the summers I worked for my father at his sand and gravel plant (I was here before, in "Derrida at the Little Big-horn"). Today people would call Red and most of his family mentally challenged, but in those days (it was 1962) Red was

Figure 4. Identification

known as the "village idiot." Red was born retarded, due to incest
it was said (none of this is written down). The Cryer family were
riding their rototiller onto the bridge crossing the Yellowstone
River. The machine had been modified to serve as the family
vehicle, which seemed pretty smart to me—blade disengaged,
removed, a wagon bed with a bench added to carry the folks. Its
speed was about that of a good walk. The Cryers could be seen
driving their rototiller all over that side of town, the wrong side
of the railroad tracks, the poor side, the working-class side, past
the grain elevators, down to the river, where mobile homes and
run-down houses clustered behind the dike built against the
spring floods.

The river is the one Lewis and Clarke navigated through that
part of the frontier. In the hills on the far side of it Chief Rain-
in-the-Face killed a sutler of the Seventh Cavalry. Just a few
miles away, near the mouth of the Tongue River, the medicine
man Black Elk once camped. I was down in the "hole," beneath
the trap where the truck dumped its load of aggregate from the
gravel pit, or quarry, up on the hill across the river—dumped it
into the bin. I was working the conveyor belt carrying the pit
gravel to the plant (the screens and washer, which used water
pumped up from the river). I had to go down in the hole every
so often to remove the aggregate that worked its way between
the belt and the rollers, causing the belt to slip. "If the belt grabs
the shovel while you have it shoved in there," Walt said, "let go
fast. Otherwise it will jerk you right into the roller, and it'll be
'Look Ma, no arms!'" (laughter).

It was Saturday, and people were hauling their trash out to
the town dump up Airport Hill. A wind was blowing over the
river, and a large piece of cardboard had blown off the back of
some pickup or trailer. I came up out of the hole about the time
the Cryers approached the cardboard. As the rototiller chugged
along, Old Man Cryer gestured and Red stepped off to pick up
the cardboard. Dad had called my attention to the scene, both of
us standing beside the plant, which made a tremendous racket,
its motor vibrating the contraption into which the pit gravel was

fed by the conveyor from the trap and out of which came four materials—three sizes of rock plus the sand.

Red picked up the large piece of cardboard, carried it over to the side of the bridge, and threw it off into the river. But he threw it *into* the strong wind, which whipped it back into Red's face, nearly knocking him over. He retrieved the cardboard, carried it over to the *same side of the bridge,* and threw it off once again (with the same result). With his hand on my shoulder, Dad pointed to the bridge, and to be heard above the roar of the machinery, he leaned closer to shout into my ear. "There's a lesson in that!" he said, gesturing toward the bridge.

Family discourse, a primary vehicle of the Cultural code, operates with these kinds of lessons, with common sense couched in maxims and proverbs, or tales with morals. What did Walt mean that day, when he raised his arm to point at the bridge (the whole scene remains in my memory as a living tableau)? Ostension I now know is notoriously ambiguous, since it is never certain exactly at what the finger is pointing. The context reduces the ambiguity only in an unstable way. In the paradigm of possibilities, I might suppose Dad intended to evoke the proverb about not spitting into the wind. At the same time, Dad also believed in perseverance in support of a cause, even if it was unpopular, so perhaps he meant just the opposite. My thought was, "Red is my stupidity."

How does Affective Memory work? I recalled this place, this physical setting, to find out how my father felt in 1939 when he received the myth of the beautiful death. What is it like to receive that kind of lesson? I refer to the theory of *chora* (Kristeva).

> That order, that glance, that voice, that gesture, which enact the law for my frightened body, constitute and bring about an effect and not yet a sign. . . . I *am* only *like* someone else: mimetic logic of the advent of the ego, objects, and signs. But when I *seek* (myself), *lose* (myself), or experience *jouissance*—then "I" is *heterogeneous*. Discomfort, unease, dizziness stemming from an ambiguity that, through the violence of a revolt *against,* demarcates a

space out of which signs and objects arise. Thus braided, woven, ambivalent, a heterogeneous flux marks out a territory that I can call my own because the Other, having dwelt in me as *alter ego,* points it out to me through loathing. (Kristeva, 1982:10)

The context of *folie* helped specify the feeling further when I recognized Red Cryer as the heir of a great tradition. His story is a kind of *Narrenspiel* in the tradition of *Hamlet*—*folie* as folly: the lesson of the traditional fool. How should I conduct myself (the logic of conduction)? In the didactic conventions of traditional (premodern) daily life the fool was opposed to the wise man, the upright man, Solomon, in a multitude of proverbs and maxims pointing out "hundreds of ways in which fools . . . may err, rebuking as folly conduct of all degrees of offensiveness." "This fool is characteristically *incircumspectus,* 'withoute any wysedome,' 'one that dooeth a thing unadvisedly or without discrecion'" (Swain, 4). At the same time, folly was also a source of amusement and recreation. The irony of approaching learning in cyberspace (in Greek the *cyber* of *cybernetics* refers to the helmsman or steersman) by means of this folly—an irony that may be a clue to the peculiar nature of *folie* as hyperrhetoric—is that the fool is precisely one whose ship (the ship of fools) *lacks* a rudder, lacks direction. The fool, living in guilt and shame, may serve to condemn the lack of prudence and right judgment, or (in the burlesques in which the fool refutes every one of Solomon's maxims) to argue that "the wise are no longer wise, their methods no longer lead to the accomplishment of their desires, and the foolish now speak with wisdom to those in authority" (35). It is the ambiguity of all proverbs (of the Cultural code as such). Either way, I recognized that in the tableau of the Yellowstone bridge I was receiving a proverb about the fool and the wise man (Red and Walt).

Red could be interpreted as the local *kynic* in the tradition going back to Diogenes. As the antiacademician, Diogenes refused to argue but performed little dramas with a spirit of gall or cheekiness. "Spirited materialism is not satisfied with words but proceeds to a material argumentation that rehabilitates the body," Sloterdijk says, discussing Diogenes' practice of relieving himself in public. "Certainly, ideas are enthroned in the academy, and urine drips discreetly into the latrine. But urine in the academy! That would be the total dialectical tension, *the art of pissing against the idealist wind*" (Sloterdijk, 105). Why, Kristeva wondered, does corporeal waste always represent "the objective frailty of symbolic order?" (Kristeva, 1982:70). In chorography, I do not choose among possibilities but enter them into the paradigm of the diegesis, creating a network in which to catch an invention.

Intuition

As I worked with the analogy of Method acting, I realized that the rehearsal technique could be used to read texts of Discipline as well as of Entertainment. Or rather, that the Method mediated between the particulars of *Beau Geste* and the abstractions of "*Chora.*" The tableau of the fool highlighted again the role of reception in my rehearsal exercises, moving from the lesson Beau practiced within the narrative (his desire to have a Viking's Funeral) and relaying the myth through a series of instructional scenes from my father to me. I was curious about how this scene functioned within Discipline discourse itself. The anecdote about Red Cryer looked at from another angle, as a rehearsal of *chora* in Derrida's essay for the Villette Park *folie,* produced an insight that is the logical and chronological source of chorography.

In the practice of Emotional Recall, the significant part of the narrative is not in the story but in the physical details of the scene, the setting that supports the action. Following the line of displacement away from the story revealed in every scene the gravel plant, crashing violently in place as it sorted the pit gravel into four piles. "I make something out of nothing," Walt used to say. "The aggregate in the pit is without value. But when we're finished with it, it's a building material. Our sand and gravel is in the concrete foundations and floors of many of the buildings in town, not to mention the guard rails, park benches, feed troughs, and septic tanks."

Once the gravel plant turned up in my memory exercise, I realized that the image Derrida selected from the *Timaeus* for the design of the folly—the *liknon* or sifting tool as an image of *chora*—also described the sand and gravel washer; I recognized that my father's plant was exactly such a machine (the *folie* is a *fabrique* in my story). The sand and gravel plant is *chora,* down to the smallest details of Plato's description—not just the winnowing device but the receptacle swaying and vibrating as it sorted out the four basic elements, Earth, Air, Fire, and Water, which matched the three sizes of rock (oversize, half-inch, pea gravel) and one of sand in the Family discourse. The commentators had suggested, in any case, that the specific technology used in the metaphor was not important, that Plato used in his metaphor the technology of his period and invited an updating of the sorting machine analogy from one age to the next. In addition, the gravel pit as quarry and the screening process involving rock, sand, and water—the materials that recurred throughout the planning sessions between Derrida and Eisenman (to be discussed later)—could be understood at once as the elements passing from nothing to something at the Miles City Sand & Gravel Company.

The memorial or monumental point of my rehearsal, then, is just where the relays provided by Lynch predicted it would be—in the invention (the machinery) of the scene (like the cup or the pencil). The convergence of images from the two different institutions of my experience shocked me nonetheless (the effect of not knowing a secret is going to be revealed), struck me as a revelation with the force of a "eureka." The connection first appeared when I wrote a mystory. The difference between my mystory ("Derrida at the Little Bighorn," in *Teletheory*) and the remake emerging here is that chorography shows what to do with mystory (how to generalize it into a method for cyberwriting). The chorographer uses the mystory to guide the exercises of the Method (actively searches for or creates repetitions among the discourses of society). And these repetitions do not produce "grand designs" but "miniaturizations" bringing the heterogeneous items of information into order around a detail or a prop (a strange attractor) in the setting.

Chorography as a method of invention writes directly the hyperbolic intuition known as the eureka experience. It is first of all a means for simulating this experience, for transfering it from the living body to an apparatus, whether print or electronic, for "writing" or artificially performing intuition "outside" the organic mind and body and entrusting this process to a machine (both technological and methodological). The study of grammatology has demonstrated in detail how print favors and supports or augments an analytical mode of thought based on the fit between the properties of verbal discourse and the abstract demands of logic. It is not that it was impossible to reason analytically in an oral apparatus, but it required the genius of a Socrates to do it. Socrates made his interlocutors look stupid because he was reasoning in an alphabetic style while they were reasoning in an oral style (Havelock). Alphabetic writing, as an "artificial memory" capable of sustaining long chains of reasoning outside living memory and making them available for spatial manipulation, democratized the skill of analytic logic. This technology required the foundation of a new institution—School—to turn analysis into a cultural habit of mind.

Intuition (to retain paleonymically this overdetermined and problematic word), in contrast to analysis, operates in a global or Gestalt mode, crossing all the sensory modalities in a way that may not be abstracted from the body and emotions. There has never been a technology capable of fully supporting and augmenting intuition in the way that print supports analysis—until now. The multichanneled interactivity of hypermedia provides for the first time a machine whose operations match the variable sensorial encoding that is the basis for intuition, a technology in which cross-modality may be simulated and manipulated for the writing of an insight, including the interaction of verbal and nonverbal materials and the guidance of analysis by intuition, which constitute creative or inventive thinking.

What exactly is the eureka experience, such that it might be simulated in writing or artificially manipulated in electronic technology? The canonical examples of scientific insight have been enumerated often enough: Newton observing the falling apple, Archimedes taking a bath, James Watt watching the kettle boil, Poincaré getting on a bus (Bastick, 352). My remake, remaining at the level of a rehearsal, tells a theory of an insight as an analogy for an electronic rhetoric.

How are such modest concrete events able to trigger an insight? As all the examples show, "eureka" results from a repetition between quotidian and disciplinary experience (it is a kind of memory), as in the fit between the machinery of the gravel plant and the metaphor for *chora* featured in Derrida's essay. The moment of sudden insight has been described in terms of "psychophysical emotion" very similar to those involved in the Emotional Recall exercise of Method acting. Bastick mentions that training in acting improves performance on empirical tests designed to measure intuitive thinking (276). It is interesting that Lee Strasberg (one of the founders of the Actor's Studio) literalized the "Aha!" exclamation traditionally associated with the eureka experience in his relaxation exercises designed to overcome the social conditioning that suppresses emotional expression: "The actor makes an easily and evenly vibrated sound from his chest: '*Ahhhhhhhhh.*' The emotion is allowed expression through this sound. . . . If the above procedure does not release the emotional experience but hampers the relaxation, the actor should then make a sharp, fully committed, and explosive sound from the chest: '*Hah!*' This allows the expression of this stronger emotion" (Strasberg, 130).

Analysis of instances of eureka shows that while environment, or place, plays an instrumental role in insight, it is in the style of an "accident" that does not have a logical relevance to the problem that an invention addresses. The definition of the eureka experience, reflecting the seeming arbitrariness of this triggering accident, resembles the basic strategy of surrealism, which was to juxtapose unrelated items. In a eureka intuition, the materials of a disciplinary problem are brought into sudden, unexpected relationship with other areas of a thinker's experience, with the mediating link being precisely a Psychological Gesture.

Eureka insights are said to arise out of the peculiar way memory stores information in "emotional sets," gathering ideas into categories classified not in terms of logical properties but common feelings, feelings that are based in eccentric, subjective, idiosyncratic physiognomic perceptions.

> When an emotional set occurs which is similar to the original "problem" emotional set, i.e. has the same "feel," then a new link is made. The pathway is opened up and the present "solution" emotional set is combined with the "problem" emotional set to produce recentering insight with its recognition of the present emotional set as the solution. This is often triggered by some slight kinaesthetic experience giving that final similarity of feeling causing recentering. (Bastick, 73)

The trigger or catalyst causing "recentering" (creating a pattern of redundancy between two unrelated sets) tends to be "a body posture or movement which has sufficient physiological components equivalent to the attributes of the requirements" (248). The Method, and the rehearsal as the search for a Psychological Gesture, is a way to bring into learning Kristeva's association of *chora* with the human body, the site mediating through certain strong feelings the relation of *subject/object* with the *abject*.

This kinesthetic thinking is a reasoning by *Geschlecht,* consisting as it does in a "mental 'feeling' of the texture, contours, and consistency of the environment. It is as though the 'mind's hands' feel the composition and the spatial relations among objects in the environment" (284). It is not that the solution set has no logical consistency with the problem set (intuitions may turn out to be "wrong" when this is the case) but that this consistency may go unnoticed until a "feeling" calls attention to it. Intuition uses emotion to encode information redundantly across all the perceptual modes, so that "problem solving" may draw upon the body as well as upon discourse (355).

Business

The appearance of *chora* as *liknon* in the story of Red Cryer could be described as a recentering of the emotional sets from two different discourses into a pattern (Discipline and Family institutions). The repetition that appeared when the discourses were juxtaposed simulated what happens in intuition—the cross-modal transfer and transposition across emotional sets that occurs because information is duplicated by different senses (variable encoding). The sudden recognition of this redundancy produces a strong feeling of certainty, of being "right," a feeling of "knowing," which Bastick names "judgment": "The correctness of an intuitive product is judged by the intuiter according to the release in tension, anxiety, and frustration afforded by the product. This judgment based on body reference is necessarily subjective. . . . As some evidence is subliminal and all experiential evidence has subconscious associations, it is not possible to verbalize all the evidence used in deriving an intuitive product" (Bastick, 154). Lacan's term, *bliss-sense,* could be used to name this pleasure cue, translating Lacan's punning play on *jouissance,* which he said was one kind of "sense," along with common sense, nonsense, and sense proper. Kristeva marks this experience as the "sublime": "As soon as I perceive it, as soon as I name it, the sublime triggers—it has always already triggered—a spree of perceptions and words that expands memory boundlessly. . . . Not at all short of but always with and through perception and words, the sublime is a *something added* that expands us, overstrains us, and causes us to be both *here,* as dejects, and *there,* as others and sparkling" (Kristeva, 1982:12).

The Method analogy, which is related to this sublime feeling, begins to clarify how chorography can make judgments reflexive

(how this giganticized memory may be inscribed within a technology). The insight of my eureka story, for example, had already
been categorized as a genre in Nietzsche's *Gay Science* (a theory
of blissense, after all), in a section entitled "On the Origin of
Scholars."

> Once one has trained one's eyes to recognize in a scholarly trea-
> tise the scholar's intellectual idiosyncrasy—every scholar has
> one—and to catch it in the act, one will almost always behold
> behind this the scholar's "prehistory," his family, and especially
> their occupations and crafts. Where the feeling finds expression
> "Now this has been proved and I am done with it," it is generally
> the ancestor in the blood and instinct of the scholar who approves
> from his point of view "the finished job"; the faith in a proof is
> merely a symptom of what in a hard-working family has for ages
> been considered "good workmanship." (Nietzsche, 290)

The interest of the passage has to do with the gathering into one
set of the matters of feeling, judgment, style, and reason. "Abjection itself is a composite of judgment and affect" (Kristeva,
1982:10). When the sons (or daughters) of clerks and office work-
ers become scholars, in Nietzsche's examples of how this feeling
of judgment works in a proof, "they consider a problem almost
as solved when they have merely schematized it," given that the
work of their family had been "to bring order into diverse materials, to distribute it over different files." The principle in such
cases—philosophers who are basically schematizers—is "for
them the formal aspect of their fathers' occupation has become
content."

Similarly, "the son of an advocate will have to be an advocate
as a scholar, too; he wants above all that his cause should be
judged right. . . . The sons of Protestant ministers and school
teachers may be recognized by their naive certainty when, as
scholars, they consider their cause proved when they have merely
stated it with vigor and warmth; they are used to being *believed,*
as that was part of their fathers' job." And as for the children of

those who dredge in quarries turning wild aggregate into domestic building materials, isn't it likely that they might tend to try to generate something "original," to invent?

The method of chorography is meant to give access to this sorting machine of judgment that determines my intuitions, what "feels" right and proper, or wrong and improper, not to leave these feelings in place but to make them available for writing. The luck of my mystory, of my particular case, which lends itself to generalization, is that my signature machine literalizes the metaphor of *chora*. "The intuitive judgment of suitability has most import for creativity and problem-solving, as these endeavours are based on the intuitive judgment of a group of 'solution' elements being suitable for a group of problem 'requirement' elements" (Bastick, 247). "Gut advertising," Bastick adds (in a point that could be extended to all "interpellations" or forms of ideological address), exploits the same judgmental process that makes insight possible: something new (an unfamiliar idea or a novel commodity) is made acceptable to my sense of judgment "by evoking related highly redundant global emotional sets, for example those centered on Mother, nostalgia, patriotism" (247). The challenge of chorography is: to remake the sense of judgment itself.

Mise en Abyme

The formal device for simulating intuition in chorography is the *mise en abyme* (placing in the abyss). If travel through an information landscape is the most venerable metaphor for method, the specific metaphor most likely to replace the book in the design of hypermedia interface (rhetoric) is filmmaking. As Ted Nelson has suggested, composing in hyperrhetoric is more like making a movie than it is like authoring an essay (Laurel, 238). The chorographer, then, borrows the devices of filmmaking and videography, such as montage (editing—relation between shots) and mise-en-scène (framing—composition within the shot). Much of the history of cinema has been told as the struggle between, and final synthesis of, these two devices. Chorography adds the *mise en abyme* to this pair of French terms as the technique that merges filmmaking and computing.

Lucien Dällenbach devoted an entire book to the *mise en abyme* in literature, noting its historical association with the styles of periods classified as "baroque." The most famous examples of the device in literature are the play within a play in *Hamlet* and the discussion of *Hamlet* in the library scene in Joyce's *Ulysses*. The device has at least two different sources, both related to the dynamics of identity: heraldry, and mirrors. In heraldry, the abyss point is at the center of the shield bearing the family coat of arms, with the inner shield "miming" the outer one. The logic of the heraldic abyss, Dällenbach explains, is that the inner shield at once supplements, exceeds, and covers a default in the outer shield (Dällenbach, 144). He explicitly cites Derrida's allusions to the abyssal, reminding us that Derrida in his early writings used the *mise en abyme* as an emblem of the notion of *différance*.

The other source of the figure derives from mirror optics, the repetition of images in facing mirrors, giving rise not to simple reflexiveness but infinite regress, or paradoxical aporias. He remarks that Lacan's mirror stage and his theory of the unconscious as the discourse of the Other, in which the sender's message returns from the receiver in inverted form, participate in the optics of the abyss (26). The operation of the device as a change of scale Dällenbach associates with "miniaturization," referring to Levi-Strauss's definition of art in *The Savage Mind*—the way art renders the world intelligible in representations that reduce, simplify, miniaturize the mass of detail in the real. One of Dällenbach's most useful definitions is his comparison of the device to a "diegetic metaphor"—an object, scene, or character serving a metaphorical or allegorical purpose but whose appearance in the work is *motivated* by the story (as when the background music in a film is shown to be coming from a radio or other source in the narrative world).

One of the more interesting aspects of Dällenbach's account is his reminder that the *mise en abyme* was one of the most common devices of the experimental (avant-garde) novel in France, with its prototype in Gide's *Counterfeiters* developing a simple reflexivity in the New Novel, and culminating in an attempt to create an "impossible literature" in the New New Novels by Jean Ricardou, Claude Simon, or Michel Butor, among others. The goal of these experiments was to disturb realism, to show that narrative could be generated entirely out of itself, out of its own resources, simulating realistic effects by means of a kind of linguistic mathematics. As with most genres, the abyssal form passed from classic to baroque versions, although the principle that "whatever resembles, assembles" remained constant. To count as an abyss, something at one level must signal the device, some repetition or resemblance must be literally manifested across the levels of text. In short, one part of the text must literally (at least in part) as well as metaphorically reproduce the other. These authors created a hybrid writing that attempted to perform the theories of literature that they described. In my remake as rehearsal, the gravel plant in the Red Cryer proverb repeats the choral machine in an abyssal way.

Miniaturization

Theorists as well as novelists have exploited the *mise en abyme*. In his own close reading of Freud's *Beyond the Pleasure Principle* (upon which Lacan's seminar on the Ego is also a commentary) Derrida located the peculiarity and particularity of Freud's writing in this text—specified as being neither logical nor dialectical but "speculative" (including the reflective metaphor in this term)—as owing precisely to Freud's use of the *mise en abyme* structuration. Even if he does not "trust" in the "abyssal" form, Derrida remarks, nonetheless he will mime Freud's use of the device, as in the famous tale of Freud's grandson playing *fort/da* with the bobbin and string. "Freud does with (without) the object of his text exactly what Ernst does with (without) his spool" (Derrida, 1987d:320). What interests Derrida in Freud's "speculation" is the ambiguity, the confusion of the boundary (not) separating subject from object (versus the pose of objective science). What is modeled in *Beyond the Pleasure Principle* in any case reflects the economy of Freud's work as a whole, which is the abyssal inscription of Freud's family in the institution of psychoanalysis. The speculator, that is, relates to the object of study in the mode of identification and projection, thus *showing* what is being theorized (transference).

Having in mind Richard Hugo's advice to pay attention to the words of the place, the importance of this example for chorography as a remake of *Beau Geste* may now be apparent. Most of the time the child played only part of the game, throwing his toy away: "As he did this he gave vent to a loud, long-drawn-out 'o-o-o-o,' accompanied by an expression of interest and satisfaction." Freud and his daughter agreed that this interjection "represented the German word 'fort' ['gone']" (Freud, 1961:9). Freud observed the complete game when the child played with a reel on a string. The reel was thrown away (*fort!*). "He then pulled the reel out of the cot again by the string and hailed its reappearance with a joyful 'da' ['there']. This, then, was the complete game—disappearance and return." Although the boy mostly played *fort,* "there is no doubt that the greater pleasure was attached to the second act." This *da* or *there* is the eureka I seek in the *fort* of *Beau Geste,* Fort Zinderneuf as the diegetic metaphor of *chora.* The *da* (Derri-*da*) is in the abyss of the *fort* at Zinderneuf. "The constituting barrier between subject and object has here [in psychosis] become an unsurmountable wall. An ego, wounded to the point of annulment, barricaded and untouchable, cowers somewhere, nowhere, at no other place than the one that cannot be found. . . . Letting current flow into such a 'fortified castle' amounts to causing desire to rise" (Kristeva, 1982:47).

The usefulness of the *mise en abyme* for choral work is that it allows one to show what cannot be stated directly in propositions.

The *Timaeus* itself, for example, resorts to the abyss structure as part of the dream reasoning needed to communicate *chora*. In his own struggle to express *chora,* Plato created a double chasm in *Timaeus*—the form of the dialogue itself, which is divided into two versions of the cosmos, one told from the side of the intelligible, one from the side of the sensible, and the abstraction of chora as space at the level of theme. "If there is indeed a chasm in the middle of the book, a sort of abyss 'in' which there is an attempt to think or to say this abyssal chasm which would be *chora,* the opening of a place 'in' which everything would come both *to take place and to be reflected* (for these are images which are inscribed there), is it significant that a *mise en abyme* regulates a certain order of composition of the discourse?" (Derrida, 1987b:276). The isotopies—"formal analogies or *mises en abyme*—organizing the dialogue constitute a closed but generative field or system: the art of the analogies across the levels of the text is important first of all, Derrida says, not so much for its formal nature but for the "constraints which produce these analogies. Shall we say that they constitute a program? A logic whose authority was imposed on Plato? Yes, up to a point only, and this limit appears in the abyss itself: the being-program of the program, its structure or pre-inscription or typographic prescription forms the explicit theme of the discourse *en abyme* or *chora*. The latter figures the place of inscription of all that is marked on the world" (Derrida, 1987b:277).

Since *chora* may not be observed directly in philosophical terms, it must be put into a story, "but a story of going outside of story." This other story is in the discourse but does not belong to it, covering over the chasm in the middle of what is missing or cannot appear (as in the heraldic shield). Its structure, then, is that of "an overprinting without a base," which functions by "figuring" what is in question in the dialogue (comparable to the suspension of the university as an institution of reason over the abyss of its foundation as event). When Socrates positions himself in the dialogue in a manner of an errant, mobile, neutral place, he "reflects" and anticipates the conceptual discussion of *chora* that follows. He possesses no metalanguage and can show the "truth" only from within the place in question. "*Chora* 'means': place occupied by someone, country, inhabited place, marked place, rank, post, assigned position, territory or region. And in fact, *chora* will always already be occupied, invested, even as a general place, and even when it is distinguished from everything that takes place in it. Whence the difficulty of treating it as an empty or geometric space" (289). My remake works with this choral figure, then, telling a theory with a narrative already invested and occupied.

This staging generally informs the nesting of stories in the dialogue, as when Critias retells the tale of Atlantis through a series of relays (from one grandfather to the next, back to Solon), and the scene of this telling is nested in several other fictions, including that of the dialogue itself: "The staging unfolds according to a setting of discoures of a narrative type, reported or not, of which the origin of the first enunciation appears to be always relayed, their mythic dimension is sometimes exposed as such, and the *mise en abyme,* the putting *en abyme* is there given to be reflected without limit" (281). *Chora* is not the object of a tale but the seat, the place of reception and unfolding in which each tale is a receptacle, a place of inscription, for another. "A structure of inclusion makes of the *included* fiction in a sense the theme of the prior fiction which is its *including* form, its capable container, let us say its receptacle. Socrates who figures as a general addressee, capable of understanding everything and therefore of receiving everything (like ourselves, even here), affects to interrupt there this mythopoetic string of events. But this is only in order to re-launch it even more forcefully" (286).

Much of Derrida's analysis of the dialogue is devoted to sorting out the relationships among the embedded narratives, from the legend of Atlantis to Plato's account itself, through the fictions of the dialogue. In the sequence of the relay, a reversal or "catastrophe" takes place, in that Athens, which appeared to be the receiver of the lesson from the Egyptian tale, turns out to be its utterer, its sender, given that the Egyptian priest was telling

Solon about ancient Athens. What is this relation between one culture and another, from one historical period to another, in which one civilization receives the heroic story of another (the way Athens learned from Egypt about its own glorious past)?

10

COLUMBUS

The Replica

I wanted to practice Emotional Recall by treating Gary Cooper as a "cult star" in my rehearsals. "Such cult figures essentially represent what Christopher Lasch terms 'ego-ideals': 'admired, idealized images,' in a most fundamental sense, *loved ones*. In their ability to capture 'the contradictory quality of unconscious mental life,' he argues, such images prove 'indispensable' for our well-being" (Telotte, 9). Cooper has not made it into the encyclopedias of actors around whom cults have formed, although *Beau Geste* could be described in terms applied to the prototype of cult films, *Casablanca*. The prototype relates to "the American cultural landscape, which has tended to idealize a romantic, highly

Figure 5. Commemoration

glamorous, and heroic past—one often located in the period surrounding World War II and visually fixed for us by the classical
Hollywood cinema that reached its peak in both production and
influence in that era" (40).

The types of characters played by Cooper have little in common with the outlaw persona of the star of *Casablanca,* Hum-
phrey Bogart. Cooper played the likes of Sergeant York and Lou
Gehrig and embodied the "everyman" type in some of Frank
Capra's films. Among the roles that make him suited for creating
a diegesis for my premises is that of Bertram Potts in *Ball of Fire*
(called during production "The Professor and the Burlesque
Queen"): Professor Potts, "writing a treatise on slang for an encyclopedia, elicits, for research purposes only, the aid of a burlesque
stripper, Sugarpuss O'Shea" (Barbara Stanwyck) (Dickens, 184).
Cooper wanted to star in *A Tale of Two Cities* (Swindell, 148). He
played an architect at least twice, Marco Polo once, and was often
cast as a "soldier of fortune" (even more often than as a cowboy).

In finding the memory to rehearse this role as soldier of fortune I was guided also by what Derrida said in his talk on "the other heading" about the "prow of the ship" as the image of European identity, and of identification as such (the head as vanguard). I was thinking also about the pattern of scenes of instruction, the tableaux of my other rehearsals, relaying the myth of the beautiful death.

The setting for this rehearsal is the Florida Museum of Natural History on the campus of the University of Florida during the first exhibit of the Columbus quincentenary (October 1989): "First Encounters: Spanish Exploration in the Caribbean and the United States, 1492–1570." The centerpiece of the exhibit was a two-thirds scale replica of the *Niña,* Columbus's favorite ship. The design for the ship was discovered in the Archives of the Indies in Seville, Spain—"the first description ever found of any of Columbus' ships"—by a researcher from the University of Florida. In my memory the ship is surrounded by children dressed in period costumes; on each Sunday a fifth-grade class from one of the local schools performed a "living tableau," populating the scene of the replica and displaying the duties of preparing for departure in 1492.

Visitors to the exhibit were encouraged to pose questions to the students about what they were doing. No questions could be answered about the outcome or aftermath of the voyage, however, because within the parameters of the drama, it had yet to happen. Still, people would ask, "What do you think of the people you met when you arrived in America?" The rehearsed response was, "I don't know; we haven't gotten there yet." A fair question was, "What do you think you will find on this voyage?" A common response was, "Spices and gold." One student said, "America."

My son was selected to represent Columbus when his class had its turn. He stood on the prow of the replica—precisely on the prow of the ship—with a serious expression on his face and explained that everyone knew the world was round and that his method would be to get to the East by going west. As I took his picture, I remembered that my father's birthday was October 12, Columbus Day. "Nice of them to fly the flags for me," he used to say. The pattern came into formation—perhaps when I depressed the button on the camera—the click of the shutter like the click of recognition, triggering the emotion of eureka. What surprised me was how unpleasant the feeling was, as I saw all at once the line of descent from Columbus to my son, or even from Solon, handed down through his grandfather and father. That was when I decided I had to perform a quincentenary commemoration in the Montana centennial.

Cultural Literacy

The fifth-grade classes participated in the exhibit because in the elementary school curriculum a unit on the "Age of Discovery" is taught in the fifth grade. The living tableau at the museum is as typical of School discourse as *Beau Geste* is of Entertainment discourse, or *"Chora"* is of Discipline discourse. School discourse functions by means of explanatory codes (the terms and concepts of specialized knowledge outside the context of Discipline expertise) in a manner similar to "cultural literacy" as described by E. D. Hirsch. To be culturally literate is to recognize and share the associations of a national culture (E. D. Hirsch, 19). Thus in school one learns not so much the common "facts" or the details of a disciplinary expertise as the stereotypes, myths, and legends that constitute American national identity. In this discourse, "Columbus" means "discovery" or "invention." Anecdotes such as those about George Washington and the cherry tree or Abraham Lincoln's log cabin boyhood (reading by the light of the fire and writing with a piece of charcoal) contribute to the formation of an ideology. "The Lincoln of folklore had a significance even beyond the Lincoln of actuality. For the Lincoln of folklore embodied what ordinary inarticulate Americans cherished as ideals" (90). The event at the Florida Museum is an example of what Hirsch says used to be done implicitly and now needs to be done explicitly (and this is the controversial aspect of his book): it teaches the schemas and scripts, the symbolic register of a certain national identity, even one defined and fixed at a given moment of American history.

The tableau format is a commonplace of the institutions of Family and Entertainment as well, where the genre of the "living tableau" has a long tradition. A handbook entitled *Tableaux, Charades and Pantomimes,* for example, first published in 1889, carries the subtitle, "Adapted alike to Parlor Entertainments School and Church Exhibitions and for use on the Amateur Stage," and includes a scenario for a tableau of "Columbus before Ferdinand and Isabella." Columbus should be "clad in dark Knickerbocker suit, over which is cast a long black cloak, thrown back from one shoulder; long stockings, low shoes with buckles; ornaments and gold chains about neck and arms; black hat with plumes, in hand; hair thrown back from forehead; full beard and mustache." In this tableau, Columbus kneels upon one knee at the foot of the double throne of Ferdinand and Isabella, with doctors in black robes standing to the left, lords and ladies to the right, and soldiers to the rear. "Indians with bows, arrows, and tomahawks stand in a group near Columbus."

The tableau form also suits the cognitive science that is the basis of Hirsch's account. In this view, School discourse develops the schemata that organize memory: "We use at least two radically different types of schemata, one analogous to static pictures and another to scripts or procedures" (56). The students at the museum were engaged in a ritual, rehearsing something the nation values, confirming the institutionalization of a habit of mind. The lesson is learned in one's very body.

Both commemorative ceremonies and bodily practices therefore contain a measure of insurance against the process of cumulative questioning entailed in all discursive practices. This is the source of their importance and persistence as mnemonic systems. Every group, then, will entrust to bodily automatisms the values and categories which they are most anxious to conserve. They will know how well the past can be kept in mind by a habitual memory sedimented in the body. (Connerton, 102)

The 1893 Columbian Exposition served to fix several such rituals, including Columbus Day and the pledge of allegiance to the flag.

Francis J. Bellamy, an editor of *Youth's Companion,* devised a plan for the fair's dedication (12 October 1892) where schoolchildren across the country could participate in the Exposition's quadricentennial liturgy by celebrating in their schools. To make the event truly national, Bellamy drafted the Pledge of Allegiance to the flag of the United States. The federal Bureau of Education circulated copies to teachers nationwide. . . . Millions of children around the country promised their allegiance, thus beginning a ritual thereafter repeated daily in the nation's public schools. (Schlereth, 288)

The account of the exhibit provided by the Florida alumni magazine reveals a dimension of experience linking the institutions of Family, School and Discipline—boosterism. As luck would have it (keeping in mind Derrida's "Other Heading"), the name of the official alumni magazine of the University of Florida is *Today.* This *Today* is to School what *Beau Geste* is to Entertainment. In a recent issue, the lead story, "First Encounters," declared: "As the world prepares to mark 500 years since Columbus reached the New World, remarkable discoveries by UF researchers are in the spotlight."

Today shows that the "Columbus" story is a feature of the continuing process of inventing the "psyche" or self that emerges in a subject through the performance of a certain logic: "A logic of the psyche, the topic of its identifications and projections warrants a lengthy discussion" (Derrida, 1989a:63). The context of "First Encounters"—its relation to the other stories in the magazine—shows the *spirit* of boosterism that is the unthought foundation or habit of mind of School, which is in turn the ground or support of Discipline research. While Discipline focuses on instilling a critical intelligence, School works to create loyal subjects, whose loyalty will be tested by their open hands rather than by open minds, by the gifts they give to the university.

Among the feature articles in the same issue of *Today* as "First Encounters," which calls attention to the innovations of UF researchers with respect to the Columbus theme, is a story on "The Test of Time": "Former U.S. Senator George Smathers' $20 million gift secures the future of his alma mater's libraries," followed by, "Sky's the Limit": "With a year of Coach Steve Spurrier's high-powered brand of football behind them, the Gators are poised to start the 1991 season." By juxtaposing the researchers with the retiring senator and the successful coach, *Today* shows the booster spirit linking the institutions by means of identification and projection. The university's "Embrace Excellence Campaign," which concluded on December 31, 1991, according to the local newspaper "broke all predictions of success and unearthed a network of alumni and friends throughout Florida and the nation that UF officials hope will continue to carry the university to its vision of greatness." Over one hundred thousand donors gave a total of $358 million to the university endowment. To write with the paradigm is to follow the heading of *Today,* to try to think research and boosterism together.

An Emblem of Invention

If School used "Columbus" on behalf of the booster spirit, what lesson did Discipline want to convey by means of the tableau with the replica? Whatever the ideological message, the analogy to Columbus had an intellectual lesson to teach as well. It concerned not the actuality but the legend of Columbus, of course, associated with the value of invention: invention, inventiveness, innovation name an American value. Columbus, excerpted as a metonym for the whole age of exploration and discovery, came to stand for the intellectual curiosity that is the basis for enlightened thought. Francis Bacon, for example, one of the inventors of scientific method, used as the frontispiece for his

Great Instauration (a book marking the epochal shift into an enlightened era) the image of Columbus's ship sailing beyond the Pillars of Hercules.

> Francis Bacon, primary theorist of a new epistemology and staunch opponent of medieval scholasticism, extrapolated Columbus himself into a symbol of bold modernity. His voyager was decidedly not the man of terminal doubt and despair whom we encounter in the Jamaica letter of 1503. He was instead a figure of hopeful departures, a man whose discovery of a "new world" suggested the possibility that "the remoter and more hidden parts of nature" might be explored with success. The function of Bacon's *Novum Organum* was to provide for the scientific investigator the kind of encouragement which the arguments of Columbus prior to 1492 had provided for a Europe too closely bound to traditional assumptions. (Franklin, 7–8)

What Bacon did with Columbus in the natural sciences, Henry David Thoreau did in the "moral sciences." *Walden* concludes with this admonition:

> What does Africa,—what does the West stand for? Is not our own interior white on the chart? black though it may prove, like the coast, when discovered. . . . Be rather the Lewis and Clarke and Frobisher, of your own streams and oceans; explore your own higher latitudes,—with hiploads of preserved meats to support you, if they be necessary; and pile the empty cans sky-high for a sign. Nay, be a Columbus to whole new continents and worlds within you, opening new channels, not of trade, but of thought. (Thoreau, 212)

Hirsch points out that "the contents of American schoolbooks of the nineteenth century were so similar and interchangeable that their creators might seem to have participated in a conspiracy to indoctrinate young Americans with commonly shared attitudes, including a fierce national loyalty and pride" (Hirsch, 87).

The *Niña* tableau continued this tradition, mounting Columbus in the curriculum in terms that resemble his appearance in *Self-Help*, Samuel Smiles's immensely popular series of conduct books first published in Britain in 1859. These books collect anecdotes from the lives of great men that illustrate the virtues of the middle class (thrift, character, duty) and stress the value of inventive contributions to one's society. They were no doubt one source for my father's motto: "You Have to Pay for Your Space."

In *Self-Help*, a lesson on the importance of close observation of detail for invention is punctuated by noting that "so trifling a matter as the sight of sea-weed floating past his ship enabled Columbus to quell the mutiny which arose amongst his sailors at not discovering land and to assure them that the eagerly sought New World was not far off" (Smiles, 100). The life of Columbus is told in *Duty: With Illustrations of Courage, Patience and Endurance,* qualities that "constitute the glory of manly character." To point this manly moral, Smiles had in mind a different part of Columbus's life—not the moment of discovery but that of "terminal doubt."

> Some men are willing to throw themselves away in the pursuit of a great object. The early martyrs, the early discoverers, the early inventors, the pioneers of civilization—all who work for truth, or religion, for patriotism—are the forlorn hope of humanity. They live and labor and die without any hope of personal reward. It is enough for them to know their work, and by the exercise of moral power to do it. The man of energy and genius is guided by his apprehension of the widest and highest tendencies. He may be thwarted and discouraged. Difficulties may surround him. But he is borne up by invincible courage; and if he dies, he leaves behind him a name which every man venerates. Death has fructified his life, and made it more fruitful to others. (Smiles, *Duty,* 112)

Orison Swett Marden, one of America's most famous authorities on "success" (he started publishing in 1894), traced his career inspiration to a reading of *Self-Help*. "The book filled me with the hope that some day, perhaps, I might be able to do something that would stimulate and encourage poor American boys like myself to develop and make the most of all the powers God had given them" (Huber, 147). In Marden's philosophy, however, hard work and perseverance were supposed to lead to financial as well as to ethical rewards.

The moment depicted in the museum tableau—the eve of departure—is the moment that the tradition of invention initiated by Bacon selected out of the total biography of Columbus. Ernst Bloch, in his study of *The Principle of Hope,* noted the association of utopian thinking with the voyages of discovery, an association that led to the use of Columbus "as a witness and emblem for *ars inveniendi.* In alchemical works of the seventeenth century, Columbus is the master who sailed out beyond the Pillars of Hercules to the golden Gardens of the Hesperides. He stands for the alchemical journey, for the magus who seeks paradise in the curse of the earth. Even in the eighteenth century, 'golden America' appears under this aspect on alchemical title-pages, as much invention as discovery" (Bloch, 751).

The curriculum features the departure, the image "of distant lands hovering in the mind at the beginning of the journey as well as during it." This drive to set forth, the motive of curiosity, and not the arrival with all of its unexpected and unintended consequences, is what counts in the folklore and legend of Columbus communicated in the cultural literacy of America.

The Effigy

One value of the Columbus story is as a reminder that "America had to be invented after its discovery" (Elliott, 16). "Columbus" as a story circulated for a long time in two versions, both of which contributed to the formation of American national identity (a third story was suppressed). Two tableaux were available for thought—"hopeful departure" and "broken dreams." The latter tableau represents Columbus at the end of his life, dying in obscure poverty. "In his writings we first detect the voice of the American exile, the unhoused wanderer left with little but open space and the pain of enduring it. This too was part of what the Genoan discovered" (16–17).

Chorography as an *ars inveniendi* addresses this process of cultural invention—the invention of culture itself and the role of cultural resources in individual thought. Analogical or figurative thinking is always selective, retaining only those parts of the vehicle considered relevant to the question while dropping other parts. Which parts of "Columbus" are *relevant* to Americans after 1992? The initiation of the Columbus legend in American cultural literacy is attributed to Washington Irving, who, during the wars for independence from Britain, offered Columbus as an alternative to our Anglo-Saxon heroes. "Columbus" is typical in this respect. The story of George Washington and the cherry tree, for example, like most of the other legendary anecdotes of American symbolic figures disseminated in textbooks (the principal medium of School discourse), is an invention that may be credited to a specified author—in this case, Mason Weems: "Weems deduced that the public needed a domesticated Everyman whose life would serve as a model for American youth" (E. D. Hirsch, 88). The story eventually found its way into McGuffey's *Reader,* which assured its place "in our permanent lore."

This process of cultural invention continues in the present with the recovery of another version of the Columbus story in circulation. If Francis Bacon selected the story of exploration for his tableau, the American Indian Movement (AIM) has selected another part of the story—the imperialist events of disease, enslavement, and massacre of Native Americans by colonial invaders. "Columbus stands as a clear example of an insane person, a killer and a cannibal, a user and abuser of his fellow human beings" (Forbes, 41). Toward the end of the exhibit at the Florida Museum, AIM organized a protest, marching outside the building and demanding that the exhibit be dismantled. The local newspaper reported the demands as "a public apology by museum officials, abolition of Columbus Day on local, state and national levels, and a telephone outside the museum for the protesters' personal use." One of the protesters explained AIM's point of view in a guest column of the newspaper.

> During the November protest, a woman emerged from the museum and berated Russell Means, leader of the American Indian Movement, and the other protesters for spoiling the children's enjoyment of the exhibit. She and others, she said, had worked many hours to present a balanced view. Russell asked how she thought the Jewish communities in America would feel if the Nazis put together an exhibit presenting a balanced view of the holocaust and then celebrated Hitler Day. . . . The blatant genocide practiced by the early invaders has become a more subtle form of genocide mandated by government policy. (Gainesville *Sun,* December 12, 1990)

Similar protests were staged at each location to which the exhibit traveled. At the Science Museum of Minnesota, in the summer of 1992, for example, Vernon Bellecourt, an AIM leader, declaring the display "racist, slanted and deceitful," boarded the replica, threw a pint of his own blood on the sail, and knocked a mannequin representing Columbus off the prow of the ship.

Adventure

What is the lesson of the *Niña* tableau? "Learning is an adventure: Go explore the frontiers of knowledge." One advantage of remaking *Beau Geste* as a discourse on method is the opportunity it provides for reviewing the metaphor of learning as "adventure." "Adventure" is not really a genre; anything can be an adventure, including inventing. "Adventure in the cinema is conditioned by a characteristic of the medium, the minuteness of its gaze. Where a few words or an exchange of glances can add up to a forceful narrative, adventure can exist on a very intimate scale. Opening up the Northwest Passage or the Chisholm Trail is evidently adventure, but so, in the movies, is the discovery of radium, or Glen Miller finding 'The Sound'" (Cameron, 16). Indeed, this association of scientific and cultural "discoveries" with opening up the western frontier is precisely the problematic addressed in my method.

A disciplinary name (however inaccurate) for the process of invention in progress here could be "deconstruction," which is to say that chorography must emerge from within the field of the old metaphors for research (such as "the frontiers of knowledge"). But this very redundancy is what will make chorography intelligible.

> Deconstruction is inventive or it is nothing at all; it does not settle for methodical procedures, it opens up a passageway, it marches ahead and marks a trail; its writing is not only performative, it produces rules—other conventions—for new performativities and never installs itself in the theoretical assurance of a simple opposition between performative and constative. Its *process* involves an affirmation, this latter being linked to the coming— the *venire*—in event, advent, invention. But it can only make it by deconstructing a conceptual and institutional structure of invention that would neutralize by putting the stamp of reason on some aspect of invention, of inventive power: as if it were necessary, over and beyond a certain traditional status of invention to reinvent the future. (Derrida, 1989a:42)

Adventure and invention are linked in deconstruction by the *vent*.

Derrida is associated with a poststructuralist rereading of Nietzsche, who is *the* philosopher of adventure. In *The Gay Science,* Nietzsche advised the thinker to "live dangerously! Build your cities under Vesuvius! Send your ships into uncharted seas! Live at war with your peers and yourselves! Be robbers and conquerors, you lovers of knowledge" (cited in Zweig, 204). Zarathustra makes explicit the ancient link between seafaring and theoretical curiosity: "Have you never seen a sail go over the sea, rounded and taut and trembling with the violence of the wind? Like the sail, trembling with the violence of the spirit, my wisdom goes over the sea—my wild wisdom" (Nietzsche, in Zweig, 206). This sail—the paradigm of all the sails, literal and figurative, in the Western tradition of knowledge—is the one the Native American threw blood on in Minnesota. I want to *receive* his gesture (and this *geste* is the entire issue), his *coup,* knocking the effigy off the prow: Eureka.

To be adequate to the agonistic qualities of knowledge, which Nietzsche believed must be won in a struggle or combat, the philosopher must recover and learn how to use the style of high adventure that high culture exiled to popular letters (205). Hans Blumenberg, clarifying what is at stake in Nietzsche's hostility to the "domestic" virtues promoted in the high-culture novel of his day, credits him with recognizing that the drive for knowledge (based on a drive of curiosity) cannot be taken for granted as "natural" or "autonomous" but has to be *achieved* in a struggle with other social demands and interests (Blumenberg, 379).

It has been recognized since antiquity that the same appetite to know the unknown that motivated philosophers to study the heavens also "drives masses of people to the spectacles, makes us rummage through what is locked up" (261). The ambivalence in Western civilization about curiosity concerns an uneasiness about "proper" knowledge and its relevance to the best interests of humanity. Augustine ranked the levels of *curiositas* from the lowest to highest, starting at the bottom with "amusement at a mutilated corpse" (314). Intellectuals have long tended to denigrate popular adventure, Martin Green observed. Nietzsche's position was that despised or degraded popular attractions constitute a refuge of theoretical curiosity in the modern age. Paul Zweig suggests in this vein that only by following our "bad taste" in pulp magazines, tabloid newspapers, second-rate movies, and the like may one grasp something of the spirit of knowledge as adventure (Zweig, 225). Derrida generalizes this attitude, finding a value in any and all types of denigrated knowledge as providing positions from which to question the premises of reason, the legitimacy of "knowledge" in the university (Derrida, 1990b:594).

Cultural Politics

As a politics of writing, chorography rehearses this problematic, polysemous association linking the metaphors of method with a "frontier" whose diegesis includes colonization and wars of imperialism. "Abjection then takes the place of the other, to the extent of affording him jouissance, often the only one for the borderline patient who, on that account, transforms the abject into the site of the Other. Such a frontiersman is a metaphysican who carries the experience of the impossible to the point of scatology" (Kristeva, 1982:54). Michael Nerlich, who believes that "good adventure-thought" is still possible (Nerlich, xx), itemized the qualities associated with "the integration of chivalric adventure-ideology into bourgeois consciousness": (1) conceiving of order in terms of change; (2) acceptance of the unknown as a positive value; (3) acceptance of risks; (4) acceptance of chance ("Chance, constituent of any adventure, becomes an essential value of adventure-ideology"); (5) recognition of the other ("Integration of the other into one's own, whether by peaceful means or not"); (6) elaboration of "search systems" (Nerlich, xxi). This integration resulted in an extension of an adventure mentality into "all domains of social practice."

Almost every discourse of the different cultural institutions, then, includes the element of "adventure" as a value. Sir Robert Baden-Powell, for example, commander of the British garrison at Mafeking during the Boer War, invented the Boy Scouts as a solution to what he saw as the problem of his nation's youth, which he described as without individuality or strength of character, utterly without resourcefulness, initiative or guts for adventure. The value of adventure is invoked today in books such as *Vacationland U.S.A.,* published by the National Geographic Society (1970), which begins with this appropriation of one of America's founding documents: "We hold this truth to be self-evident, that leisure leavens life. So take off! Measure your leisure in days or months but wrap it in excitement. Spice it with challenge, fun, adventure. Begin with a questing spirit. End with the discovery that here in America there's world enough—and time."

In the ancient world, the search for truth was indeed thought to depend on the availability of leisure time (made possible by the class system and slavery). And in contemporary Discipline discourse the rhetoric of adventure is practiced as much as it is in Entertainment discourse. "We have not produced a 'designed' landscape," Bernard Tschumi said of his park for creativity— Parc de la Villette. "Instead we have devised a framework capable of absorbing an infinite number of intentions and extensions of meaning. Our strategy is to confer on the simple the dimension of adventure" (Tschumi, 1983:77). We still need "inventive, adventurous, more or less solitary experimentation and research." Derrida stated, in a way that acknowledges the risks of adventure-thought. "The assault on the so-called 'individual signature,' with all its accusations of narcissism, elitism, solipsism, and so on, under the pretext of the 'good political conscience,' seems to me disastrous" (Derrida, 1991b:44).

Martin Green noted the association of adventure with masculinity, and also with nationalism, due in part to the gender folklore assigning the realm of violence to men and of law to women. "Today it is women who have the initiative in the world of ideas. And the more antimasculinist literature becomes, the more hostile it will be to adventure writing" (Green, 1991:4). Yet some women also write the conjunction of adventure and method, such as Kathy Acker, who invokes the myth of the pirate, which she associates with being tattooed. "For me tattooing is very profound. The meeting of body and, well, the spirit—it's a *real* kind of art, it's on the skin. It's both material and not material and it's also a sign of the outcast. So that's what I'm saying about looking for the myth with people like that—tattoo artists, sailors, pirates" (Friedman, 18).

Acker's view includes a commitment to experimentation and

method: "Method has become supremely, politically important. For example, the novelist who writes about the poor Cambridge vicar who can't deal with his homosexuality is giving us no tools for survival. Whereas William Burroughs's writing methods, his uses of psychic research, are weapons in the fight for our own happiness" (34). One of her own experiments uses the diegesis of "Algeria" to juxtapose the dramas of sexism and colonialism, forming a passage between institutions of the private and public spheres. It is entitled *Algeria: A Series of Invocations Because Nothing Else Works.*

Similarly, in the Discipline discourse of theory, a feminist critic of poststructuralism, showing the patriarchal nature of the "crisis of modernity," still invokes the masculinist metaphor of research as adventure in terms that might be described as "deconstructive." She states the problematic in a way that reflects the drama of Zinderneuf. The feminist critique of Western philosophy, that is, shows the complicity linking rationality, masculinity, and war: "According to this critique, philosophy defends an image of thought where rationality is like a besieged fortress that must be defended by a tactical arsenal of well-armed arguments so as to mark very clear frontiers in the domain of thought and to keep up boundaries or distinctions that function as frames of self-legitimation" (Braidotti, 278).

Meanwhile, what Braidotti admires in the feminist critics of the Western tradition of abstract reason is "the element of risk that these thinkers introduce into intellectual activity. Theirs is a more daring, risky form of intelligence; their approach to enunciation and to discursive practice is freer and more disrespectful than the established norms. Veritable adventuresses into the field of theory—as I have described them, they reveal remarkable acrobatic talents as they trace mental routes across the void, without falling victim to gravity" (280). "Risk" is perhaps *the* quality of both intellectual and physical adventure, as defined by Sir Edmund Hillary ("conqueror of Everest," climbed "because it was there"), in a foreword to the Rand McNally *Almanac of Adventure:* "To most of us, adventure is synonymous with danger, difficulties, and fear. I believe that, young or old, you have the right to risk your life in a challenge if you wish to do so" (Hillary, 11).

To translate her metaphor into the diegesis of Zinderneuf, Braidotti's feminist adventuresses are not on the side of the soldiers of fortune in the foreign legion (who must be defending the fort of rationalism) but on the side of a "new nomadism" (277)—in short, on the side of the Touaregs attacking the fort. But are these the only choices in the scenario? To rehearse a remake of *Beau Geste* as *chora* is to bring directly into the invention process the metaphor for research that has been the unacknowledged support of a certain *feeling* of thought. What is this feeling—the one guiding the judgments upon which invention depends? Is it anything other than that the X of an unknown marks a mystery, an enigma, whose solution is Truth? Chorography seeks an alternative to this gesture (to re-mark the X).

11

THE SQUARE

Le Cafard

By this time I realized that the rehearsal process had produced
a rule for the remake: to perform *Beau Geste* as "*Chora.*" In my
Emotional Recall exercises, my Discipline discourse appeared as
often as did memories from Family or School experience—especially the theory of psychoanalysis. It was time in my rehearsal of
the event at Fort Zinderneuf to remember the *folie* of Villette
Park in Tschumi's hybrid sense, evoking not only the music hall
but "madness."

Madness serves as a constant point of reference throughout the
Urban Park of La Villette because it appears to illustrate a char-

Figure 6. Fort Da

acteristic situation at the end of the 20th century—that of dis-
junctions and dissociation between use, form, and social values.
This situation is not necessarily a negative one, but rather is
symptomatic of a new condition, as distant from 18th-century
humanism as from this century's various modernisms. . . . In this
analogy, the contemporary city and its many parts (here La Villette) are made to correspond with the dissociated elements of
schizophrenia. (Tschumi, 1987:16–17)

There is a madness specific to the foreign legion both in its
historical reality and in Wren's narrative. The name for this
madness is *le cafard*. The usage is slang. *Cafard* literally means
"bug"—a man who has the *cafard* has "gone bugs" (Mercer, 147).
It entered the vocabulary of the legion in the latter part of the
nineteenth century to describe the effect of service in the "true

desert" of North Africa. The conditions of the blockhouses or forts in the desert created an atmosphere of the *cafard,* "a collective name for all the inconceivable stupidities, excesses and crimes which tormented nerves can commit"—murder, suicide, mutiny, self-mutilation, flights into the desert, desertion, madness, despair. A man with the *cafard* is continually irritated, easily enraged, prone to spew insults, as likely suddenly to put a bayonet through his neighbor as to tear up his own uniform into rags.

The *cafard* is always present in some form, according to veterans' reports, and "is the cause of the horrible tattooing, of drinking and brawling, of the longing for continual change." In desert conditions, the "harmless peculiarities" of many of the men who joined the legion quickly grew into madness. "A Legionnaire is gloomy, sitting sullenly on his bed for hours, speaking to no one. If you ask him what is the matter, he will answer with gross insult. He sits thinking all the time and does the queerest things. He has the *cafard*" (148). In *Beau Geste,* one soldier dies of the *cafard,* and a veteran warns John Geste about this mood. "'We call it *le cafard.* The cockroach. It crawls round and round in the brain, and the greater the heat, the monotony, the hardship, the overwork, the over-marching, and the drink—the faster goes the beetle and the more it tickles. . . . And do you know what is the egg of this beetle? No? It is absinthe'" (Wren, 178). This mood or feeling is as important to my tableau as the event and the myth of the beautiful death. But does it name the feeling of research?

The setting giving rise to this mood was any one of the many forts built throughout North Africa, typified in Fort Zinderneuf. When the legion was not fighting, the soldiers were kept busy building roads and forts. Building their own forts gave the soldiers a chance to use the skills they learned in civilian life. "As invariably happened, the Legion produced its experts from the ranks—draftsmen, masons, carpenters, and other craftsmen. It is said that one Legion company turned out five qualified architects" (Mercer, 35). One of the chief antidotes to the *cafard* was the practice of handicrafts (along with music and gardening) (150).

The design of the forts became standardized, each one being square in shape, with walls made of stone and mud one hundred yards long, three yards high, and one yard thick. There was a tower at each corner, a single entrance wide enough for a cart, a heavy oak gate, and crenelated parapets (140). A rock quarry was an essential part of legion work: "for the basic elements of life had been reduced to rock and sand and water, and it was as essential that a fort be built near the site of a suitable rock quarry as near a source of water" (141).

The design for the Villette *folie* that unfolds through the meetings between Derrida and Eisenman bears remarkable similarities to a legion fort. The elements of their invention are the same as those essentials of the North African desert—sand, water, and a rock quarry. It also has to do with a certain Sand & Gravel plant. To convey the absence of *chora,* that *chora* itself cannot appear; the designers worked with the metaphor of writing embodied in architectural elements that might produce marks that could then be erased. "I think the idea of writing something new is good. I also think there should be the possibility of erasing," Eisenman observed in the second meeting. "One possibility is to use sand and water—sand for writing, water for erasing. Physically the architecture will have to deal with these issues" (Eisenman, in Kipnis).

The "quarry" (along with the labyrinth and the palimpsest) became one of the central features of the design discussions. "We have a quarry, from which stones have obviously been taken and moved to a palimpsest, where they leave their mark. They are moved to this other thing, leaving a trace on the palimpsest," Eisenman adds in the third meeting. "The whole thing becomes a mental operation concerning the history of the stones as they are moved by the people from the quarry to form the palimpsest and return eventually to the quarry. I know it's not so easy." Building the fort is an emblem of *inventio* (retrieving arguments stored in the places).

The fort forms a link, in the pattern of my diegesis, with the folly of the traditional fool, depicted in illuminated manuscripts with a stone in his hand or in his mouth: "Throughout the Middle Ages the stone remained the main symbol of folly—hard, impenetrable, stolid" (Zijderveld, 39). The "Blue Water" sapphire participates in this set as well, along with the stones of the Miles City Sand & Gravel and the status of the subject in Lacan's theory of *folie:*

> When a subject is confronted with an enigmatic, impenetrable Other, the thing he has to grasp is that his question to the Other is already the question of the Other itself—the impenetrability of the substantial Other, the hindrance which is preventing the subject from penetrating the heart of the Other, is immediately an index of the fact that this Other is already in itself hindered, structured around a certain "indigestible" rock, resisting symbolization, symbolic integration. (Zizek, 178)

These "rocks" figure my stupidity ("blockhead!"). The uncanny experience of electronic rhetoric is that invention is impossible without this stupidity, and if computers are going to be smart (used by speaking subjects) they will need as much artificial stupidity as artificial intelligence (cognitive science must absorb the logic of *folie*).

The visitors to the Eisenman *folie,* had it ever been built, could have imagined themselves as legionnaires building a fort. The design, represented in the model offered at the sixth meeting, is fortlike, involving a moat and a wall "as thick as it is high." "You could sense it as a battlement" (Eisenman, in Kipnis). It is a memorial to the "wall of language." One of Plato's images for *chora* as the receptacle that allowed becoming to appear as a reflection of being was that of the stars reflected in a mirror. Lacan used a similar optic metaphor to discuss the formation of the ego as a "mirage." The wall of language is reflected in the mirror of the subject, allowing the ego to appear and to appear to itself as coherent. The "unconscious" is one name for this relationship of the individual ego to the collective institutions of society: the ego as mirage is a delusion constructed in the field of consciousness the way an optical illusion is an effect in the field of light. The "self" is like a mirage in the desert of North Africa.

The Unconscious

Rehearsing the scene at Fort Zinderneuf in terms of Discipline discourse reminded me of psychoanalysis as a theory of memory. Julia Kristeva's *Revolution in Poetic Language* is a study of how to take into account the function of the unconscious in poetic discourse. Her insight is that inventive writing (categorized in modern culture as artistic or creative writing) is the result of an interference between two different orders of signification—the "semiotic" (referring to the drives of the primary processes, the rhythms of the body in its gestural and vocal materiality) and the "symbolic" (the languages or discourses of social institutions, whose constraints, imposed on the body, "arrange" the semiotic). Recalling Derrida's preference for a metaphor of the "mark" to that of "light," Kristeva understands the semiotic order "in its Greek sense of distinctive mark, trace, index"; like Derrida, she names this order *"chora"*:

We borrow the term *chora* from Plato's *Timaeus* to denote an essentially mobile and extremely provisional articulation consti- tuted by movements and their ephemeral stases.... Our dis- course—all discourse—moves with and against the *chora* in the sense that it simultaneously depends upon and refuses it.... The *chora* is not yet a position that represents something for someone (it is not a sign); nor is it a *position* that represents someone for another position (it is not yet a signifier); it is, however, generated in order to attain to this signifying position. Neither model nor copy, the *chora* precedes and underlies figuration and thus specu- larization, and is analogous only to vocal or kinetic rhythm. (Kristeva, 1984:26)

Kristeva uses *chora* as an analogy for the unconscious to characterize its quality as prior to discourse but already ordered (as in *Timaeus,* in which space is prior to the work of the Demiurge craftsman, but is not "chaos"). In discursive terms, she uses the mediating character of *chora* to theorize a space that is neither that of propositional knowledge nor commonsense opinion. This boundary or frontier (interface) function of *chora* on the verge of language is glimpsed through artistic, poetic practices that perform the irruption of the semiotic order into the symbolic order. "By *reproducing signifiers*—vocal, gestural, verbal—the subject crosses the border of the symbolic and reaches the semiotic *chora,* which is on the other side of the social frontier" (79). Kristeva is concerned with thinking that which produces or generates the "I" or self that makes judgments (36) comparable to what I have called my premises.

The part of Kristeva's theory most important for chorography is her understanding of the *chora* function as a process or movement of invention conducted as a transgression of rules (the burlesque principle) that undermines the plausibility and verisimilitude of classic mimesis, argumentation, judgment, realism. Choral writing is a kind of dreamwork (hence the usefulness of psychoanalysis for theorizing her poetics) drawing not only on condensation and displacement (metaphor and metonymy) but especially on a third process—"the *passage from one sign system to another.*" The choral order may be discerned in this "passage" as a "mechanism of innovation" (as generative), distinct from something that is directly intelligible or sensible. "The new signifying system may be produced with the same signifying material; in language, for example, the passage may be made from narrative to text. Or it may be borrowed from different signifying materials: the transposition from a carnival scene to the written text, for instance" (59). The novel, Kristeva adds, was invented out of just such a transpositional process, a hybrid made from the redistributing of "carnival, courtly poetry, scholastic discourse." The emerging mode of hypermedia writing is similarly a complex, unstable hybrid.

In hypertext, multivocalism is popular, graphic elements, both drawn and scanned, have been incorporated into the narratives, imaginative font changes have been employed to identify various voices or plot elements, and there has also been a very effective use of formal documents not typically used in fictions—statistical charts, song lyrics, newspaper articles, film scripts, doodles and photographs, baseball cards and box scores, dictionary entries, rock music album covers, astrological forecasts, board games and medical and police reports." (Coover, 25)

The mechanism of innovation is described in psychoanalytic terms as an evasion or subversion of the censoring superego. It is a kind of "memory," an "anamnesis" recalling the semiotic drives into the symbolic. This "subject in process" (marking the frontier or interface joining the physical and cultural orders) may be discerned in a "rhythmicity" traversing a text's organization (structure and completion). The best metaphor for conveying this traversal or passage, according to Kristeva, "would not be the grammatical categories it redistributes, but rather a piece of music or a work of architecture" (126). In short, a *folie*.

Quadripodes

Having located the trace of the body in culture and associated it with the practice of textual poetics, Kristeva sought to locate this practice in turn in the symbolic order of institutions. The psychoanalytic theory of discourse provided the instructions. "Lacan has delineated four types of discourse in our society: that of the hysteric, the academic, the master, and the analyst. Within the perspective just set forth, we shall posit a different classification, which, in certain respects, intersects these four Lacanian categories, and in others, adds to them. We shall distinguish between the following signifying practices: narrative, metalanguage, contemplation, and text-practice" (88).

Kristeva's approach is useful for chorography first of all for relating her textual version of *chora* to Lacan's four discourses.

In fact, Lacan's theory of the four discourses has much in common with Plato's cosmology in the *Timaeus*. A comparison of Lacan's seminars, such as the ones on "The Ego in Freud's Theory and in the Technique of Psychoanalysis" (Lacan, 1988) and "The Inverse of Psychoanalysis," with Plato's *Timaeus* (both authors make liberal use of "bastard reasoning") displays a correlation between Lacan's symbolic order and Plato's *chora*. *Chora* as "active receptacle" contains the four fundamental elements— Earth, Air, Fire, and Water—from which everything else is composed. The receptacle sorts the elements and also facilitates their combination. "Plato's position was nearer to that of Heraclitus, who alone had rejected the notion of substance underlying change and had taught the complete transformation of every form of body into every other. We are now to think of qualities which are not also 'things' or substances, but transient appearances in the Receptacle. The Receptacle itself alone has some sort of permanent being" (Cornford, 178).

Lacan conceived of the symbolic as a four-part, four-sided order whose character he explored at several levels of modeling from apologues and images to mathemes. He once referred to this representation of the symbolic as his "apparatus on four paws," associated with his own pet dog, "Justine," who greeted him with a wag of her tail when he returned home. This four-pawed machine was also his answer to the riddle the Sphinx posed to Oedipus (concerning what goes on how many limbs at different times of the day).

To explain the status of psychoanalysis as a discourse (and hence subject to the same operations of the unconscious in the symbolic order as any other discourse) and its relation to the other institutions of society, Lacan supplemented the image of his dog with a matheme that he named *quadripodes,* involving four signifiers: "S1 or the primordial signifier; S2 or unconscious knowledge; \$ or the barred or unspeakable subject; and finally *a,* the object, fissure, quest, residue, or lack." The purpose of the formula was "to show the organization of the same within the different, of multiplicity within unity" (Roudinesco, 561)—in short, the problematic of *chora*. The four terms were placed successively in four positions: "the agent or appearance, work or sexual bliss, truth, and surplus enjoyment" (561). A rotation of the signifiers through each of the positions, a quarter turn at a time, generates the formulas for the four fundamental discourses: of the master, the hysteric, the psychoanalyst, and the university. Roudinesco indicates how the procedure works, describing for example how the discourse of the university is represented in the combinatory. Pivoting to university position from the master position produces the following situation:

> Unconscious knowledge then finds itself in the position of agent, *a* in that of work, S_1 in that of truth, and S in that of surplus enjoyment. The moral: university discourse produces subjects it addresses as though they were "course credits." It pretends to master truth through technique and conceives of knowledge as a multidisciplinary distribution. In addition, it acts in the name of knowledge itself and not of a master capable of producing knowledge. (Roudinesco, 562)

As for the position of master, Roudinesco credits Lacan with foreseeing a mutation in the status of knowledge in which the master would be replaced in the circuit of discourses by the computer.

The *quadripodes* models a theory of memory. As Lacan noted, memory changes from one epoch to another, being both conceived of and practiced by means of machinery (the "apparatus" as social machine, at once technological and ideological). Plato's Socrates designed a pedagogy of "reminiscences." Because the soul had a life before birth, the subject already knew everything, according to this doctrine, so that education could be conducted through anamnesis, a technique of reminding. This doctrine, being pre-Christian, ignored the phenomenon of guilt and is therefore inadequate for figuring modern memory, Lacan stated. To take guilt into account, modern memory supplements recollection with repetition (compulsion—beyond the pleasure principle).

Plato's images were borrowed from the devices and crafts of his day, such as metal work or agriculture, among others, used to convey the sense of *chora,* which contributed eventually to the alchemical psychology of humors. The machine guiding Freud's hypotheses about the pleasure principle, Lacan noted, was the steam engine, which conceptualized energy in terms of thermodynamics, entropy, and homeostasis. Lacan explained that his own image of memory comes from a more recent generation of equipment, "that most modern of machines, far more dangerous than the atom bomb." The name of this machine is *la machine à calculer,* which the dictionary translates as "computer" [but which the translator of the seminar gives as "adding machine"] (Lacan, 1978:111; 1988:88).

In the theory of memory modeled on the computer, a person's situation is not a matter of fate, destiny, luck, or chance but a cultural condition that may be represented cybernetically as a syntax of possibilities. The revolution or turning of the *quadripodes* or "square," as it is sometimes called, is a discursive analogy of what in machine language is an exercise of the combinatorial possibilities of 0 and 1 (00, 11, 10, 01). Everything that Freud was trying to theorize as "the death drive" may be reformulated as this combinatorial, Lacan suggested. The rules of the combinatorial are accessible through discourse ("outside the mirror is the wall [*le mur*] of language") representing the operations of the institutions of society (the symbolic order). "In other words, even if the word of my life had to be sought in something as long as an entire recital of the *Aeneid,* it isn't unthinkable that a machine [computer] would in time succeed in reconstituting it. Now, any machine can be reduced to a series of relays which are simply *pluses* and *minuses.* Everything, in the symbolic order, can be represented with the aid of such a series" (185).

To become reflective and reflexive about judgment is to realize that much of one's thinking takes place "outside" the "self" and within the symbolic order. "The important thing here is to realize that the chain of possible combinations of the encounter can be studied as such, as an order which subsists in its rigour, independently of all subjectivity. Through cybernetics, the symbol is embodied in an apparatus—with which it is not to be confused, the apparatus being just its support. And it is embodied in it in a literally trans-subjective way" (304). Thus whatever specific situation or combination arises in practice, "it manifests a strict symbolic pattern" (Muller and Richardson, 69). "Memory" in this system is an effect of the constraints of a "law" or a "syntax" (70). And the "shape" (*Eidos*) of this law is square:

> Wiener posits two beings each of whose temporal dimensions moves in the opposite direction from the other. To be sure, that means nothing, and that is how things which mean nothing all of a sudden signify something but in a quite different domain. If one of them sends a message to the other, for example a square, the being going in the opposite direction will first of all see the square vanishing, before seeing the square. That is what we see as well. The symptom initially appears to us as a trace. (Lacan, in Zizek, 55)

The square—that is the pattern appearing in the field or network of my diegesis: the pattern that is a message about invention.

Lacan clarifies his theory of memory, and the relation among the discourses of the square, by asking if it is possible for any person to "know" psychoanalysis *intuitively*. He uses the example of the slave from Plato's *Meno,* who according to the doctrine of reminiscences could use his common sense to solve the riddle of science (could construct a proof in geometry by merely answering certain questions Socrates put to him). It is significant in my context that the proof in *Meno* concerned the square: "The problem was to determine how long the side of a square must be if its area is to be twice the area of a given square. Socrates diagrams a square and arbitrarily sets the side equal to two units. The area of the original square is, of course, four square units. Using the diagram Socrates next shows the boy what the diagonal is. Then he asks the boy how many units long the sides of a square twice the area of the original square will be [etc]" (Magill, 66). That the boy is able to work out the problem is meant as a justification of theoretical curiosity and its expression in inquiry, against the skeptic's denial that learning was possible.

Lacan shows the limits of the Platonic model of memory by observing that the slave lacks an important piece of information. "Don't you see there is a fault-line between the intuitive element and the symbolic element? One reaches the solution using our idea of numbers, that 8 is half of 16. What one obtains isn't 8 square-units. At the center we have 4 surface units, and one irrational element, the square root of 2, which isn't given by intuition. Here, then, there is a shift from the plane of the intuitive bond to a plane of symbolic bond" (Lacan, 1988:18). The slave needed a knowledge of Discipline discourse (of mathematics) to solve the problem. The geometric figure of the square in this ancient problem marks the place of the quadripodes—the square of four discourses—of the symbolic order in psychoanalysis. In my rehearsal, Lacan's square provides the subtext for the square fort of the French foreign legion, place of *le cafard*. Choral work, Frances Yates might say, is an example of "the square art of memory," relying on "images of corporeal things, of men, of animals, of inanimate objects. When its images are of men or of animals, these are active, engaged in actions of some kind" (Yates, 327).

The Heraldic Erasure

The "fort" is a place of passage—a switch—in my diegesis, its square design marking *en abyme* the psychoanalytic theory of *folie*. Susan Stewart reminds me why Derrida mistrusted the abyssal form, resembling as it does "microcosmic" thought. "In Plato we find the broad outlines of a microcosmic theory. The *Timaeus* asserts that the cosmos is a living organism and that, as such, it is a copy of the transitory world of 'becoming'" (Stewart, 128). Plato drew analogies between the state and the soul in a way that informed the tradition of Neoplatonism and all thinking of correspondences, from the cabalists and the "signature" (human body equals cosmos) theory of Boehme to modern anthropology's finding correspondences between village layout and the cosmology of a tribe.

Sharon Crowley has shown that this cosmology of correspondences found its way into conventional School rhetoric and thus has explained the "strange" prominence given to the writing of paragraphs that emerged in the modern era:

> In its maturity, current-traditional rhetoric tended to see a composition as a nest of Chinese boxes, in which the smaller parts of discourse—words and sentences—were contained inside, and reflected by, the structure of increasingly larger parts—the paragraph and the essay. In treatises on method, this microcosmic to macrocosmic view of discourse was often illustrated by analogy with the study of grammar, which began with letters, syllables, and words since these were the smallest discernible units and supposedly the least difficult to understand. (Crowley, 132)

Stewart distinguished microcosmic thought from "miniaturization": "But whereas miniaturization involves the juxtaposition of object and representation, of everyday and extraordinary scale, microcosmic thought is a matter of the establishment of correspondences between seemingly disparate phenomena in order to demonstrate the sameness of all phenomena. Such thought therefore always tends toward theology and the promulgation of a 'grand design'" (128). Derrida is not interested in "grand designs" or metanarratives. His return to the *Timaeus,* and specifically to *chora,* is an attempt to extract something other from this tradition, to think what is gathered in *Geschlecht* not in terms of sameness but of difference, and thus his own usage of the "abyss" has more in common with what Stewart calls miniaturization.

Derrida appropriates and deconstructs the correspondences of the "signature" tradition, as in his reading of Francis Ponge's poetry as generated out of the poet's proper name. This experiment is part of the continuing struggle within the *trivium* in which rhetoric, reduced in the modern period essentially to nothing but style, recovers the functions usurped from it by grammar and logic. This recovery must begin within the possibilities of style itself (to show the logical operations of which style is capable).

Every text may be identified both by the name signed to it and the style of its composition. Ponge's lesson is to use the first signature as the formula for the second, a formula that is signaled *en abyme,* creating a third dimension that must be comprehended neither as the intelligible nor the sensible but the generative (*chora*) (Derrida, 1984:54). The same basic figure that is dear to burlesque—the pun—informs the linguistics of the signature *en abyme.* The correspondence at the level of the signifier of the thing, *éponge* (sponge), as object and the proper name, "Ponge," figures a theory of writing that uses the *mise en abyme* to direct the devices of mise-en-scène and montage.

In hyperrhetoric the pattern formed by the signature *en abyme* functions as the electronic alternative to concept formation for gathering heterogeneous materials into a set (the paradigm). The effect of inserting the signature into the abyss of the text is to "monumentalize, institute, and erect it into a thing or a stony object. But in doing so, you also lose the identity, the title of ownership over the text" (56). This "catastrophe" opens an exchange between the proper and the common, the personal and the public domains, that may be generalized into a new style of abstraction that links particulars without the aid of a covering concept or generalization (no more generals). Derrida learned from Ponge, that is, how to use style (rhetoric, rather than grammar or logic) to generalize by means of the absolutely particular. At this level, the name signing the abyss of my remake is "ulmer," monumentalized as *le mur* ("the wall," by macaronic anagram): the wall of Fort Zinderneuf; the wall of language; the crenelated parapet of "Choral Work." That is how *folie* receives: The Other writes *le mur,* and I read *ulmer.*

Chorography orders a diverse body of information by an extension of this miniaturized signature: the *da* emerges from the *fort* as an outline for a kind of heraldic shield, a family crest of the subject. Lacan's heraldic device, for example, was (topologically) the Brunian knot, although as Elizabeth Roudinesco explains, "the structure in which three rings are linked together without being linked two by two, so that, if one untied, the others are freed" is often referred to as "Borromean rings" (Roudinesco, 564).

Lacan had been tying knots privately for years, as a hobby. In the 1970s he introduced knot tying into his seminars, calling the knots his *ronds de ficelles,* which he used to model his topological account of the psyche. The Borromean knot demonstrated neatly "the triangulation of the Symbolic, the Imaginary, and the Real," embodying what his abstract formula or matheme articulated, that "every discourse had its meaning as a result of another discourse" (564). His decision to integrate the *ficelle* or string into his teaching came in 1972 due to his discovery, at a dinner party, of the heraldry of the Borromeo family, who constituted "the principal signifiers of his intellectual itinerary: the Roman Catholic Church, the Reconquest [driving the Moors out of Europe], the struggle against a 'bastardized' psychoanalysis, and the plague" (563).

> Something was triggered when Lacan heard the story of the Borromeo family, or at least a few scraps of its story. The armorial bearings of the Milanese dynasty were constituted by three circles in the form of a cloverleaf, symbolizing a triple alliance. If one of the rings is withdrawn, the two others are set free. Each circle evoked the power of one of the three branches of the family. One of its most illustrious representatives, Saint Carlo Borromeo, was a hero of the Counter-Reformation.... He reformed clerical morals, moving toward a greater discipline. During the plague of 1576 he distinguished himself through his charity. (563)

The *inventio* directing the selection of information for writing the rehearsals of the remake (or for ordering a database), may be a simulation of this search for a mystory, for the knot or pattern binding together the emotional sets that are the foundation of one's judgment (of one's intuitions, and hence of one's creativity): the signature signs my premises. That Lacan found his pattern by accident, in the crest of the Borromeos, shows that one's "family" is open to history, a chiasmus of public and private.

PART FOUR

YELLOWSTONE
DESERT

This always takes place as part of collective conditions, although minor, the conditions of minor literature and politics, even if each of us had to discover in himself or herself an intimate minority, an intimate desert.

Gilles Deleuze and Félix Guattari

12

TUNING

Mnemonics

What will writing be like in an electronic apparatus in whose memory information is stored and retrieved in the manner of the *folie* square? The simple answer is that learning in hyperrhetoric is conducted more with memory than with argument or narrative (argument and narrative are subordinated to the patterns of memory). Any research project may be programmed by the diegesis of an Entertainment work (such as *Beau Geste*) rewritten as an actor's rehearsal of a Discipline work (such as "*Chora*"). "*Chora*" is in the abyss of *Beau Geste*. The paradigm set by this juxtaposition is completed in rehearsal by matching the pattern

Figure 7. The Categorical Imperative

with materials from the other discourses of the institutions of education (Family and School).

The analogy for my method is "Method acting." Method acting is first of all a way to "memorize" a script: "By determining the actions, the actor is able to build a logical, consecutive performance and to assimilate his role—and this practice will also be exceptionally helpful to him in memorizing the part" (Moore, 46). The Method is an art of memory, the chief surviving heir of the mnemonic systems that dominated education in the preprint era. The connection between classical and modern mnemonics may be seen in Lee Strasberg's comment on Stanislavski's comparison of the emotional memory exercise (seeking a Psychological Gesture for a character) to an actor remembering his house.

It is easy to find the house, the room, the cupboard, the drawer, the boxes, and even the smallest box of all. But it will take a very sharp eye to find the tiny bead that fell out of the box and, flashing for a moment has gone for good. If it is found, it is by sheer accident. The same is true with the storehouse of an actor's memory. . . . But how is the actor to find one of the beads of his emotional memory which flashed across his mind and then vanished, seemingly forever? Stanislavsky maintained that this is really the true task of the actors. This was the task I was to devote myself to in establishing the Method. (Strasberg, 60)

The Greeks developed mnemonic picture writing as a supplement to the alphabet in order to deal with the information overload that resulted from manuscript culture (Bolter, 56). It survived through to the Renaissance but became obsolete with the advent of the book (and hence served as an example of the cycle of invention in the institutional dimension of the apparatus). The practice was codified in the *Rhetorica ad Herennium,* whose equivalent today might be something like the Saint Martin's handbook. As part of his reform of education aimed at simplifying the complexities of scholasticism, Peter Ramus eliminated the mnemonic art. "Ramus abolished memory as a part of rhetoric, and with it he abolished the artificial memory," replacing it with his own method of dialectical order (Yates, 232). *Heuretics* is part of a movement that will be to the Saint Martin's handbook what the handbook is to the *ad Herennium.* To adapt a phrase from McLuhan and Ong, electronics is not secondary orality but secondary mnemonics.

A brief version of how mnemonics worked is that an orator trained in the art and needing to commit to memory a body of information (Roman law, the lives of the saints, the virtues and vices) called to mind a mnemonic scene, a mental diegesis, representing the places of invention. This imaginary space consisted typically of some familiar part of the orator's hometown or childhood house serving as the place of storage. The orator memorized the information by placing basic units of data at regular intervals throughout the space and associating each unit with a striking image (something sexual, violent, or bizarre) or else a very familiar image (a family member, a friend, a famous person). When delivering the speech, the speaker retrieved the data as needed by taking an imaginary walk through the place, recalling first the image, and then the associated data. The audience, of course, received only the information or argument; the memory scene was not externalized, although it may have contributed to nonverbal aspects of the delivery.

The practice of oratorical mnemonics—conceived of as travel or navigation through an information landscape, thus literalizing the metaphor of method as a journey—is a useful historical relay for a remake of method for an electronic apparatus. The practice has changed functions several times, according to Frances Yates, to meet the needs of different institutions (oratory for Greek politics; devotional meditation for Christianity; nature investigation for Renaissance science). In the electronic apparatus in a culture dominated by Entertainment, the function of mnemonics changes once again. Moreover, the convergence of media in hypermedia suggests that the present moment of video technology institutionalized in television is a temporary stage in which the culture is exercising a "pure" mnemonics. TV is pure memory in the sense that it includes two of the three elements of artificial memory—the familiar settings and the striking or familiar images or agents. What is missing is the specialized knowledge of Discipline (or, TV remembers "ideology"—it is the treasure house of contemporary mythology). But this lack may not be supplied only in terms of form: the institutions responsible for these different discourses must enter into communication as well.

Hypermedia provides the equipment capable of bringing the three elements together, and mnemonics offers a relay for solving the interface problem: the electronic citizen may negotiate the data environment of cyberspace the same way an orator memorized immense quantities of written material, or the way an actor learns a play. The difference between chorography and oratory or acting is that what the latter two memories suppress (the performance of a tour through the places) is made manifest in the former. A more obvious difference is that in chorography the mnemonic scene is entrusted to writing, where it may be manipulated critically, not kept in the head (and body).

The Popcycle

Lacan's square suggests a choral practice—writing as the revolution or turning of the square. Or, to put it in Derridean terms, the X of the erasure that marks a concept for deconstruction may be recognized as the implanting of the square in a semantic field. This insight moves my eureka experience from a feeling into a rule. The rehearsals have shown that chorography as a rhetoric gathers information together by means of a square or *quadripodes* composed of the discourses articulating the *Geschlecht* of my culture. Following Kristeva's lead, the strategy is to accept Lacan's notion of the four discourses as the structure of the symbolic order but to provide my own account of the operation of those discourses.

In chorography, the four discourses appearing in the choral square are not necessarily the same ones named by Lacan or Kristeva (even if there is an overlap). Indeed, part of the power of the square as the figure of my premises is that it marks the convergence of the major traditions of logic that, as Schleifer and his colleagues have shown, produces binary opposition as the dominant form in modern thought. The structuralist A. J. Greimas, working with an operation dating back to Aristotle, devised the "semiotic square," a schema of logical relationships that exhaust the possibilities of binary opposition: "A *contrary* relationship creates a double relation of conjunction and disjunction in terms of the presence or absence of some shared *feature* [e.g., "reason" versus "irrationality"]; a *contradictory* relationship creates that double relation in terms of a shared *function* [e.g., "reason" versus "intuition"]; and a *complementary* relationship creates that double relation in terms of a shared *situation* (that is arbitrarily defined) [e.g., "reason" re "discourse"] (Schleifer et al., 8, 69).

The operation of the logical square, from Aristotle to Baudrillard, revealed the relationship of linguistic to political opposition:

> The attempt to understand opposition questions why conflicting interpretive possibilities move along particular lines and not others. If such *particular* conflict did not arise, oppositional critics assert, change—and especially important political changes—could not be understood, subject to cognition. Without the understanding generated by the oppositional metaphor, differences would be lost in the ongoing iteration of heterogeneity and chance and would have no ideological markings—no signs. (136)

Schleifer and his co-workers show that Lacan's "schema L" of the four agencies or positions of the subject participates in this same tradition of the semiotic square (135). The "subject" is dispersed through all four corners of the X.

> This schema [L] signifies that the condition of the subject S depends on what is being unfolded in the Other A. . . . How would the subject be an interested party in this discourse, if he were not taking part? He is one, in fact, in that he is drawn to the four corners of the schema, which are: S, his ineffable and stupid existence; a, his objects; a', his *moi*—that is, what is reflected of his form in his objects; and A, the locus from which the question of his existence may be put to him. (Lacan, 1968:107–108)

The immediate point of interest for my method is the recognition that the tradition of the square is invented within the alphabetic apparatus of literacy. Schleifer and co-workers ignore the grammatological dimension (which relates the triumph of binarity to the time of Peter Ramus and his break with the tradition of the memory palace) and focus instead on twentieth-century Discipline discourse. The grammatological frame shows that the square needs to be adapted to an electronic apparatus in which the routes of linkage (the narratives inscribing logical relations into the ideologies of specific cultures) go beyond the given options for moving between the particular and the general: abduction moves from "thing" to "rule"; deduction moves from "rule" to "case"; and induction moves from "case" to "thing" (Eco and Sebeok). In electronic logic, however, it is necessary to reason directly from "thing" to "thing," from particular to particular, supplementing the inferential detour through conceptual reasoning. Hence the importance of *folie:* French poststructuralism in general, including Lacanian psychoanalysis, provides the best outline of such a logic as a guide to inventing the *premises* for a logic of invention. This electronic path of "inference" is called "conduction" (*Teletheory*) and its operations show that "chance" has its own order that makes "opposition" thinkable in another way (a new gesture).

The square in chorography, then, redefines the *quadripodes* of discourse, which are derived from the circulation of signification through the institutions in what may be called a "popcycle": Family, Entertainment, School, Discipline. Each of these institutions has its own discourse, including a matrix of logic, genres, modes, and forms relevant to its function in the society. A rough analysis of the four discourses produces the following chart:

	Family	*Entertainment*	*School*	*Discipline*
Reason	common sense	mythology	cultural literacy	logic
Proof	self-evidence	fashion	authority	argument
Medium	oral	book + electronic	oral + book	book
Form	anecdote	pop genres	textbook	treatise

Although reductive, the chart clarifies the materiality of communication across institutions. In our culture there is a symbiotic (some would say parasitic) relationship between the two institutions on the left side of the chart and between the two on the right side. It is important to note in this respect that School and

Discipline are distinct institutions, each with its own organization and tradition, in the same way that Family and Entertainment obviously are distinct.

Perhaps the distinctness of the two institutions on the right is less recognized because they have been closely associated for so long, as in the integration of the sciences with the university and the continuing absorption of every knowledge practice into School, including every field from agriculture to creative writing. A symptom indicating that the fit between the two is not perfect, however, is the recurring debates about the balance between research (Discipline) and teaching (School). If the nesting of Discipline in School now tends to be taken for granted, the more recent nesting of Entertainment in Family (with the mass importing of television sets into the home as required appliances) is still controversial (as in Dan Quayle's attack on *Murphy Brown*).

These institutions are more or less the ones Louis Althusser once described as constituting the "ideological state apparatus."

> While engaged in social practices each individual is addressed or 'interpellated' in various terms that confer a social identity.... Interpellation occurs primarily through ideological state apparatuses—church, family, educational system, trade unions, media, etc.—and it is these rather than the repressive state apparatus of police and courts that play the major role in securing the reproduction of social relations. Through them people gain both their sense of identity and their understanding of reality. (Lapsley and Westlake, 8)

The four institutions featured in the popcycle represent the predominant (if not the only) ones involved in "education." Althusser thought that misrecognition of one's determined condition as freely chosen condemned a subject to be the dupe of ideology.

Chorography is a rhetoric for writing with these interpellations that follows Lacan's insight that each of the discourses of the square provides a position for speaking in which one is at once subject and object. Unlike the method of critique professed by Althusser, however, which presumed the possibility of attaining a scientific perspective external to ideology (a position of truth outside of mere opinion), chorography must be written within the popcycle of ideology, without any certainty of truth. Chorography is designed to put the cycle fully in motion and thus to facilitate exchanges in all directions without restriction and anticipate the emergence of an institution capable of integrating the left and right pairs of the popcycle (whose technology will be hypermedia). Such is the "long march through the institutions" understood now as a formula for invention—the migration of meanings through the popcycle.

Manhattan Relay

An idea of how a choral rhetoric, operating with a square of discourses, might function in practice may be observed in Bernard Tschumi's *Manhattan Transcripts*. This experiment demonstrates how to operate a combinatorial machine (the formal operation of the square) within the diegesis of a narrative. It is a relay, in other words, of how to write by turning the square. He applies, moreover, the filmic devices of framing and editing to the composition of an architectural theory (anticipating many of the ideas used in the Villette design): "As in those film books in which the illustrations are enlargements of frames from the film, the *Transcripts* consist of frame-by-frame descriptions of an architectural inquest" (Tschumi, 1981:6).

In principle any form may be assigned the choral function of mediation. Tschumi first experimented with the abstract grid as a coupler or switcher zone of spacing for transducing heterogeneous items—the same grid used in Villette Park to bring together three heterogeneous systems—in a project entitled *Joyce's Garden*, which appropriated *Finnegans Wake* as the program for a garden design: "The point grid functioned as a mediator between two mutually exclusive systems of words and stones, between the literary program and the architectural text. *Joyce's Gar-*

den in no way attempted to reconcile the disparities resulting from the superimposition of one text on another; it avoided synthesis, encouraging instead the opposed and often conflicting logics of the different systems" (Tschumi, 1987:v–vi). Nor is there any necessity for the structure of the mediation to be a "grid," since the grid is but one of many possible organizing formations. Other possibilities include the spiral, wheel and spokes, lattice, branching tree, and rhizome. The choral function, here, is the grid as interface between the sensible and the intelligible.

Manhattan Transcripts—a "tool-in-the-making"—is not *about* architecture but research *of* architecture. The notations are organized in sets of three—three tracks running simultaneously treating independently the three dimensions of objects, movement, event. The whole is divided into four scenes or acts, each treating a different location in Manhattan: a park, a street, a building ("tower"), a block. "The effect is not unlike an Eisenstein film script or some Moholy-Nagy stage directions" (7).

Another feature of the experiment that makes it relevant to my remake is that the program for *Manhattan* is based on "the most common formula plot: the archetype of murder" (7) (continuing the convention of including a corpse in a discourse on method). Kristeva suggested the link of the detective story—or its subgenre, the murder mystery—to *chora* in terms of "sacrifice" as the founding moment of civilization *marking* the frontier or interface between nature and culture: the founding violence marked in the murder of the sacrificial victim, the rupture that sets the symbolic economy going, still resonates in the irruption of the semiotic into the symbolic in the practice of textuality (Kristeva, 1984:77). The ritual performance accompanying sacrifice, identified as the laboratory of all art, repeats the symbolic economy itself: "The reenacting of the signifying path taken from the symbolic unfolds the symbolic itself and—through the border that sacrifice is about to present or has already presented on stage—opens it up to the motility where all meaning is erased" (79). The purpose of inscribing the combinatorial square of discourses into the diegesis of a popular formula narrative is to make appear the trace of this *frontier.*

Using this program of "murder" allows Tschumi to address the relation of design to social context, of structure to event. The first "episode," then—a drawn and photographed notation of a murder—evokes the formula plot: "The one figure stalking its victim, the murder, the hunt, the search for clues building up to the murderer's capture—is juxtaposed with an architecture inextricably linked to the extreme actions it witnesses" (8).

Tschumi is playing with the fact that in certain popular, formulaic genres, such as the Western or the hard-boiled detective thriller, the setting itself (the atmosphere or mood of the place, premises, or grounds) immediately evokes the conventions of the story). In my remake the formula involves "adventure," although the theme of sacrificial death is still prominent, even while the mood of mystery is put under erasure.

In *Manhattan* representations of the three series are juxtaposed: objects (buildings abstracted from maps, plans, photographs); movements (abstracted from choreography, sports, or other movement diagrams); events (abstracted from news photographs). Crossing the terms of the real city of Manhattan and a popular genre, Tschumi's experiment is not to tell a story but to "invent," to open up all the possibilities generated by these confrontations but conventionally excluded by the constraints of traditional discourses. The *Transcripts,* that is, functions as a combinatorial machine (and hence as a model for the inscription of the abstract square in a particular diegesis and as a way to conduct paradigm writing). It evokes a linear narrative that is then transformed through four acts into a decomposing, interfering, recombining, "deconstructive" program for the generation of improbable, irrelevant, unexpected patterns and logics.

Each horizontal sequence (made of five frames, notated A, B, C, D, E) is part of a simultaneous vertical relation that contains the three equal conditions of object, movement, and event (notated

1, 2, 3). All combinations of the resulting matrix are then possible
... A1, A2, A3, where object-reinforces-movement which
reinforces-event in a sort of architectural tautology favored by
most functionalist doctrines; or they can, alternatively, be fully
disjunctive and heterogeneous, whereby A1, E2, B3 announces
that there is no relation whatsoever between form, program, and
movement. Further scrambling can be applied in the guise of a
sort of poststructuralist questioning of the sign, whereby movement, object, and event become fully interchangeable, where
people are walls, where walls dance the tango, and tangos run for
office. (12)

Tschumi adds that the combinations "are nothing but a form
of editing, of montage," including the filmic possibilities of the
"jump-cut, where space is carefully broken apart and then reas-
sembled 'at the limits,'" and the Kuleshov effect, in which "the
insertion of any additional space within a sequence can change
the meaning of the sequence." And while the operations for the
transformations are systematic (drawing on all the formal possibilities of geometry and dreamwork), the application is not. The
choices proceed from "subjective moves" depending on the pleasure of the person making them.

The relevance of *Manhattan* to chorography may be observed
in Derrida's debriefing interview at the conclusion of the Villette
project, in which he said that invention would not be stated as a
set of rules but would be a process of relationships confronting a
field with its outside (as demonstrated in *Manhattan Transcripts*
and in the Villette Park itself). At the same time, he suggested a
deconstruction of the tradition of method on the order of the
deconstruction of architecture undertaken at Villette. Method,
that is, traditionally has been understood as the "elimination of
accidents" established against the power of fortune or fate,
allowing people to gain control over their own destiny (Desan,
12–13). The history of science traces this gradual triumph of
method over chance. Derrida's attitude, however, is that this pro-

cess overreached itself and that the lack of appreciation for contingency in modern method needs to be reconsidered.

> Interesting coincidences are necessary coincidences, they reveal the law. . . . Let's just say that the event of the coincidence is a place where the innumerable threads of causality fall together, coincide, begin to cross and reconfigure. They are the moments in which the greatest numbers of possibilities produce the economic effect of an event. By economic I mean that all of a sudden, at one point or with one word, a huge storehouse of forces and motifs begin to reassemble themselves and the structure which they articulate. In the economy of one event the unfathomable threads of causality cause unpredictably. (Derrida, in Kipnis)

The square marks the *chi* and *ich* of this crossing, articulating each of the institutions of the popcycle. Much of his work, Derrida adds, is devoted to an examination of how philosophy has tended to repress just this compatibility between necessity and accident, pretending instead that these elements are opposed to one another. Chorography is a method of chance.

Fortune

With Tschumi's example in mind, I realize that my remake is not a "copy" of *Beau Geste* but another text, which thus requires its own title: "Yellowstone Desert." "Yellowstone Desert" is a mnemonic tableau set in a concert saloon in frontier Miles City and whose image agent is Gary Cooper. To function as electronic memory, this scene must receive a graft of Derrida's theory of *chora*. Moreover, the scene is not an aesthetic spectacle but a cognitive schema: it must be "tuned" (made dynamic) in order to allow me to write with it, to map and classify a database.

Fort Zinderneuf is in the abyss of this scene, evoking in miniature the intelligibility of the whole. The fort makes a square pattern, lining up the squares in each discourse of the popcycle from the formation the legion used against cavalry through the square rigged sails that made the *Niña* oceanworthy to the *quadripodes* of Lacan's symbolic order (for these happen to be the domains of my memory). In chorography, the construction of a pattern replaces the creation and resolution of enigmas and enthymemes as the means for managing curiosity at the level of composition. In subordinating mystery to memory, and arguments to paradigms, chorography promises something more than just an alternative to concept formation as a way to organize data into meaningful sets. It promises also to engage the users' premises in the process of learning, opening a mutually transforming circuit between judgment and theory, and hence to affect not only the institutional practices of the apparatus but human subjectivation as well.

Why is adventure still justified as the mode for writing an invention? Because of the *risk* that accompanies the possession of a technological prosthesis augmenting my stupidity:

> The knowledge at work here is knowledge concerning the most intimate, traumatic being of the subject, knowledge about the particular logic of his enjoyment. . . . Psychoanalysis brings about a dizzy experience of how this given positivity exists and retains its consistency only in so far as somewhere else (on another scene) some fundamental non-knowledge insists—it brings about the terryfying experience that if we come to know too much, we may lose our very being. (Zizek, 68)

The chief difference between "Yellowstone Desert" and *Beau Geste* is the grafting in the former of a Heuretic code onto the Hermeneutic code structuring the latter. In my remake, I place the square X at the moment of enigma (what happened at Fort Zinderneuf?). This cross marks the place (*chora*) of my premises. I am aware that this X overlaps with the question of desire (the sublime), of how an empirical object "begins to contain some X, some unknown quality, something which is 'in it more than it'" (Zizek, 119). The X of desire is rationalized in realist empistemology by a hermeneutic enigma constituting a "royal road" of passage among the discourses of the popcycle: each discourse has its own version of "mystery." In School the learner is taught to approach the unknown as a mystery, to be investigated and solved using the methods of one kind or another of detective (one of the chief modern types of adventurer, according to Martin Green). That School should invoke detection as a metaphor for research is consistent with the apparatus of print, for, as Walter Ong demonstrated, the detective story thematizes the analytical essence of print technology (Ong, 144).

It is a commonplace of pedagogy to teach problem solving by analogy with the sleuth, as is apparent in the existence of such books as *The Historian as Detective* and *The Sociologist as Detective*. "I suppose it can be best characterized as a 'soft' introduction to research methods," William Sanders said of the collection he intended as a "field manual" for sociology.

> The 'softness' is designed to gently bring students into research without scaring them half to death and letting them get their feet wet in a little research of their own. Once they get in they'll find it isn't as bad as they had feared and will be eager and willing to go in deeper.... Since I had been doing my own research on police detectives and found many natural parallels between what they were doing and what I was doing in the research, and because detectives have held the public's attention ever since Sherlock Holmes came to the scene, detectives seemed like a natural group to compare with sociologists." (Sanders, ix)

Why is research so terrifying? In the migration or transduction across institutions, from Entertainment to School, the dead body in the mystery, the victim, the murder, is usually forgotten, suppressed. In chorography, the sign of this X is changed from "Unknown" to "invention," marking a new operation—no longer the solving of a mystery but the making of a pattern (gathering a paradigm rather than following a path) that can be written *without* the violence of truth.

Gary Cooper, the agent of my (discursive) unconscious, is a

soldier of fortune defending Zinderneuf. That he so often played a soldier of fortune is crucial to his role in a discourse on method, keeping in mind that the history of method from its invention by Plato through Derrida's remake of that history displays a contest between "fortune" and *virtu* (in the Renaissance sense of the term). The contest is between fate (destiny), on one side, and the free will of the autonomous individual (hero), on the other (De-san, 27). The historical goal of methodologists has been to eliminate accidents, to wrest away from fate the power to predict and to control the future.

One of the most influential texts in this tradition of method is the *Timaeus,* one of the founding documents of the mathematical episteme that ultimately overcame Fortune as the arbiter of human affairs (68). The turning point in the contest is represented in Machiavelli's *Prince,* which defines *virtu* in terms of the self as an actor: by the prudent application of human "virtues" (which during the chivalric era slid from referring to the qualities of wisdom, temperance, justice, to mean valor and heroism) to action, one might take control of one's own destiny. This new "virtue" was masculine; men make history, and "Fortune is a woman whom one must abuse!" (16). A "virtuoso" in this tradition, which treated history as a reservoir of examples that could be generalized into principles guiding future conduct, was one able to recognize the pattern in any situation (59).

That Derrida gave the title *"Fors"* to his introduction to Abraham and Torok's work on the Wolf Man case signals his interest in this ancient contest. As the translator, Nicholas Rand, pointed out, sorting through the paradigm of this term, *"le for intérieur* designates the inner heart, 'the tribunal of conscience,' subjective interiority," while *fors* means "outside" or "outdoors" (in Derrida, 1986c:xii). This spatial paradox is relevant to *chora,* but so is another part of the *fors* paradigm—its association with fortune and *Fortuna.* In the Roman era *Fortuna* included the qualities of *Tyche* (Greek *Nemesis*). *"Fortuna* is itself an adjective of *fors* (derived from *ferre*), and it signified in the beginning the principle or thing that carries off or diverts the incalculable elements of nature and of human affairs" (Desan, 27). Oedipus's story, in which everything that seemed to happen by chance was actually foretold, was noted sometimes as an example of *Fortuna*. Montaigne, in contrast, emphasized the relation of *Fortuna* to chance, mediating between destiny and free will (Martin, 18). He translated *"Fors Fortuna"* as *"Bonne adventure"* (16).

Derrida's discussion of *"Fors"* is offered as an introduction to *Cryptonomy*, which treats the psychology of "mourning" (related to the castration complex and the formation of the superego)— the process of internalizing images of "loved ones" or objects of identification to deal with their loss (initially, separation from the mother, the pre-oedipal relation Kristeva discusses in terms of "abjection"). When the "normal" process of "introjection" is blocked (as in the case of postwar Germany, which denied its collective identification with Hitler), the subject defends itself by means of "incorporation," forming a "crypt" within the psyche that marks a "refusal to mourn" (denial of the loss). This crypt is described as a psychic "fortress" and "monument," a fortress as monument where a secret commemorating a catastrophic inaugural event is buried. "The cryptic fortress protects this analysis resister by provoking the symbolic break. It fractures the symbol into angular pieces, arranges internal partitions, cavities, corridors, niches, zigzag labyrinths, and craggy fortifications" (Derrida, 1986c:xx). The lesson of the Wolf Man case concerns how an encrypted secret still manages to communicate itself: how to pass a word/thing out of the crypt (how to pass through the wall). Beau's gesture depends upon Aunt Pat receiving his letter. And the secret of this crypt first showed itself as a "frozen" tableau in the Wolf Man's dream of white wolves sitting quite still and without making any movement on the branches of a walnut tree (Freud, 1971:173). This scene was a way to remember a feeling— a paralyzing terror.

The square fortification of Fort Zinderneuf is the switching place for moving from one register of the popcycle to another. "One possibility we are considering," Eisenman noted in the planning meetings, "is using Tschumi as a sort of switch. At each site, Tschumi would be at a different level. We are also considering switching on the quarry. Paris is a quarry used by both of us, particularly the abattoir and the walls" (Eisenman, in Kipnis). The switching point (or strange attractor) operates in rhetoric the way the slide rule operated in mathematics. "All there is to the slide rule," Howard Margolis observed, "are some scratches on two pieces of wood, tuned to the properties of the number system" (Margolis, 68). Yet precisely because of this "tuning" this simple device produced roughly accurate versions of certain complex calculations with extraordinary ease (replaced now by the computer). Referring to the patterns of inferential reasoning, Margolis compares human cognition to the slide rule: "It is a device that gets things roughly right, and there is no reason to suppose that the means by which it does so look at all like the manipulation of propositions in logic or like the algorithms that run contemporary computers." Chorography is a kind of slide rule of intuition using the square to tune writing to the materiality of language and the human subject, to the sliding of the signified under the signifier. This "rule" is what I seek; it turns the *law* of the square into a tool—like the measuring device used by carpenters or joiners.

13

AGENT COOPER

Cooper's Gest

Choral rhetoric (cyberwriting) organizes information the way a Method actor builds a character. Preparing to perform "Yellowstone Desert" for Montana's centennial, I started work on the part of Beau, as played by Gary Cooper. "General" Custer was responsible not only for the founding of my town (Fort Keogh was authorized as a direct response to the Custer catastrophe), but according to one biography, for Gary Cooper as well. "If General George Armstrong Custer and his more than 200 men had not been killed by Sitting Bull and his Sioux warriors on June 25, 1876, in Montana, there might have been no movie star

Figure 8. Analogy

named Gary Cooper" (Kaminsky, 7). Charles Cooper, Gary's father, followed his older brother, Walter, from England to America, where the latter, "an avid consumer of legends of the American West through pulp novels and distorted newspaper accounts," had gone "with the goal of becoming an Indian fighter and avenging the death of Custer and his men." After Charles joined Walter in Helena in 1885, he met and married Alice Brazier, the sister of a man who had immigrated from England for exactly the same reason as Walter: he was "moved by the tales of Custer's defeat" (9).

Since Miles City was founded by sutlers, one possibility for a place of passage in the popcycle between *Beau Geste* and Miles City might be the figure of the sutler moving between Fort Keogh and Fort Zinderneuf. "Occasionally a sutler, who had no traffic in women, penetrated into the desert with his cart of wines, sweets, and trinkets. Many of the sutlers were venturesome Jews who had discovered, to their surprise, that the Arabs tolerated them as they never would tolerate Christians. In time nearly every Legion unit in northern Algeria and Morocco had a favorite sutler who followed it from place to place and became a kind of unofficial Legionnaire" (Mercer, 144). Sutlers, moreover, were responsible for spreading tales of adventure of the sort called in German *Kolportageliteratur* (*"Kolportage* refers to the way such books were distributed, by pedlars and notably at fairs" [Green, 1991:161]). A cameo role for the real Derrida, then—as the sutler.

I believed that I left Miles City behind when, as a student, I went to the most exotic place I could think of—Paris, France. I am looking now for a link between two of the cities anchoring my premises (formatting cyberspace for me)—Paris and Miles City (crossing the axis of Gainesville and Sidi-bel-Abbes). What is the link? It has something to do with the Northern Pacific Railroad (which brought the follies to the saloons of Montana). Stanislavsky, in any case, compared the playscript to the railroad line connecting Moscow to Leningrad:

The Salvini, or genius-like actor can board an express train directly to the old capital because his role comes to him completely and intuitively on first reading. The average performer, however, must take a plodding mail train and stop along the way, get a feel for his part at each station, and then continue up the line until he has fully sampled the textual countryside. Most performers need to be filled with a large amount of detail before the total landscape of their role takes shape. Yet not all the information can be digested at once. The road to Leningrad starts in Moscow, and often very short stop-and-go trips must be made before completing the journey. (Gordon, 192)

Chorography, writing with the logic of conduction (in the family of dreamwork), emphasizes in this analogy of the "train of thought" not only the local over the express route but also the possibility of changing directions, or *headings*. Titles of concepts are replaced in this logic by "choral words," which function like words in dreams: "Dreams are 'laconic,' as is the dream text itself in relation to its later interpretation. Condensation represents the 'nodal point' (*Knotenpunkt*) of the dream and will be like a railroad switch in the dream work, always allowing multiple interpretations (overdetermination)" (Anthony Wilden, in Lacan, 1968:109).

Gary Cooper is the active image or agent in the tableau of "Yellowstone Desert," serving as a guide to the popcycle, a role for which he is qualified, considering that one of his summer jobs during his college years was as a tourist guide driving a bus in Yellowstone Park (Swindell, 35). His task is to help me find a Psychological Gesture for my tableau. The secondary effect of this search for a gesture is *learning,* gathering into a set whatever is associated with the gesture. That Method acting is the proper style for rhetoric's *reconquista* of logic is suggested by one of its trademarks—the use of the body to display the mental, in what has been called "affective thinking": "The faces of certain actors ... seem to be acutely inner-reflective. These actors seem to be doing a good deal of thinking. Their faces look preoccupied, as if attending to some inner voice, or memory" (Lawrence Schaffer, cited in Naremore, 71).

Can the face of Gary Cooper convey or evoke the thought of *chora* (for this is my ambition, linking Montana to France, to serve as *theoria* for my community)? Although Cooper was not trained as a Method actor, Strasberg said in an interview that "movie stars like Gary Cooper who always behaved naturally and who seemed to be drawing on their true personalities were unconsciously using the Method" (F. Hirsch, 162). Other commentators described Cooper's gest as that of *thinking,* which is the quality that might have prompted Strasberg's observation: "One cannot imagine John Wayne philosophizing about his lot as one could Gary Cooper. Though Cooper's hero was a man of fewer words than Wayne's, his silences were more than hiatuses between 'Yup' and 'Nope'—they were the interval in which he confronted himself" (Walker, 314). Cooper had a knack, it was said, of "turning momentarily into a totem—but a *thinking* totem" (315). In my remake, he is thinking about Derrida.

What is it to write chorography by means of Gary Cooper? In an electronic apparatus, the fact that rhetoric has been reduced to style is not the weakness it was in literacy. When rhetoric served face-to-face oratory, speakers studied with actors to learn *pronunciatio* (delivery), whereas in the representational conditions of the electronic, acting serves *elocutio* (style); this is indicative of the specific way that rhetoric is replacing logic in the postmodern *trivium.* One commentator noted the convergence of argument and style in the Hollywood celebrity: "In the electronic media, style shows itself in a variety of ways. . . . Often the idiosyncratic mannerisms of a performer will become an overnight smash, and a particular style will be attributed to that person's performance. Hollywood, television, and professional sports are built on that kind of celebrity status. Much style in the electronic media is a product of the star system itself" (Primeau, 63). "Proof" in Entertainment discourse, that is, is an effect of fashion. And by rotating the square (electronically or conceptually, in a thought experiment) this proof may be brought into contact with and serve as a relay for the other modes of proof operating in the popcycle. Each proof *supplements* (questions) the other.

One obstacle to electronic cognition is the attitude, widespread among cultural critics, "that the vast majority of commercial TV is irredeemable junk and that celebrity worship has reached such vast proportions and has infiltrated our society to such a degree that it constitutes an unhealthy sore on the body politic" (Mitroff and Bennis, 184). In chorography, the actor's style, whose emblem is the legendary gest of Marlon Brando—mumbling, scratching, talking too softly when far away, and too loudly when nearby, hesitating, looking off into space or down at the floor—becomes a map to insight and invention. If rhetoric was reduced to style in the print era, then it is in the actor's style in particular that rhetoric's recovery of the powers it lost to logic will begin (the means of the recovery must be invented).

As an actor, Cooper was famous for understatement, for being a laconic type, possessed of a stillness that was perfect for cinema. Defending him against a director who complained that Cooper wasn't *doing* anything, Charles Laughton declared, "You don't see it, but the camera does!" (Swindell, 144). Cooper's acting "grammar" has been analyzed into five basic gestures: evasive yet penetrating glances; a casual lean in the saddle; slight eyebrow movement; a calculated shifting of weight; pursing of the lips (Tatum, 69). His "signature" scene—the one that made him a star—is in *The Virginian* (the novel in which Owen Wister codified the myth of the cowboy) during a poker game in the Medicine Bow saloon. "When Trampas says, 'Your bet, you longlegged son of a ... ,' the Virginian *purses his lips* and says, after an eloquent pause, 'When you call me that ... *smile!*'" (Swindell, 110).

Cooper was also known for the sensitivity and expressiveness of his hands.

> Another Cooper trademark was his ability to refer to spaces in the film as if they were real, not just sets or nonexistent reference spots just beyond the end of the frame.... He would gradually

play with this until he could point some place off the screen without looking at it and give the impression that the farm, office,
ship or battle was so clearly there that it needed no reference beyond his character's assertion of its existence. (Kaminsky, 46)

In "Yellowstone Desert," Cooper points to my diegesis becoming
chora, a hybrid of Miles City, Paris, Gainesville, Sidi-bel-Abbes,
affirming the existence of this place, an anywhere that is everywhere, for me.

Chorography as rhetoric is a way of gathering dispersed information into an unstable set (like the TV set or *poste*) held together
by a *pattern* that is the trace of understanding or learning. This
pattern absorbs and remotivates the other two principal means
of releasing information in a discourse—enigma (narrative) and
enthymeme (exposition)—thus inverting the arrangement governing literacy. As a rehearsal it follows the path of a "want."
What do I want in this scene? To witness my own foundations?
My premises? Following a variant of Richard Hugo's advice (including the shifting of attention from the referent to the words
of the scene), agent Cooper takes me to the past of my hometown,
in search of a Psychological Gesture that might be a guide to the
future, to American national identity after 1992.

The Differend

The Psychological Gesture remembers an emotion: the body
remembers, and this is the kind of Memory augmented by hypermedia. Can "Yellowstone Desert" still be composed as an "adventure"? "Auschwitz," as many cultural critics have argued, has
put in question, if not completely destroyed, the "adventure" of
invention by undermining the credibility of *theoria.* It is very difficult, if not impossible, that is, to "witness" foundational events.

A witness, the addressor of an ostensive phrase validating a description, attests through this phrase to the reality of a given aspect of a thing. But he or she should by that very score recognize

that other aspects which he or she cannot show are possible. He
or she has not seen everything. If he or she claims to have seen
everything, he or she is not credible. . . . Either you were not
there, and you cannot bear witness; or else you were there, you
could not therefore have seen everything, and you cannot bear
witness about everything. (Lyotard, 45)

Chorography assumes that citizens of an electronic apparatus
will have to make judgments in conditions in which *theoria* has
been rendered ambiguous, uncertain, undecidable. Judgment, in
any case, resembles a choral event ("It too serves to articulate the
sensible with the concept" [44]). After Auschwitz the legitimation process in the public sphere has broken down. It is no longer
certain how to move through the popcycle, how to link one genre
to another, or one phrase to another: such linkages remain to be
invented in a radical crisis of genre. Nor is it a matter of deciding
whether or not to reason through the crisis using objectivist con-
ceptuality, since there is no concept for this condition. What remains, however, even as knowledge falls silent, is a "feeling" that
is "a sign for the common person." These are the conditions of
the differend ("a case of conflict, between at least two parties,
that cannot be equitably resolved for lack of a rule of judgment
applicable to both arguments").

They will say that history is not made of feelings, and that it is
necessary to establish the facts. But, with Auschwitz, something
new has happened in history (which can only be a sign and not a
fact), which is that the facts, the testimonies. . . . all this has been
destroyed as much as possible. Is it up to the historian to take into
account . . . not only the testimony but also what is left of the
testimony when it is destroyed (by dilemma), namely, the feeling? (57)

As an effort to write the premises of my judgment, "Yellowstone Desert" is an experiment of the sort Lyotard calls for
when he says that "the historian must break with the monopoly

over history granted to the cognitive regimen of phrases, and he or she must venture forth by lending his or her ear to what is not presentable under the rules of knowledge." A new competency is required for beginning the work of this idiom, whose nature may only be signaled by a *feeling* (an intuition). "A lot of searching must be done to find new rules for forming and linking phrases that are able to express the differend disclosed by the feeling, unless one wants this differend to be smothered right away in a litigation and for the alarm sounded by the feeling to have been useless. What is at stake in a literature, in a philosophy, in a politics perhaps, is to bear witness to differends by finding idioms for them" (13). Chorography adds that these "intuitions" are not "natural" and bear no closer relation to "truth" than that possessed by the cognitive regimen, which is why a Heuretic code must be added to the Hermeneutic code. I cannot negotiate the differend by means of argument.

Abduction

Lacan's analogical matrix of the symbolic order, the computer, and Poe's detective story suggesting the suitability of the detective's style of reasoning for the new apparatus make it possible to locate precisely the function of a Heuretic code in chorography. The detective, thematizing or personifying the Hermeneutic code, achieves insight by means of abduction (as C. S. Peirce called it). An abductor comes upon a "result," the observed facts of a situation (the first position, the time of looking). Poe's Dupin, whom Conan Doyle later imitated, assumed nothing, and letting the object dictate the inquiry and keeping the whole in mind, proved *that impossibilities were really possible* (Harrowitz, 193). What was "surprising" or unexpected in the observed phenomena was rendered "necessary" by the hypothesis. The observation—details, fragments construed as clues—seen but not yet understood was rendered intelligible by an informed guess, through evaluating it in terms of a rule.

The difference between the detective's abduction and the philosopher's induction and deduction is that the detective reasons with memory rather than argument. In memory information is organized associationally, so that the "address" of an item is another item related to the first item by its content (Campbell, 158). Knowledge is not in a place, it is not *there,* except as a "ghost"— as the pattern of activity of the whole. A key issue of this ghost economy concerns its shortcuts, its efficiency, the selection process by which the user judges what is and is not relevant to the case. "Remembering is not essentially different from solving everyday problems, because in each case, fragments of incoming information wake up networks of interacting knowledge, resulting in a pattern of activity that represents a memory, or the answer to a problem, that is most consistent with the evidence" (160).

In this discussion of "The Purloined Letter," Lacan focused on one aspect of Dupin's abductive method that is not the one usually associated with solving a crime. Rather, Dupin's method resembles the Emotional Recall exercises of Method acting: the search for the Psychological Gesture. In contrast to the police, who applied their investigative method without taking into account the character of the criminal, Dupin *identified* with the criminal. In the example that Lacan refers to repeatedly in his seminar, Dupin illustrated this tactic by the example of a child whose success at winning the guessing game of "even-odd" does not depend on "luck" (as his friends suppose) but is due to "an identification of the reasoner's intellect with that of his opponent":

> "When I wish to find out how wise, or how stupid, or how good, or how wicked is any one [the boy says], or what are his thoughts at the moment, I fashion the expression of my face, as accurately as possible, in accordance with the expression of his, and then wait to see what thoughts or sentiments arise in my mind or heart, as if to match or correspond with the expression." This response of the schoolboy lies at the bottom of all the spurious profundity which has been attributed to Rochefoucault, to La Bruyere, to Machiavelli, and to Campanella. (Poe, 15–16)

The authors Dupin cites are all major contributors to the history of "method," anticipating the later Stanislavski's Emotional Recall and confirmed by contemporary neurophysiology. The Heuretic code (the logic of conduction) may be distinguished from the Hermeneutic code (abduction) by this difference in the use of Lacan's example, emphasizing not the enigma of mystery as the device organizing curiosity but the "aha!" or *da* of an actor's identification.

Choral work, in other words, begins *within* enigma (or enthymeme), based on the stereotypes of a culture. The commentators agree that abduction relies on "intuition" and that the intuitions rely on the stereotyped thinking of common sense (ideology). How did Holmes, for example, know that the stranger across the street was a retired sergeant of marines?

> Clearly, Holmes did not prove a "theorem" about the stranger's military career by deriving propositions from axioms using general rules of inference, or searching all conceivable possibilities by brute force. Instead, he summoned up, at lightning speed, relevant knowledge about the world that was evoked by a few fragments of information. He generalized from the clues he observed in the stranger's manner and bearing to the concept, fully formed in his mind, of a typical sergeant of marines. (Campbell, 87)

For the detective working in everyday life, the "rule" for the abduction comes from what Barthes called the Cultural or Referential code, the *doxa* or opinion organizing the common sense of a culture, its general knowledge or proverbial wisdom (including the "explanatory" concepts of School discourse that E. D. Hirsch named "cultural literacy"). By knowing the *topoi* of the culture and subcultures peculiar to the environment of the crime the detective could formulate an hypothesis (case) that would then be tested against the observed facts (induction).

The discussion of the importance of stereotypes as knowledge schemas in a connectionist model of memory should be related to the recent renewal of interest within the philosophy of science in the logic or method of discovery or invention as an alternative to teaching science always from the side of verification or justification. The inventive strategy treats "scientific problems as structures of constraints" accompanied by the instruction that certain types of gaps in those structures be filled" (Nickles, 37). Rules, results, and cases are related in this inferential method neither inductively nor deductively but abductively, with abduction being the one mode of inference capable of inventing a new idea:

> The choice of the major premise, or more precisely of its protasis or antecedent, exercises the whole creative imagination of the researcher, and it is here that we have the root of the major or minor novelty of the abductive conclusion. Roughly, it may be said that the more unusual the mating of consequent and antecedent, or the more distant their semantic fields are from one another, the more pregnant the abduction will be. (Bonfantini and Proni, 132)

The difference between "Baker Street reasoning" and scientific creativity concerns the source of the "rule." Whereas Holmes's puzzles could be solved by recourse to the typologies of daily life, a "revolutionary" scientist might have to invent a new law (a new major premise, generated within Discipline discourse) (133). In this context, theories and stereotypes are not sharply distinguished: "Scientific theories, like schemas and even stereotypes, make sense of the world by excluding certain ways of interpreting ambiguous or incomplete information. This is a form of cognitive economy" (Campbell, 128). Stereotypes are redescribed as patterns, schemas, knowledge structures, even "theorems" collecting or clumping multistep reasoning into one-step units of meaning.

If a logic of invention replaces explanations with acts of judgment (Wartofsky, 2), then Trinh Minh-ha's warning about the stereotypes of science must be taken into account: "At no time, while he sets out scientifically to interpret the natives as bearers of a stamp imprinted on them 'by the institutions in which they

live, by the influence of tradition and folk-lore, by the very vehicle of thought, that is, by language,'" Trinh says, citing an an-
thropologist in a way that resonates with the problematic of
Geschlecht, "does he feel the scientific urge to specify where he
himself stands, as a stereotype of his community, in his interpretation" (Trinh, 72). To take into account my own stereotypes, I
need to write from all four corners of the square at once.

Artificial Stupidity

My premises come into appearance in the diegesis of my remake as stereotypes. Once they have appeared, however, they are
available for "debugging." To learn how this process works, I
explored the link between Method acting and the abductive reasoning of the detective as a place to graft the Heuretic code onto
the Hermeneutic code, in the person of the actor I identify with
as the protagonist in my remake: Gary Cooper.

In "Yellowstone Desert," Cooper acquires the function of "interface agent," indicating how stereotypes and celebrities take on
a cognitive role in an electronic apparatus. As an alternative to
the book metaphor for the computer interface, it has been proposed that some components of AI (artificial intelligence) in the
form of "agents" be included in a database (conceived as an information environment or landscape represented in an annotated
movie). Personifiable as residents of the environment, an agent
may operate as guide, coach, tutor, to help the user manage the
overload of information. The choice of personification is specific
to each user, in line with the principle governing interface design
to adapt the model of the system to the cognitive style of the user.
The agent would be dramatized as some legendary character,
perhaps as a movie star with cult status. The advantage of this
personification is its predictability and consistency of performance—its *legibility:*

> The case for modeling interface agents after dramatic characters
> is based on both the familiarity of dramatic characters as a way

of structuring thought and behavior and the body of theory and methodology already in place for creating them. Most cultures have a notion of dramatic form, and people are quite familiar with both the differences and the similarities between characters and real people. Character traits function as stereotypic "shorthand" for understanding and predicting character behavior. (Laurel, 363)

Consider the example of the encyclopedia of American history (the early moment of hypermedia is devoted to reproducing encyclopedias in the same way that the early moment of the printing press turned out Bibles).

After deciding that the interface should have an historical look and feel, we moved towards embedding the "travel guides" in the database. Each guide would be a stock character of the period itself. They would have a set of specific interests in the historical period and could suggest different things for the user to view. . . . A list of "interests" for each guide was built using the master topic list (a hierarchical topical index of over 200 items). A program then compared each guide's interest list with the specific index terms for each article. The more terms that appeared in both, the more interest the guide would have in a particular article. (371)

Configuring the interface by means of a popular, formulaic work is precisely what makes the environment "legible." In *Beau Geste,* for example, everyone explicitly operates according to stereotypes, as in the scene when John Geste meets an American, whose nationality he recognizes from the following evidence: "'*Sure ting, Stranger.*' . . . Don't care who owns the earth. . . . Great contempt for effete English. . . . Tar and feathers . . . Stars and Stripes. . . . '*I come from God's Own Country and I guess it licks Creation*'" (Wren, 183). The American recognized John as British in the same way: "Pink and white. . . . Own the earth. . . .

'*Haw! Who's this low fellah? Don't know him, do I?* . . . Dude '*Open all the windahs now I've come!*'"

Relevance Sieve

The function of the guide is to cull the information environment for items *relevant* to the user's projects. "Relevance" is the crucial notion, concerned with *chora* as "sorting machine": "The user is presented with a collage of contingencies—information, not necessarily understanding. This tangle of linkages becomes an even more critical limitation to the user when navigation in hypertext is unmediated by an instructor or experienced guide. . . . How does the uninitiated learner distinguish between wheat and chaff if access to the system is purely solitary? How will hypertext help the learner 'think with' on-line information?" (Barrett, xx). The winnowing metaphor (recalling the *liknon* of Plato's metaphor) in this passage identifies the need for a sorting device, a function to be automated in my agent, who is my liaison with the symbolic order.

In psychoanalytic terms, the agent is my *chorus*. As Zizek explains, the "illusions" of ideology are objective, on the side of reality, not knowledge, externalized in the relations among things themselves. "The most intimate emotions such as compassion, crying, sorrow, laughter, can be transferred, delegated to others without losing their sincerity" (Zizek, 34); this is the significance of the chorus in tragedy: "We feel the required emotions through the medium of the Chorus: 'You are then relieved of all worries, even if you do not feel anything, the Chorus will do so in your place'" (35). Chorography is a way to learn from the chorus.

The challenge of chorography (whether in hypermedia or in its paper simulation) is to design an agent whose "judgment" or intuitions of relevance include the unconscious in its psychoanalytic (*folie*) as well as in its connectionist sense. What does the agent need to "know" about the user to tune attention, in order to *supply* what the writer *wants,* especially when the motive is learning, and even invention? How can users customize the agent, instructing it what to look for, since by definition they are unaware of the object of the search at that level? The database needs to be made "stupid," as well as smart, to take into account the operation of the unconscious. I cannot *define* the specifics of my stupidity, but I recognize its features in Gary Cooper. My search, then, is guided not by a concept (truth) but by "Gary Cooper." The procedure is "automated," even without equipment, in that my writing tactic is to take what Cooper gives me.

Agent Cooper takes me on a tour of my premises beyond the conventional limits of inference. Relevance involves an aspect of thinking that is inferential more than communicational, that depends not only on knowing a language but on being situated in a culture, being able to fill in information gaps by means of inference to "the most likely explanation." Inference does not convey precise messages but "focuses attention in a certain direction" (Sperber and Wilson, 8). Communication by inference, then, depends on the recognition of intentions, judging what is relevant based on shared cognitive environments, no two of which are exactly alike (38). What makes information worth processing?

> Some information is old: it is already present in the individual's representation of the world. Unless it is needed for the performance of a particular cognitive task, and is easier to access from the environment than from memory, such information is not worth processing at all. Other information is not only new but entirely unconnected with anything in the individual's representation of the world. It can only be added to this representation as isolated bits and pieces, and this usually means too much processing cost for too little benefit. Still other information is new but connected with old information. When these interconnected new and old items of information are used together as premises in an inference process, further new information can be derived: information which could not have been inferred without this combination of old and new premises. When the processing of

new information gives rise to such a multiplication effect, we call it *relevant*. (48)

The agent can be the means by which the linking of new to old information may overcome the user's "censor," which filters out "irrelevant" items, since the erueka experience of invention works precisely by the surprise shifting of an item from the category of "irrelevant" to "relevant." Nor is abduction alone adequate to this work on relevance, considered as an inferential recognition of patterns triggered by cues or clues. As Howard Margolis points out, the nature of a "clue" in intuitive judgment is not easy to predict.

> Since there is no reason why only (normatively) good cues should enter the nonconscious mechanisms that guide our attention, affective responses, and intuitive seeing-that, clear intuitions may have (normatively) absurd foundations. The relation between cues and patterns is only one of correlation, not necessarily of causation, and sensitized cues will not necessarily be causally important cues or rationally defensible cues. (Margolis, 130)

This normatively absurd quality of my foundations is precisely the obstacle to an electronic *theoria* inhibiting the witnessing of my premises. Margolis's insight is all the more important, keeping in mind that invention often requires *counter*-intuitive thinking (as Paul Feyerabend once demonstrated using the example of Galileo). The problem with abduction, unassisted by choral logic, concerns the fact that intuitive judgment of what "fits" or what "goes together" does not recognize any fundamental difference between stereotypes and theories. Margolis suggests that the feeling of discomfort affecting one who sees a logical contradiction as intolerable is similar to a feeling that it is intolerable (for example) to mix races at a hotel. As *normatively* different as these two thoughts are, they are similar cognitively, Margolis argues, in that they concern the judgment "fits/doesn't fit." Yet it is also this very continuum at the level of feeling that makes possible a dialectical communication between belief and logic.

In chorography (and here is the site of *risk*), intuitive judgments based on stereotypes offer a way, open a passage for negotiating the differends separating the discourses of the popcycle (exactly the opposite of the effect of stereotypes in the print apparatus). The Method, performed by my agent (Cooper), supplements the conscious inferences of abduction with the "automated" machine of the square (the logic of *conduction*). Hypermedia is the technology, and chorography the institutional practice, for augmenting the intuitions of inference, for writing with the logic of the unconscious.

Gary Cooper holds the proxies of the other ego-ideals constituting my superego—Walt Ulmer (Family), Christopher Columbus (School), Jacques Derrida (Discipline). To say that these men figure my superego is to say that I identify with them in a profound way, for better or worse, having to do with the mark of *Geschlecht* in my body. According to the theory of mourning and melancholy, a child resolves the Oedipal conflict by internalizing the authority of parental figures (the parents themselves at first, reinforced throughout development by those responsible for the child's cultural training). Freud characterized the superego as a kind of "internalized monument," suggesting an analogy with Mount Rushmore: my signature as a "stoney thing" collects a personalized Rushmore—one talking head for each of the quarters of the popcycle.

"Freud stressed the fact that the superego is not only a product of parental identifications, but it functions also as a mode of expression of the most powerful id drives. By constructing the superego, the ego places itself in subjection to the id. Indeed, Freud says 'the ego forms its superego out of the id'" (Sandler, 21). In popular psychology the superego is best known in its censorial role ("the dread of the superego persists from the earlier fear of castration"), although according to Discipline its positive or productive role as "guide" is equally important (17). Perception, that is, involves an active coordination of internal and external stimuli, whose coordination is the key to intuition, such that it should be described as perception work to call attention to the directive role of the inner schemas formed by identification in guiding a person's attention (3).

Intuitive judgment, Bastick argued, relies less on inference and more on empathy and projection—the operations of identification (Bastick, 288). And "serious attempts to conceptualize empathy have generally only been made by theorists with a psychoanalytic orientation" (294). Comparisons of these two operations—descriptions of defense mechanisms and of intuition—show a remarkable resemblance, however differently they might be evaluated. The two form a hybrid experience in the annotated movies of cyberspace, in which the initial act of identification of a spectator with a film diegesis is "digitized," so to speak, choralized, incorporated and augmented in the prosthesis, and given back to the subject by means of hyperrhetoric as a generator of thought.

In my research, I don't *know* anything about this *virtual* unconscious: I take what Cooper brings me (this is an analogy). In a computerized memory palace the actor using the Method goes to the physical setting, the triggering towns, and finds not only emotions but beliefs, ideas, concepts, theories. This initial trip to the premises allows me to map cyberspace. Once I have the map I can go anywhere (if I *want* to).

14

THE CHORAL WORD

Passage

In chorography, the actor's memory is automated, letting inference be guided by a generative paradigm. The chorographer
is like the poet who takes the side of language, subordinating the
nostalgic return to the places of memory, to Miles City or to Paris.
Derrida's version of this strategy is the device of the choral word,
the word that tunes a database to the materiality of language, sets
the square in motion, and opens a passage through the popcycle.
The choral word is a miniaturization of the popcycle, being to
language what the square is to discourse—that which links the
parts of my tableau and transforms it into a cognitive schema.

To locate the choral word, one must be "attuned to coincidence. Not just any relationship can produce a work, an event. Coincidence must be loved, received, treated in a certain way. The question is, in which way?" (Derrida, in Kipnis). Derrida answers his own question by indicating the nature of the "event" that emerged during the planning sessions with Peter Eisenman—the discovery of "choral" for the name of the project, demonstrating the operation of the "trace" manifested in "the uneasy dependence of necessity on accident":

> In this one word is fused all the necessities, the object, the metonyms, the structures as well as the psychological, personal, material and linguistic aspects of the project. But it is—coincidentally—much more. Hence it is a unique event which will leave a trace independent of the intentional forces which led to its emergence. My thematic suggestion—*chora*—led to Peter's play—choral work. But it is evident that the thing is as independent in its existence as a piece of coral one might find along the seashore. It is independent of Peter's existence and my own. (Derrida, in Kipnis)

The choral word (event functioning as abstraction) sets a series going, a movement or passage through language, a spreading memory, drawing to itself an associated range of meanings. The choral word produces the paradigm, the combinatorial of possibilities, from which the inventor selects, and the selections made by Derrida and Eisenman do not limit the subsequent influence of the series. When he introduces the name into the discussion, Eisenman lists the meanings it generates for him: "There is togetherness. For me it means corral as enclosure, coral as stone and coral as color, choral as a group musical work, and choral as of *chora*." Derrida adds, "It reminds me also of 'firework'—choral work, fire work, something work" (Kipnis). The associations continue to spread through the encyclopedia, carried by the "core" syllable of *chora*.

The choral word will be different for each project. Because Derrida maintains this part of the speculative tradition, he holds that Hegel, who discovered and elaborated an equivocation in *Aufheben*, is at once the close of the old era and the beginning of the new. Hegel learned how to exploit the idiomatic materiality of natural languages for the purposes of philosophy. Lyotard described the point succinctly:

> It is an "advantage" for the mind to find multiple senses for the words of a natural language. This advantage is at its height when the senses are opposed. The more frequently this is the case in a language, the more it is inhabited by the "speculative spirit." . . . If thought's delight culminates in *aufheben*, it is because this term from ordinary language is also the name *par excellence* of the speculative operation. The *Selbst*, or subject of the ordinary phrase is *circulated* by speculative discourse among the various instances presented by that phrase. (Lyotard, 93)

Dialectics, however, imposes specific rules of *linking* onto the meanings thus generated to produce a "result" expressing the passage between opposites in a third term, a synthesis that "eliminates the dilemma" (94). Chorography continues the speculative circulation of meaning through equivocal words but introduces a different style of linkage (hence a different "method")—one that is "punceptual" rather than conceptual—in which conduction (passing from thing to thing in the real, "external" to my conscious reasoning) reorganizes abduction, deduction, and induction.

The pun, which simulates in writing the effect of intuition (the convergence of emotional sets) may be visual as well as verbal. As Ronald Schleiffer reminds us, the pun is one of the most basic linguistic units for creating redundancies, the condition that gives rise in experience to a feeling of eureka. "Isotopies are 'discoverable' in the apprehension of redundant semes in discourse that create 'the principle of the equivalence of unequal units'" (Schleiffer, 76). Thus, the formal point at which the Heuretic code may be grafted onto the Hermeneutic code is located in the mystery's reliance on the pun as part of its *inventio*. Victor

Shklovsky noted this feature of detective writing, for example, in his discussion of Conan Doyle's "Speckled Band": "The writer looks for a case where two incongruous things overlap, at least in one respect. Of course, even in detective stories this coincidence often takes the form of something quite other than a word. In *The Innocence of Father Brown,* Chesterton employs as a device the coincidence of a gentleman's dress coat with the uniform of a valet" (Shklovsky, 108).

Derrida often uses the strategy of the choral word to organize his compositions, not just passively, but as an *inventio,* setting the criteria of selection and combination for his composition. The use of *cap* in *L'autre cap* is one example, or the phrase *droit à la philosophie* in the collection by that name, whose unpacking provides the subheading for his commentary: the relation of law (*droit*) to philosophy? who has a right (*droit*) to philosophy? can one go directly (*droit*) to philosophy? (Derrida, 1990b:14).

During the Eisenman meetings, Derrida supplied a choral word that organizes my rehearsal of a Psychological Gesture for performing Gary Cooper thinking *chora.* Eisenman had been receiving the notion of *chora* in terms of the story of *Romeo and Juliet,* which informed his design in the Canareggio project (architecture as a remake of Shakespeare). "If you force me to compare the Romeo and Juliet project with this one," Derrida responded, "I would say that it is still very historical and emotional, not naked enough. The atmosphere of *chora* is naked; there is no love, no story; it's *desert.*" "It's a zero?" Eisenman asks. "A zero," Derrida replies, "yes" (in Kipnis).

Elsewhere Derrida has suggested what "desert" evokes for him—the place of ascetic monks in a Semitic tradition who withdrew from the temptations of the city to live in the desert. "Logologically, speech goes with the Father, with the mind, while writing is relegated to the desert of externality and illegitimacy" (Harpham, 8). To allude to these monks, Derrida says, is to suggest how a discussion of negative theology could become his autobiography: "In other words what about Jewish and Arab thoughts on this matter? For example, and in everything that I will say, a certain void, the place of an interior *desert* will resonate with this question" (Derrida, 1987a:562).

The "desert" (the place of mirages—Algeria or Montana) in "Yellowstone Desert" resonates also with Jean Baudrillard's view that "America" is "heir to the deserts" because it shows that culture itself is a "mirage" (Baudrillard, 63). The best embodiment of this mirage is cinema: "It is not the least of America's charms that even outside the movie theaters the whole country is cinematic. . . . This is why the cult of stars is not a secondary phenomenon, but the supreme form of cinema, its mythical transfiguration. . . . *They embody one single passion only: the passion for images,* and the immanence of desire in the image" (56).

In Lacan's psychoanalysis this desire is associated specifically with the image of "desert": "We have already said that the signifier dismembers the body, that it evacuates enjoyment from the body, but this 'evacuation' is never fully accomplished; scattered around the desert of the symbolic Other, there are always some leftovers, oases of enjoyment, so-called 'erogenous zones,' fragments still penetrated with enjoyment—and it is precisely these remnants to which Freudian drive is tied: it circulates, it pulses around them" (Zizek, 123). This allegory is available in *Beau Geste* (Fort Zinderneuf is next to an oasis), not as its interpretation but as one item of a set.

Desertion

Derrida's theory of the crypt, and of blocked mourning, is dramatized in the situation at Fort Zinderneuf leading up to the pyrrhic victory that wipes out the legion garrison. As conditions deteriorated at the fort, the men planned to mutiny and desert the legion. Desertion is a major theme in *Beau Geste* and a major problem for the real foreign legion, which countered it with extreme measures so that escape was all but impossible. Englishmen and Americans seemed least adaptable to the brutal conditions of the legion. One Adolphe Cooper, an Englishman, deserted twice unsuccessfully and was submitted to the tortures of the penal camp—the *tombre* (imprisoned in a hole the size of a grave) and the *crapaudine* (bound in a "toad" shape, hands and ankles wired behind his back) (194).

Although both sides in the struggle inside the fort—the brutalized men and the evil sergeant—try to enlist Beau, painting the choice as an absolute either/or, Beau takes up a position in between, neither "butcher" nor "pig" in the scenario evoked by the two sides. The moment of highest drama in the story is when, having aided the sergeant in stopping the rebellion, Beau refuses the order to act as firing squad against the leaders of the deserters. Beau foresaw the possibility of such an impasse, as he explained when his brother demanded, "What is to be done?" "*Nothing,* I tell you. We've got to 'jump lively when we do jump,' as Buddy [his American friend] says; but we can only wait on events and do what's best, as they arise" (Wren, 292). At the fateful moment, just as the sergeant is about to shoot Beau, the Arabs attack: "But for Gronau's coming up and diverting attention from the inside of the fort to the outside, there probably would not have been a man of the garrison alive in the place by now.... As I loaded and fired, loaded and fired, I wondered if these things were 'chance'" (320). Another allegory, perhaps, entitled "*aporia.*"

In my remake this scene of impasse at the fort has to be presented not in terms of the Action and Hermeneutic codes as it is in all the extant versions, but in terms of the Symbolic code, to be written directly with mythology. In stripping away Action and Enigma the point is not to "demystify" the narrative, translating the story into the language of critique, but to write directly with the rhetoric of the symbolic order, for which dreamwork supplies an analogy. The resolution of the double bind in the unfolding of a narrative is achieved *superficially* in terms of the codes of Action and Enigma (the heroism of Beau's gest). Under the cover of the plausibility created by these codes, the (illusory) resolution is actually accomplished with the mechanisms of dreamwork. The explanatory effect of actions organized by puzzles to be solved ("who stole the Blue Water?") pass off as reasonable the paradox or logical contradiction informing the narrative myth, such as the "die in order not to die" of *Beau Geste*.

Bill Nichols believed that the open articulation of the mythical paradoxes structuring the Symbolic code had a critical potential based on their similarity to the creative logic of "bisociation" described by Arthur Koestler:

> Bisociation involves "perceiving of a situation or idea, in two self-consistent but habitually incompatible frames of reference." . . . In the case of humor our intellect recognizes the sudden bisociation and comprehends it, but the suddenness catches our emotions unprepared: they cannot shift to the new frame of reference rapidly enough and so spill out into the gutter of laughter. In scientific discovery the "aha" moment brings fusion of incompatible frames and intellectual synthesis; in art bisociation involves the juxtaposition of, or the confrontation between, incompatible frames and an aesthetic experience. (Nichols, 97)

The experience of eureka is inherent in the structure of mythology, in other words, and makes it possible to invent with stereotypes. The strategy for making a myth function critically is to avoid resolving the paradox but instead to expose this cultural "optical/conceptual" mirage as an invention machine. The feeling of "aha!" or eureka is the feeling chorography introduces into the process of subject formation in order to short-circuit the melancholy of *guilt* linking the Hermeneutic code to the superego.

The impasse at Zinderneuf, suspending Beau between two enemies (his fellow legionnaires inside and the Touareg tribesmen outside), dramatizes the antithetical organization of the Symbolic code. Barthes described the situation of this code:

> The two terms of an antithesis are each *marked*: their difference does not arise out of a complementary, dialectical movement: the Antithesis is the battle between two plenitudes set ritually face to face like two fully armed warriors: the Antithesis is the figure of

the *given* opposition, eternal, eternally recurrent: the figure of the inexpiable. Every joining of two antithetical terms, every mixture, every conciliation—in short, every passage through the wall of the Antithesis—thus constitutes a transgression: to be sure, rhetoric can reinvent a figure designed to name the transgressive; this figure exists: it is the paradoxism. (Barthes, 1974:27)

This "passage through the wall" (the walls of the crypt, or of the fort) by finding a medium that interrupts the confrontation, is part of the choral linguistics needed to write directly with the Symbolic code. Derrida, referring to his "fable" of invention, stated his own version of the question of passage in the context of mourning.

Fable tells of allegory, of one word's move to cross over to the other, to the other side of the mirror. Of the desperate effort of an unhappy speech to move beyond the specularity that it constitutes itself. We might say in another code that *Fable* puts *into action* the question of reference, of the specularity of language *or* of literature, and of the possibility of stating the other or speaking *to* the other. We shall see how it does so; but already we know the issue is unmistakably that of death, of this moment of mourning when the breaking of the mirror is the most necessary and also the most difficult. The most difficult because everything we say or do or cry, however outstretched toward the other we may be, remains *within us*. A part of us is wounded and it is with ourselves that we are conversing in the travail of mourning and of *Errinerung*. (Derrida, 1989a:31)

A Macaronic Gesture

Desert is the choral word of "Yellowstone Desert"; it operates at the micro level of language, the way writing with the paradigm operates at the level of discourse, and provides the *inventio* that gathers differences into a set. There are several obvious ways in which *desert* relates *Beau Geste* to "*Chora,*" but the puncept or paradigm of the choral word guides me to the gesture I need to write my rehearsal and to find the "idiom" for the feeling that motivated my search for the rules of this discourse on method. The tableau staged at the saloon is based on that scene of impasse at the fort, which is ripe with the luck of *timing,* the *kairos* of opportunity or occasion that is fundamental to *Fortuna.* American stories do not so much disguise a social cause as individual initiative, as many critics insist, as they openly declare a primary value of the culture—*luck.* When an individual's *virtu* does not prevent failure, *luck* and not *society* is the "cause." The materiality of luck.

The methodological role of luck in chorography concerns making a link between the paradigms of Cooper and Derrida. Considering that Cooper is the guide of my *inventio,* the choral method directs me to look for a match between Cooper's repertoire of gestures and Derrida's French paradigm (my research is "automated" in the sense that I am guided by this pattern). A semiotic study of French gestures shows that the fundamental distinction organizing signification for a French speaker is that between straight-line and curved movement: "We shall see that the dichotomy between straight-line and curved movements which has been exposed in the physically relevant components of gestures will also be found on the symbolic level" (Calbris, 43).

This situation is related to Derrida's interest in the grounding of philosophy in a national language, in the idioms of a natural language, including its nonverbal or gestural dimension. What is the status of "gesture" in philosophy? Derrida argues against Kant on the classifying of the straight and the curved into a hierarchy of value. "How to pass from the principles of this philosophical pedagogy to a doctrine of right [*droit*]? How to pass, more precisely, to this value of 'right' constructed on the analogy between that which the name designates (*le droit, jus, right, das Recht*) and that which the adjective or adverb signifies (direct, rigid, rectilinear)? (Derrida, 1990b:76). Kant distinguishes the rectilinear from the curved or oblique, which signifies false, improper, erroneous (77). Kant's notion of "right," that is, "lacks any *for intérieur;* its 'objects' (*Objecte*) must exhibit themselves in actions. It is a domain of visibility or of theatricality without fold [in which] everything is exposable—in a discourse or in expressive gestures" (77). But what may not be exposed in this theater, Derrida insists, is the *foundation* of right, or (in chorography) the premises of judgment (hidden like the secret each legionnaire carries to the grave).

To make his point Kant used the image of the Prussian soldier, which Derrida adapts to this discussion of what he calls the "philosophical gesture" (Germans, moreover, were the largest national group in the French foreign legion). Kant argues for the superiority of the right over the left, using the analogy of the Prussian soldier, who was "trained to lead off with the left foot ... for he puts this foot forward as on a hypomochlium, to give the right side a greater impetus of attack, thus executing the movement with the right against the left" (Kant, in Rand). Derrida comments:

> This footnote enables me to recall what Kant says elsewhere about the paradox of symmetrical objects and about the difference between the two hands, whose orientation cannot be defined in purely conceptual or logical terms, but must instead be defined as a function of a topology of the senses, and of a subjective position of the human body. I have used this figure so as to suggest that the political opposition between right and left must, when it concerns a strategic lever, be handled with the greatest care, even with vigilance. (Derrida, 1992a:226)

This analogy of the soldier that Derrida finds in Kant, when mediated by the music hall, strengthens the link between Cooper and *chora*. It reminds me of Cooper's role as a legionnaire in *Morocco* (1930). Directed by Josef von Sternberg in his American debut and Marlene Dietrich's first Hollywood film, *Morocco* tells the story of an affair between Amy Jolly (Dietrich), a "cabaret" singer, and Tom Brown (Cooper), an American in the foreign legion. Amy's act at the cabaret (Lo Tinto's vaudeville concert saloon) involves dressing in a man's tuxedo—a cross-dressing that was her trademark and that resonates with the tradition of burlesque (Allen, 116).

"Dietrich," the actress explained in *Marlene Dietrich's ABC,* means "a key that opens all locks" (Dietrich, 53). She describes herself as a "Kantian," explaining that she was brought up on Kant's categorical imperative: "Logic was demanded at all times. If there was no logic in my deductions, I was ruled out of any conversation. To this day I cannot get away from this strict adherence to logic, and I demand it now of others as it was demanded of me" (102). Kant's laws were her "roots": "A man must first appreciate the importance of what we call duty, the authority of moral law, and the immediate worth that obeying it gives a person in his own eyes, before he can feel any satisfaction from consciousness of his conformity to it, or can feel the bitter remorse that accompanies consciousness of transgressing it" (93). In my diegesis the two films merge, so that Beau Geste and Amy Jolly meet at the music hall in *Morocco* and discuss "duty" (responsibility) in the different institutions of the popcycle.

At the end of *Morocco* the Dietrich character decides to join the women following Cooper's regiment as it marches off into the desert. Her fate is a cautionary tale of the fallen woman, whose choices are reduced to predatory "gold digger" or self-destruction. An officer on the ship carrying her from France to Morocco, recognizing her as a "vaudeville actress," observes: "We carry them every day. We call them 'suicide passengers'—one-way tickets. They never return" (Sternberg, 13).

Putting Amy's choice into a historical context (to write the paradigm) brings up the "Mobile Military Brothel" (*B.M.C.* in French abbreviation):

> As entertainment we had—if one's mind was sufficiently twisted to permit him to participate—the B.M.C. The females following the military columns were generally Mauresques; sometimes a European woman who had reached the last degree of decadence mixed with the crowd of colored whores; every single one was

the refuse of Moroccan brothels, old battle horses who, feeling the hour of retreat approach, tried to make a few francs by any possible means. At Ou-Terbat they numbered ten to twelve, exposed to the fury of 5,000 solid young males. (Mercer, 245)

Dietrich is not a leading character in my diegesis. She is in the "Chorus" (the chorus line), from where she teaches me how to open up the identification process, to pack the Supreme Court of my judgments. She is there, along with the three thousand Sioux rounded up in the 1880s, put on river steamers at Miles City, and deported to a reservation. My premises are patriarchal, echoing with the shout of the superego (I hear myself speaking it): "Are you at your post?" (Zizek, 77). Like Beau, I am at my *poste*. Can I learn something from 1939? Is that the end of the story (Beau dead, Amy in the brothel, Sioux on the reservation)?

"Desert"

The Psychological Gesture for my tableau has to be understood not in singular terms, but as evoking a paradigm, a field of possibilities (*inventio*). It invents; it does not verify. What does this paradigm convey? The discussion of *droit* suggests that it has to do with the dimension of *desert* concerning justice, what is *deserved* (just desert). The question of action associated with the debate over rights is that of "responsibility." In the article under discussion ("The Conflict of Faculties"), Derrida names his topic as that of "responsibility":

If we could speak of ourselves as WE—but have I not already done so?—we might be tempted to ask: where are we? And, indeed, who are we in the University where we apparently are? What do we represent? Whom do we represent? We might ask ourselves whether we are responsible; if so, for what and before whom? Assuming there is such a thing as academic responsibility, then it must at least begin with the moment one feels it necessary to hear these questions, to take them up with oneself, to issue a response. This 'responsive imperative' is the initial form and minimal prerequisite of any responsibility. (Derrida, 1992b:3)

The gesture of "desert," then, includes the paradigm of responsibility, in all its possibilities, and suggests specifically that the fundamental question of a postconventional identity (a notion generated in a debate about how taking responsibility for genocide might affect national identity) could be approached not in terms of "right" but of "desert" (the justice of just deserts). The purpose of "Yellowstone Desert" is not to dramatize or argue this case but to evoke it.

The commonsense example for a discussion of the distinction between *right* and *desert* is found in George Sher's *Desert:* "One case concerned a man who carelessly left his umbrella at home despite predictions of rain. Of this man, we said that he does deserve the soaking he gets, but that nobody is obligated to see to it that he gets wet" (Sher, 203). Derrida found in Nietzsche's notebooks (written in the state of *folie*) the phrase, "I have forgotten my umbrella." Taking the position that all the phrases of Nietzsche's disciplinary books are as ambiguous as this sentence in the notebooks, Derrida declares, in a burlesque mood, "Suppose that in some way the totality which I (so to speak) have presented is also an erratic, even parodying, graft. What if this totality should eventually be of the same sort as an 'I have forgotten my umbrella'?" (Derrida, 1978:135). And he adds, "What if even I fail to see the transparent reason of such a history and code?" In the context of "Yellowstone Desert" Derrida's *oeuvre* does indeed come down to the question signaled by the dilemma of a forgotten umbrella—the problematic of desert. What are the deserts of Amy, Beau, the Touaregs, America itself, after 1992?

The Psychological Gesture performed in the music hall tableau evokes postconventional identity in terms of *desert*. As Sher explains, *desert* concerns a responsibility for action, in terms not of obligation (related to *right*) but of value. Values are reflected in "free actions": "Treating people as they deserve is one way of treating them as autonomous beings, responsible for their own conduct" (37). The problem is that there is no consensus on values, that values cover prejudices, which has been the vulnerable point of a "liberal" society (understood as one in which individuals are free to set their own values) (209).

One view is that a just society promotes deserved outcomes. The difficulty (*aporia*) is that desert is bound up with "identity," a sorting out of traits and acts. How a person ought to fare "must specify some suitably intimate relation that holds between a person and his acts and traits, but not between him and the tides, the movements of the stars, or the acts and traits of others. It must license a distinction between factors that are external to a person and the acts and traits that are, in some appropriately strong sense, his own" (151). Yet this distinction is just what is in question, what is undergoing metamorphosis in the combinatorial of a new apparatus, on the part of a subject known as "other." What is inside and proper to a "self," and what is external and accidental?

When subjects were "parrots," Lacan noted, referring to totemic identity in tribal civilization, they were responsible to the stars (oral apparatus). When subjects were "selves" they were autoresponsible (book apparatus). These are the two subjectivations Sher figures in his account of justice. But a third subjectivation is coming into formation. How will electronic identity hold subjects responsible? I saw an ad placed in an airline magazine by a consulting firm (Karrass): "In business, you don't get what you deserve, you get what you negotiate." *Negotiate?* Its paradigm includes "to move through, around, or over in a satisfactory manner," as well as to bargain, arrange, transact (conduct), to dispose of, to transfer (negotiable paper). The interface metaphor for cyberspace in chorography is not "navigate" but "negotiate": to negotiate the popcycle. The boundary or interface zone mediating the inside/outside dimension of the human subject has shifted before in history, and it is shifting again. Its terms are being renegotiated.

"Desert" is the name of a problematic because the distinction between inside and outside (the issue of *chora*) is a *founding* distinction. It is cultural or institutional, political in a profound sense, involving the choral zone between fate and freedom, an irreducible zone of luck, chance, risk, and timing. This zone is also the region of invention. To speak of it, to "interpret" it, as Derrida says of presuming to interpret the "totality" of Nietzsche's work (or of Derrida's work), "exposes one, roofless and unprotected by a lightning rod as he is, to the thunder and lightning of an enormous clap of laughter" (Derrida, 1978:135). "Luck" may not be accessed hermeneutically, then, but heuretically.

Dessert

In my mnemonic tableau the Hermeneutic code of truth is interrupted by a Heuretic code of invention, diverting the narrative sequence of the square of opposition with a conductive turn of the popcycle. "Yellowstone Desert" does not propose an argument about justice (the question of the differend) but evokes a paradigm. This evocation is done by a gesture that Cooper can teach me. Reviewing Cooper's repertoire of gestures, I selected his expressive use of *pursed lips* as the Psychological Gesture to rely on for recalling the feeling of "the beautiful death." To embody what has to be remembered, however, Cooper's pursed lips have to be understood as speaking in French as well as in English (the sign that escapes from the crypt and passes through the wall is macaronic).

What may be said with pursed lips in French? According to *Beaux Gestes: A Guide to French Body Talk,* pursed lips belong to a family or paradigm of gestures classified as *le Jemenfoutisme:* boredom, indecision, and rejection (Wylie and Stafford, 22) and associated with an attitude described as the national life-style of France.

> It is inevitable in the land of *Le Jemenfoutisme* that there should
> be a long list of gestures indicating a rejection of responsibility,
> the belittling of one's errors, the affectation of indifference. One

says *Je m'en fous* with the whole body. A person or a problem or
a responsibility is symbolically expelled. The hands are washed
clean of responsibility. Responsibility is ejected from the mouth
with the thumb or flicked away with the fingers. Above all it is
ejected as a stream of air from the lungs; the shoulders shrug and
compress the lungs, while the lips pout as the air is expelled making the sound "bof!" (23)

In my remake, Gary Cooper pouts his lips and says "bof!" thus
fixing mnemonically my francophilia by inmixing the stereotypes
of two national spirits. Cooper's face, it was said, "was the map
of America. In it, we read our past" (Kaminsky, 221). Derrida
suggested that Thomas Jefferson might have preferred substitut-
ing for his original draft of the Declaration of Independence a
map of America with his signature as legend (Derrida, 1986b:13).
This map for me would be Cooper's face making *the* French gesture ("Bof!"). The figure could be identified as a representation
of "John Q. Public," one of whose best embodiments was said to
be Gary Cooper (Zelinsky, 24). "Brother Jonathan," as this "first
significant masculine image of America" was known, originated
as a "derisive epithet," as did Yankee Doodle. The French equivalent is "tourist Dupont" (Calbris, 98).

Given that *chora* can only be touched upon indirectly or
obliquely, it is not a matter of expressing it fully in Cooper's gesture. The French idiom, in any case, has far more "negative" than
"positive" gestures—more gestures that indicate "faults"
(Calbris, 84). As for the "zero" offered as a synonym of "desert,"
just being a legionnaire constitutes a reference to the ruthless and
brutal training designed to reduce the recruit to the status of
"Monsieur Zero" (Mercer, 33). The plot of *Beau Geste,* moreover,
traces a temporal circle around the enigma of the fort. The pushing out of the lips in French concerns judgments, varying degrees
of scepticism and doubt, which may be accompanied with the
hand gesture of "zero," the thumb and forefinger in a circle "il-
lustrating a monocle in front of the eye" (capable of signifying
either nothingness or perfection) (Calbris, 53). This ambivalence

in the gestural circle reflects the risks of the "wheel" of Fortune. "Charles Sanders Peirce"—rhymes with "purse."

The "pursed lips of doubt" depict emptiness, related to protecting oneself by a "refusal of responsibility," an "evasion reflex":

> The fact that doubt and reprobation, i.e., intellectual and emotional refusal respectively, are expressed by pushing out the pursed lips, in addition to knitting one's brow, suggest that this type of moue is equivalent to the outwardly pushed palm. Indeed, the lips are puckered for various physical reasons: to kiss, to snap up, to hold onto, or to reject. Thus moving the lips out in one way or another, one can transpose to the mouth the acts of pushing away, taking, or touching. (159)

As Derrida said regarding the "hand" in the metaphor of "concept" (in German, to grasp and to hold tightly), the gesture may be changed, the hand as vehicle may do something else, such as offer a gift (a contribution to the excellence fund of my university), with real consequences for the tenor, the notion of thinking.

In the Method, the physical action evokes the feeling. I pursed my lips as a metonymy for this paradigm of analogies, to propose all the gestures as an archive for invention. That was my plan for the tableau of "Yellowstone Desert," elaborating in one scene a music hall in frontier Miles City, Gary Cooper's acting, Derrida's theory of justice, offered in commemoration of "The Discovery of America," as it was called in 1939. Facing the forced choice of the beautiful death, suspended among mutineers, sergeants, and Touaregs, Beau, in 1992, says: "Bof!"

Would the citizens recognize this gesture as a switch? I should have had more confidence in the amateur burlesque troupe, who learned quickly how to turn the square (the choral word), how to switch the tableau from *desert* to *dessert,* to keep the show moving. The next act was ready to come on—a man whose career consisted of sitting down to play a grand piano, noticing that the stool was too far away from the keys, and spending the rest of his considerable time on stage struggling unsuccessfully to push the piano closer to the stool. The jest was on me, who should have known that the dessert would not come comfortably after dinner, the pleasure of the text, but in the style of blissense, as a victim of one of the oldest, most stereotyped bits in the clown's repertoire—a custard pie in the face, spilling all over my rented uniform, knocking off the white *képi*. Playing the fool, the clown yelled to the audience, "There ya go, General Custard! Just a desert from your friend Sioux!" (laughter).

Meanwhile, the "professor" stops playing the piano, interrupts his soliciting, and wonders, "What is that—for me, today?"

The face licks its lips, tastes the custard. "Let me guess. A French recipe, no?"

An electronic recipe.

WORKS CITED

Abel, Robert. 1992. "Synapse and Columbus." *Design World* 24:28–37.

Abraham, Nicolas, and Maria Torok. 1986. *The Wolf Man's Magic Word: A "Cryptonymy."* Translated by Nicholas Rand. Minneapolis: University of Minnesota Press.

Acker, Kathy. 1984. *Algeria.* London: Aloes.

Adas, Michael. 1989. *Machines as the Measure of Men: Science, Technology, and Ideologies of Western Dominance.* Ithaca: Cornell University Press.

Allen, Robert C. 1991. *Horrible Prettiness: Burlesque and American Culture.* Chapel Hill: University of North Carolina Press.

Ambron, Sueann, and Kristina Hooper, eds. 1988. *Interactive Multimedia: Visions of Multimedia for Developers, Educators, & Information Providers.* Redmond, Wash.: Microsoft.

———. 1990. *Learning with Interactive Multimedia.* Redmond, Wash.: Microsoft.

Appignanesi, Lisa. 1976. *The Cabaret.* New York: Universe Books.

Ashbaugh, Anne Freire. 1988. *Plato's Theory of Explanation: A Study of the Cosmological Account in the Timaeus.* Albany: State University of New York Press.

Aylwin, Susan. 1985. *Structure in Thought and Feeling.* London: Methuen.

Barilli, Renato. 1989. *Rhetoric.* Translated by Giuliana Menozzi. Minneapolis: University of Minnesota Press.

Barrett, Edward, ed. 1988. *Text, ConText, and HyperText: Writing with and for the Computer.* Cambridge: MIT Press.

Barthes, Roland. 1972a. *Mythologies.* Translated by Annette Lavers. New York: Hill & Wang.

————. 1972b. "The Structuralist Activity." In *The Structuralists from Marx to Levi-Strauss.* Edited by Richard and Fernande DeGeorge. New York: Doubleday.

————. 1974. *S/Z: An Essay.* Translated by Richard Miller. New York: Hill & Wang.

————. 1988. "The Old Rhetoric: An Aide-memoire." In *The Semiotic Challenge.* Translated by Richard Howard. New York: Hill & Wang.

Bastick, Tony. 1982. *Intuition: How We Think and Act.* New York: John Wiley.

Baudrillard, Jean. 1988. *America.* Translated by Chris Turner. New York: Verso.

Bechtel, William, and Adele Abrahamsen. 1991. *Connectionism and the Mind: An Introduction to Parallel Processing in Networks.* Cambridge: Basil Blackwell.

Benjamin, Walter. 1978. *Reflections: Essays, Aphorisms, Autobiographical Writings.* Translated by Edmund Jephcott. New York: Harcourt Brace Jovanovich.

Bergman, Herbert, ed. 1983. *Writing and Genre Films.* East Lansing, Mich.: Film Research.

Bloch, Ernst. 1986. *The Principle of Hope.* Vol. 2, translated by Neville Plaice et al. Cambridge: MIT Press.

Blum, Richard A. 1984. *American Film Acting: The Stanislavski Heritage.* Ann Arbor: University of Michigan Press.

Blumenberg, Hans. 1985. *The Legitimacy of the Modern Age.* Translated by Robert M. Wallace. Cambridge: MIT Press.

Bolter, Jay David. 1991. *Writing Space: The Computer, Hypertext, and the History of Writing.* Hillsdale, N.J.: Erlbaum.

Bonfantini, Massimo A., and Giampaolo Proni. 1983. "To Guess or Not To Guess?" In Eco and Sebeok.

Boorstin, Daniel J. 1985. *The Discoverers: A History of Man's Search to Know His World and Himself.* New York: Vintage.

————. 1987. *Hidden History.* New York: Harper & Row.

Bowen, Catherine Drinker. 1966. *Miracle at Philadelphia: The Story of the Constitutional Convention.* Boston: Little, Brown.

Braidotti, Rosi. 1991. *Patterns of Dissonance: A Study of Women in Contemporary Philosophy.* Translated by Elizabeth Guild. Cambridge: Polity Press.

Breton, André. 1969. *Manifestoes of Surrealism.* Translated by Richard Seaver and Helen R. Lane. Ann Arbor: University of Michigan Press.

Brown, Mark H., and W. R. Felton. 1955. *The Frontier Years: L. A. Huffman, Photographer of the Plains.* New York: Bramhall.

Buchler, Justus. 1961. *The Concept of Method.* New York: Columbia University Press.

Bullock, Alan, and Oliver Stallybrass, eds. 1977. *The Harper Dictionary of Modern Thought.* New York: Harper & Row.

Burgin, Victor. 1990. "Geometry and Abjection." In *Abjection, Melancholia, and Love: The Work of Julia Kristeva.* Edited by John Fletcher and Andrew Benjamin. New York: Routledge.

Burnet, John. 1957. *Early Greek Philosophy.* Cleveland: World.

Calbris, Genevieve. 1990. *The Semiotics of French Gestures.* Translated by Owen Doyle. Bloomington: Indiana University Press.

Cameron, Ian. 1973. *Adventure in the Movies.* New York: Crescent.

Campbell, Jeremy. 1989. *The Improbable Machine: What the Upheavals in Artificial Intelligence Research Reveal about How the Mind Really Works.* New York: Simon & Schuster.

Carrouges, Michel. 1950. *André Breton et les données fondamentales du surréalisme.* Paris: Gallimard.

Castle, Charles. 1985. *The Folies-Bergère.* New York: Franklin Watts.

Connell, Evan S. 1979. *A Long Desire.* New York: Holt, Rinehart & Winston.

Connerton, Paul. 1989. *How Societies Remember.* New York: Cambridge University Press.

Coover, Robert. 1992. "The End of Books." *New York Times Book Review,* June 21, 1, 23–25.

Corliss, Richard. 1990. "Czar of Bizarre." *Times,* Oct. 1.

Cornford, Francis MacDonald. 1937. *Plato's Cosmology.* London: Routledge.

Corrigan, Timothy. 1991. "Film and the Culture of the Cult." In Telotte 1991.

Crary, Jonathan. 1984. "Eclipse of the Spectacle." In *Art after Modernism.* Edited by Brian Wallis. Boston: Godine.

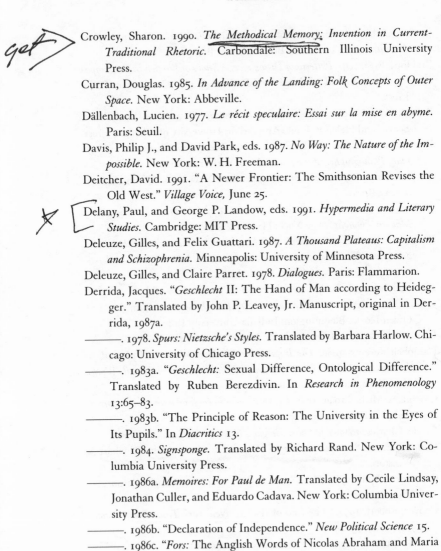

Crowley, Sharon. 1990. *The Methodical Memory: Invention in Current-Traditional Rhetoric.* Carbondale: Southern Illinois University Press.

Curran, Douglas. 1985. *In Advance of the Landing: Folk Concepts of Outer Space.* New York: Abbeville.

Dällenbach, Lucien. 1977. *Le récit speculaire: Essai sur la mise en abyme.* Paris: Seuil.

Davis, Philip J., and David Park, eds. 1987. *No Way: The Nature of the Impossible.* New York: W. H. Freeman.

Deitcher, David. 1991. "A Newer Frontier: The Smithsonian Revises the Old West." *Village Voice,* June 25.

Delany, Paul, and George P. Landow, eds. 1991. *Hypermedia and Literary Studies.* Cambridge: MIT Press.

Deleuze, Gilles, and Felix Guattari. 1987. *A Thousand Plateaus: Capitalism and Schizophrenia.* Minneapolis: University of Minnesota Press.

Deleuze, Gilles, and Claire Parret. 1978. *Dialogues.* Paris: Flammarion.

Derrida, Jacques. "*Geschlecht* II: The Hand of Man according to Heidegger." Translated by John P. Leavey, Jr. Manuscript, original in Derrida, 1987a.

———. 1978. *Spurs: Nietzsche's Styles.* Translated by Barbara Harlow. Chicago: University of Chicago Press.

———. 1983a. "*Geschlecht:* Sexual Difference, Ontological Difference." Translated by Ruben Berezdivin. In *Research in Phenomenology* 13:65–83.

———. 1983b. "The Principle of Reason: The University in the Eyes of Its Pupils." In *Diacritics* 13.

———. 1984. *Signsponge.* Translated by Richard Rand. New York: Columbia University Press.

———. 1986a. *Memoires: For Paul de Man.* Translated by Cecile Lindsay, Jonathan Culler, and Eduardo Cadava. New York: Columbia University Press.

———. 1986b. "Declaration of Independence." *New Political Science* 15.

———. 1986c. "*Fors:* The Anglish Words of Nicolas Abraham and Maria Torok." Translated by Barbara Johnson. In Abraham and Torok.

———. 1987a. *Psyche: Inventions de l'autre.* Paris: Galilée.

———. 1987b. "Chora." In *Poikilia: Etudes offertes à Jean-Pierre Vernant.* Paris: EHESS.

———. 1987c. *The Truth in Painting.* Translated by Geoff Bennington and Ian McLeod. Chicago: University of Chicago Press.

————. 1987d. *The Post Card: From Socrates to Freud and Beyond.* Translated by Alan Bass. Chicago: University of Chicago Press.

————. 1989a. "Psyche: Inventions of the Other." Translated by Catherine Porter. In *Reading de Man Reading,* edited by Lindsay Waters and Wlad Godzich. Minneapolis: University of Minnesota Press.

————. 1989b. "Biodegradables: Seven Diary Fragments." *Critical Inquiry* 15.

————. 1990a. "Some Statements and Truisms about Neo-Logisms, Newisms, Postisms, Parasitisms, and Other Small Seismisms." In *The States of "Theory": History, Art, and Critical Discourse,* edited by David Carroll. New York: Columbia University Press.

————. 1990b. *Du droit à la philosophie.* Paris: Galilee.

————. 1990c. *Mémoires d'aveugle: L'autoportrait et autres ruines.* Paris: Réunion des Musées Nationaux.

————. 1991a. *L'autre cap.* Paris; Minuit.

————. 1991b. "The Status of the Individual." In *Anyone.* New York: Rizzoli.

————. 1992a. "Canons and Metonymies: An Interview." In *Logomachia: The Conflict of the Faculties,* edited by Richard Rand. Lincoln: University of Nebraska Press.

————. 1992b. "Mochlos; or, The Conflict of the Faculties." In *Logomachia: The Conflict of the Faculties,* edited by Richard Rand. Lincoln: University of Nebraska Press.

————. 1992c. *The Other Heading: Reflections on Today's Europe.* Translated by Pascale-Anne Brault and Michael B. Naas. Bloomington: Indiana University Press.

Desan, Philippe. 1987. *Naissance de la methode: Machiavel, La Ramée, Bodin, Montaigne, Descartes.* Paris: Nizet.

Descartes, René. 1960. *Discourse on Method.* Translated by Laurence J. Lafleur. Indianapolis: Bobbs-Merrill.

Dickens, Homer. 1970. *The Films of Gary Cooper.* Secaucus, N.J.: Citadel.

Dietrich, Marlene. 1962. *Marlene Dietrich's ABC.* Garden City, N.Y.: Doubleday.

Dixon, Peter. 1971. *Rhetoric.* London: Methuen.

duBois, Page. 1991. *Torture and Truth.* New York: Routledge.

Eco, Umberto. 1986. *Travels in Hyperreality: Essays.* Translated by William Weaver. San Diego: Harcourt Brace Jovanovich.

Eco, Umberto, and Thomas A. Sebeok. 1983. *The Sign of Three: Dupin, Holmes, Peirce.* Bloomington: Indiana University Press.

Elliott, Emory, ed. 1988. *Columbia Literary History of the United States.* New York: Columbia University Press.

Ellis, John M. 1989. *Against Deconstruction.* Princeton: Princeton University Press.

Elsaesser, Thomas. 1989. *New German Cinema: A History.* New Brunswick: Rutgers University Press.

Engelbart, Doug, with Kristina Hooper. 1988. "The Augmentation System Framework." In Ambron and Hooper, 1988.

Entrikin, J. Nicholas. 1991. *The Betweenness of Place: Toward a Geography of Modernity.* Baltimore: Johns Hopkins University Press.

Erdoes, Richard. 1979. *Saloons of the Old West.* New York: Alfred Knopf.

Fell, John L. 1974. *Film and the Narrative Tradition.* Berkeley and Los Angeles: University of California Press.

Fiske, John. 1982. *Introduction to Communication Studies.* New York: Methuen.

Florin, Fabrice. 1990. "Information Landscapes." In Ambron and Hooper, 1990.

Flynn, Charles P. 1977. *Insult and Society: Patterns of Comparative Interaction.* Port Washington, N.Y.: Kennikat.

Forbes, Jack D. 1992. *Columbus and Other Cannibals: The "Wetiko" Disease of Exploitation, Imperialism and Terrorism.* Brooklyn: Autonomedia.

Franklin, Wayne. 1979. *Discoverers, Explorers, Settlers: The Diligent Writers of Early America.* Chicago: University of Chicago Press.

Freud, Sigmund. 1961. *Beyond the Pleasure Principle.* Translated by James Strachey. New York: W. W. Norton.

———. 1971. "The Case of the Wolf-Man." In *The Wolf-Man,* edited by Muriel Gardiner. New York: Basic Books.

———. 1989. *The Freud Reader.* Edited by Peter Gay. New York: W. W. Norton.

Friedlander, Paul. 1958. *Plato: An Introduction.* Translated by Hans Meyerhoff. New York: Harper & Row.

Friedman, Ellen G. 1989. "A Conversation with Kathy Acker." *Review of Contemporary Fiction* 9:12–22.

Gardner, Martin. 1957. *Fads and Fallacies in the Name of Science.* New York: Dover.

Gilbert, Neal Ward. 1960. *Renaissance Concepts of Method.* New York: Columbia University Press.

Ginzburg, Carlo. 1983. "Morelli, Freud, and Sherlock Holmes: Clues and Scientific Method." In Eco and Sebeok.

Godzich, Wlad. 1986. "The Tiger on the Paper Mat." In Paul de Man, *The Resistance to Theory.* Minneapolis: University of Minnesota Press.

―――. 1987. "In-Quest of Modernity." In Nerlich.

Goff, John V., Susan R. McDaniel, and Dena L. Sanford. 1988. *Miles City, Montana: An Architectural History.* Miles City, Mont.: Custer County Society for Preservation.

Gordon, Mel. 1987. *The Stanislavsky Technique: Russia. A Workbook for Actors.* New York: Applause.

Graham, W. A. 1953. *The Custer Myth: A Source Book of Custeriana.* Lincoln: University of Nebraska Press.

Green, Martin. 1979. *Dreams of Adventure, Deeds of Empire.* New York: Basic Books.

―――. 1991. *Seven Types of Adventure Tale: An Etiology of a Major Genre.* University Park: Pennsylvania State University Press.

Greenhalgh, Paul. 1988. *Ephemeral Vistas.* Manchester, England: Manchester University Press.

Guzzetti, Alfred. 1981. *"Two or Three things I Know about Her": Analysis of a Film by Godard.* Cambridge: Harvard University Press.

Habermas, Jürgen. 1987. *The Philosophical Discourse of Modernity: Twelve Lectures.* Translated by Frederick Lawrence. Cambridge: Polity.

―――. 1989. *The New Conservatism: Cultural Criticism and the Historians' Debate.* Cambridge: MIT Press.

Harpham, Geoffrey Galt. 1987. *The Ascetic Imperative in Culture and Criticism.* Chicago: University of Chicago Press.

Harrowitz, Nancy. 1983. "The Body of the Detective Model: Charles S. Peirce and Edgar Allan Poe." In Eco and Sebeok.

Havelock, Eric A. 1986. *The Muse Learns to Write.* New Haven: Yale University Press.

Hayles, N. Katherine. 1990. *Chaos Bound: Orderly Disorder in Contemporary Literature and Science.* Ithaca: Cornell University Press.

Higgins, Lynn A. 1984. *Parables of Theory: Jean Ricardou's Metafiction.* Birmingham, Ala.: Summa.

Hillary, Sir Edmund. 1982. "An Adventurer Speaks out about the Art." In Whittingham.

Hindle, Brooke. 1981. *Emulation and Invention.* New York: W. W. Norton.

Hirsch, E. D., Jr. 1987. *Cultural Literacy: What Every American Needs to Know.* Boston: Houghton Mifflin.

Hirsch, Foster. 1984. *A Method to Their Madness: The History of the Actors Studio.* New York: W. W. Norton.

Hoberman, J., and Jonathan Rosenbaum. 1983. *Midnight Movies.* New York: Da Capo.

Huber, Richard M. 1971. *The American Idea of Success.* New York: McGraw-Hill.

Hugo, Richard. 1979. *The Triggering Town: Lectures and Essays on Poetry and Writing.* New York: W. W. Norton.

Huyssen, Andreas. 1987. "Foreword: The Return of Diogenes as Postmodern Intellectual." In Sloterdijk.

"Hypercard Software." 1987. *Whole Earth Review* 57:102–103.

Kaminsky, Stuart M. 1980. *Coop: The Life and Legend of Gary Cooper.* New York: St. Martin's.

Katz, Ephraim. 1979. *The Film Encyclopedia.* New York: Perigee.

Keller, Evelyn Fox. 1985. *Reflections on Gender and Science.* New Haven: Yale University Press.

Kipnis, Jeffrey. Forthcoming. *Choral Work.* London: Architectural Association.

Kristeva, Julia. 1982. *Powers of Horror: An Essay on Abjection.* Translated by Leon S. Roudiez. New York: Columbia University Press.

———. 1984. *Revolution in Poetic Language.* Translated by Margaret Waller. New York: Columbia University Press.

Lacan, Jacques. 1968. *Speech and Language in Psychoanalysis.* Translated by Anthony Wilden. Baltimore: Johns Hopkins University Press.

———. 1972. "The Insistence of the Letter in the Unconscious." In *The Structuralists from Marx to Levi-Strauss,* edited by Richard and Fernande DeGeorge. Garden City, N.Y.: Doubleday.

———. "L'envers de la psychanalyse: Les quatre discours, 1969–1970." Photocopy.

———. 1978. *Le seminaire. Livre II. Le moi dans la theorie de Freud et dans la technique de la psychanalyse, 1954–1955.* Paris: Seuil.

———. 1988. *The Seminar of Jacques Lacan. Book II. The Ego.* Translated by Sylvana Tomaselli. New York: W. W. Norton.

Laplanche, J., and J.-B. Pontalis. 1973. *The Language of Psychoanalysis.* Translated by Donald Nicholson-Smith. New York: W. W. Norton.

Lapsley, Robert, and Michael Westlake. 1988. *Film Theory: An Introduction.* Manchester: University of Manchester Press.

Laurel, Brenda, ed. 1990. *The Art of Human-Computer Interface Design.* Reading, Mass.: Addison-Wesley.

Leupin, Alexandre, ed. 1991. *Lacan and the Human Sciences*. Lincoln: University of Nebraska Press.

Lewis, Helena. 1988. *The Politics of Surrealism*. New York: Paragon.

Lynch, David. 1987. "Interview." *The Face,* Feb.

Lyotard, Jean-Francois. 1988. *The Differend: Phrases in Dispute*. Minneapolis: University of Minnesota Press.

McCabe, Viki, and Gerald J. Balzano, eds. 1986. *Event Cognition: An Ecological Perspective*. Hillsdale, N.J.: Lawrence Erlbaum.

McDonagh, Maitland. 1988. "The Enigma of David Lynch." *Persistence of Vision* 6:67–82.

McNamara, Brooks, ed. 1983. *American Popular Entertainments: Jokes, Monologues, Bits, and Sketches*. New York: Performing Arts Journal.

Magill, Frank N., ed. 1961. *Masterpieces of World Philosophy*. New York: Harper & Row.

Margolis, Howard. 1987. *Patterns, Thinking, and Cognition: A Theory of Judgment*. Chicago: University of Chicago Press.

Marsh, Ken. 1982. *The Way the New Technology Works*. New York: Simon & Schuster.

Martin, Daniel. 1977. *Montaigne et la fortune*. Paris: Champion.

Mercer, Charles. 1964. *Legion of Strangers: The Vivid History of a Unique Military Tradition — The French Foreign Legion*. New York: Holt, Rinehart & Winston.

Miller, Daniel. 1987. *Material Culture and Mass Consumption*. Cambridge: Basil Blackwell.

Miller, J. Hillis. "Should I Teach Kleist?" In Rand.

Mitroff, Ian I., and Warren Bennis. 1989. *The Unreality Industry: The Deliberate Manufacturing of Falsehood and What It Is Doing to Our Lives*. New York: Carol.

Mohr, Richard D. 1985. *The Platonic Cosmology*. Leiden, Netherlands: Brill.

Moore, Sonia. 1984. *The Stanislavski System: The Professional Training of an Actor*. New York: Penguin.

Muller, John, and William Richardson, eds. 1988. *The Purloined Poe: Lacan, Derrida and Psychoanalytic Reading*. Baltimore: Johns Hopkins University Press.

"Multimedia: About Interface." 1989. *Macuser,* Mar.

Murray, Simon. 1978. *Legionnaire: The Real Life Story of an Englishman in the French Foreign Legion*. London: Sidgwick & Jackson.

Naremore, James. 1988. *Acting in the Cinema*. Berkeley and Los Angeles: University of California Press.

WORKS CITED

Nelson, Theodor Holm. 1987. *Literary Machines.* Palo Alto, Calif.: the author. Distributed by the Distributors, South Bend, Ind.

Nerlich, Michael. 1987. *Ideology of Adventure: Studies in Modern Consciousness, 1100–1750.* Vol. 1, translated by Ruth Crowley. Minneapolis: University of Minnesota Press.

Nichols, Bill. 1981. *Ideology and the Image.* Bloomington: Indiana University Press.

Nickles, Thomas, ed. 1980. *Scientific Discovery, Logic, and Rationality.* Dordrecht: Reidel.

Nietzsche, Friedrich. 1974. *The Gay Science.* Translated by Walter Kaufmann. New York: Vintage.

Ong, Walter J. 1983. *Ramus: Method, and the Decay of Dialogue.* Cambridge: Harvard University Press.

Pederson-Krag, Geraldine. 1983. "Detective Stories and the Primal Scene." In *The Poetics of Murder: Detective Fiction and Literary Theory,* edited by Glenn W. Most and William W. Stowe. San Diego: Harcourt Brace Jovanovich.

Peters, Edward. 1985. *Torture.* New York: Basil Blackwell.

Peters, F. E. 1967. *Greek Philosophical Terms: A Historical Lexicon.* New York: New York University Press.

Peterson, Ivars. 1988. *The Mathematical Tourist: Snapshots of Modern Mathematics.* New York: W. H. Freeman.

Petroski, Henry. 1990. *The Pencil: A History of Design and Circumstance.* New York: Alfred Knopf.

Plato. 1963. *The Collected Dialogues.* Edited by Edith Hamilton and Huntington Cairns. Princeton: Princeton University Press.

Poe, Edgar Allan. 1988. "The Purloined Letter." In Muller and Richardson.

Poole, John. 1980. "Hamlet Travestie." In *Nineteenth-Century Dramatic Burlesques of Shakespeare,* edited by Jacob B. Salomon. Darby, Pa.: Norwood.

Primeau, Ronald. 1979. *The Rhetoric of Television.* New York: Longman.

Protopopoff, Daniel, and Michel Serceau. 1989. "Le remake et l'adaptation." *CinemAction* 53:37–45.

Ramage, Edwin S., ed. 1978. *Atlantis: Fact or Fiction?* Bloomington: Indiana University Press.

Rand, Richard, ed. *Our Academic Contract: "The Conflict of Faculties" in America.* Manuscript.

Ray, Robert. 1985. *A Certain Tendency of the Hollywood Cinema, 1930–1980.* Princeton: Princeton University Press.

Rickels, Laurence A. 1991. *The Case of California.* Baltimore: Johns Hopkins University Press.

Roach, Joseph R. 1985. *The Player's Passion: Studies in the Science of Acting.* Newark: University of Delaware Press.

Rosenblum, Mort. 1988. *Mission to Civilize: The French Way.* New York: Doubleday.

Roudinesco, Elisabeth. 1990. *Jacques Lacan and Co.: A History of Psychoanalysis in France, 1925–1985.* Translated by Jeffrey Mehlman. Chicago: University of Chicago Press.

Rummelhart, David E., and Donald A. Norman. 1981. "Introduction." In *Parallel Models of Associative Memory,* edited by Geoffrey E. Hinton and James A. Anderson. Hillsdale, N.J.: Erlbaum.

Sack, Robert David. 1980. *Conceptions of Space in Social Thought: A Geographic Perspective.* Minneapolis: University of Minnesota Press.

Sanders, William B., ed. 1976. *The Sociologist as Detective: An Introduction to Research Methods.* New York: Praeger.

Sandler, Joseph. 1987. *From Safety to Superego.* New York: Guilford.

Santner, Eric L. 1990. *Stranded Objects: Mourning, Memory, and Film in Postwar Germany.* Ithaca: Cornell University Press.

Schleifer, Ronald. 1987. *A. J. Greimas and the Nature of Meaning: Linguistics, Semiotics and Discourse Theory.* Lincoln: University of Nebraska Press.

Schleifer, Ronald, Robert Con Davis, and Nancy Mergler. 1992. *Culture and Cognition: The Boundaries of Literary and Scientific Inquiry.* Ithaca: Cornell University Press.

Schlereth, Thomas J. 1990. *Cultural History and National Culture: Everyday Life, Landscapes, Museums.* Ann Arbor: University of Michigan Press.

Sennett, Ted. 1989. *Hollywood's Golden Year, 1939: A Fiftieth Anniversary Celebration.* New York: St. Martin's.

Sher, George. 1987. *Desert.* Princeton: Princeton University Press.

Shklovsky, Victor. 1990. *Theory of Prose.* Translated by Benjamin Sher. Elmwood Park, Ill.: Dalkey Archive.

Sloterdijk, Peter. 1987. *Critique of Cynical Reason.* Translated by Michael Eldred. Minneapolis: University of Minnesota Press.

Slotkin, Richard. 1990. "The Continuity of Forms: Myth and Genre in Warner Brothers' *The Charge of the Light Brigade.*" *Representations* 29:1–23.

Smiles, Samuel. n.d. *Self-Help: With Illustrations of Character and Conduct.* Philadelphia: J. P. Lippincott.

————. n.d. *Duty: With Illustrations of Courage, Patience, and Endurance.* New York: A. L. Burt.

Speck, Gordon. 1979. *Myths and New World Explorations.* Fairfield, Wash.: Galleon.

Sperber, Dan, and Deirdre Wilson. 1986. *Relevance: Communication and Cognition.* Cambridge: Harvard University Press.

Sternberg, Josef von. 1973. *"Morocco" and "Shanghai Express."* New York: Simon & Schuster.

Stewart, Susan. 1984. *On Longing: Narratives of the Miniature, the Gigantic, the Souvenir, the Collection.* Baltimore: Johns Hopkins University Press.

Strasberg, Lee. 1987. *A Dream of Passion: The Development of the Method.* Boston: Little, Brown.

Swain, Barbara. 1932. *Fools and Folly during the Middle Ages and the Renaissance.* New York: Columbia University Press.

Swindell, Larry. 1980. *The Last Hero: A Biography of Gary Cooper.* Garden City, N.Y.: Doubleday.

Syberberg, Hans-Jurgen. 1982. "Introduction." In *Hitler: A Film from Germany.* Translated by Joachim Neugroschel. New York: Farrar, Straus, Giroux.

Tatum, Stephen. 1987. "The Classic Westerner: Gary Cooper." In *Shooting Stars: Heroes and Heroines of Western Film.* Ed. Archie P. McDonald. Bloomington: Indiana University Press.

Telotte, J. P., ed. 1991. *The Cult Film Experience: Beyond All Reason.* Austin: University of Texas Press.

Thoreau, Henry David. 1966. *Walden.* Edited by Owen Thomas. New York: W. W. Norton.

Trinh T. Minh-ha. 1989. *Woman, Native, Other: Writing Postcoloniality and Feminism.* Bloomington: Indiana University Press.

Tschumi, Bernard. 1981. *The Manhattan Transcripts.* New York: St. Martin's.

————. 1983. "Parc de la Villette, Paris." *AA Files* 4:76–80.

————. 1987. *Cinégramme folie: Le Parc de la Villette.* Princeton: Princeton University Press.

Tuan, Yi-Fu. 1990. *Topophilia: A Study of Environmental Perception, Attitudes, and Values.* New York: Columbia University Press.

Ulmer, Gregory L. 1985. *Applied Grammatology.* Baltimore: Johns Hopkins University Press.

———. 1989. *Teletheory: Grammatology in the Age of Video.* New York: Routledge.

———. 1991a. "The Spirit Hand." In *Theory/Pedagogy/Politics.* Edited by Donald Morton and Mas'ud Zavarzadeh. Urbana: University of Illinois Press.

———. 1991b. "The Euretics of Alice's Valise" *Journal of Architectural Education* 45:3–10.

Walker, Alexander. 1970. *Stardom: The Hollywood Phenomenon.* New York: Stein & Day.

Walter, Eugene Victor. 1988. *Placeways: A Theory of the Human Environment.* Chapel Hill: University of North Carolina Press.

Wartofsky, Marx W. 1980. "Scientific Judgment: Creativity and Discovery in Scientific Thought." In *Scientific Discovery: Case Studies,* edited by Thomas Nickles. Dordrecht: Reidel.

Weber, Eugen. 1991. "The French Foreign Legion." *TLS,* Nov. 8.

West, Cornel. 1990. "The New Cultural Politics of Difference." In *Out There: Marginalization and Contemporary Cultures,* edited by Russell Ferguson et al. Cambridge: MIT Press.

Weyer, Stephen A. 1988. "As We May Learn." In Ambron and Hooper, 1988.

Whittingham, Richard. 1982. *Almanac of Adventure: A Panorama of Danger and Daring.* Chicago: Rand McNally.

Wilson, Samuel M. 1991. "White Legends, Lost Tribes." *Natural History,* Sept., 16–20.

Wollen, Peter. 1982. *Readings and Writings: Semiotic Counter-Strategies.* London: Verso.

Wren, Percival Christopher. 1925. *Beau Geste.* New York: Frederick Stokes.

Wylie, Laurence, and Rick Stafford. 1977. *Beaux Gestes: A Guide to French Body Talk.* New York: Dutton.

Yankelovich, Nicole, et al. 1988. "Issues in Designing a Hypermedia Document System." In Ambron and Hooper 1988.

Yates, Frances A. 1966. *The Art of Memory.* Chicago: University of Chicago Press.

Zelinsky, Wilbur. 1988. *Nation into State: The Shifting Symbolic Foundations of American Nationalism.* Chapel Hill: University of North Carolina Press.

Zijderveld, Anton C. 1982. *Reality in a Looking-Glass: Rationality through an Analysis of Traditional Folly*. London: Routledge & Kegan Paul.

Zizek, Slavoj. 1989. *The Sublime Object of Ideology*. London: Verso.

Zweig, Paul. 1974. *The Adventurer*. Princeton: Princeton University Press.

Index

Library of Congress Cataloging-in-Publication Data
Ulmer, Gregory L., 1944–
    Heuretics : the logic of invention / Gregory L. Ulmer.
        p.   cm.
    Includes bibliographical references (p.) and index.
        ISBN 0-8018-4717-6 (acid-free paper). — ISBN 0-8018-4718-4 (pbk. :
acid-free paper)
        1. Creation (Literary, artistic, etc.)   2. Creative ability.   3. Aesthetics.   4.
    Humanities—Study and teaching.   5. Interactive media.   I. Title.
    BH301.C84U46   1994
    001—dc20   93-31726
                                                                              CIP